SKETCH & FINISH

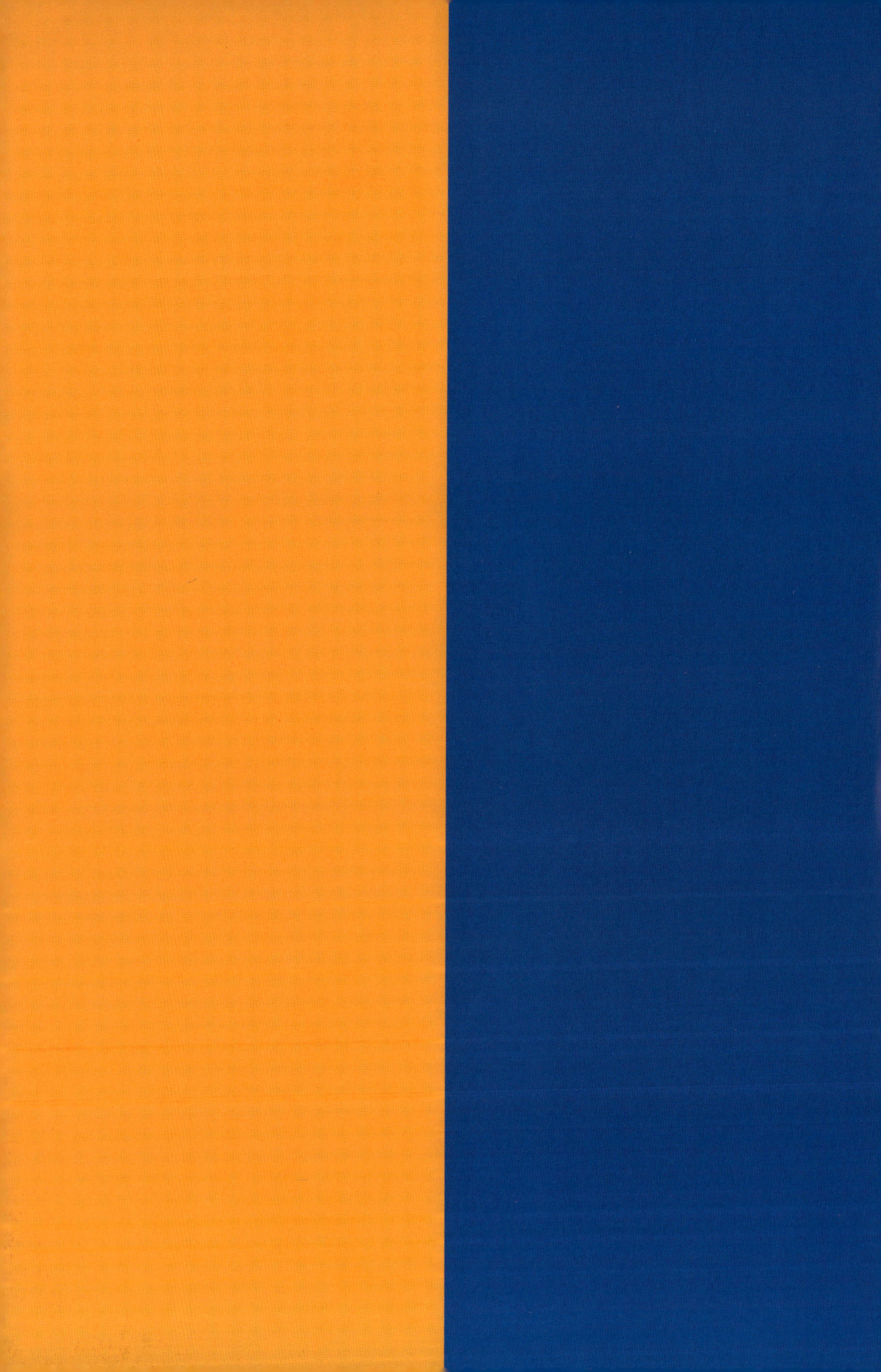

SKETCH & FINISH

THE JOURNEY FROM HERE TO THERE

Milton Glaser

PRINCETON ARCHITECTURAL PRESS · NEW YORK

SKETCH

A sketch is typically understood to be a rough drawing. It raises the questions of what a drawing is and, even more, what do we mean by "rough"? If we consider "rough" to simply be the opposite of "smooth," the definition is useless.

I'd rather consider a sketch as the mind's introduction to a creative journey. It is, by many standards, ambiguous. Its primary purpose may be to create an opportunity for a path to emerge. You don't know where you're going, but the answer lies in your brain. It just needs to be uncovered.

The tentativeness in the act of sketching is crucial. Doubt is essential. If you already know the answer before you start, why bother? Conviction is the killer of imagination.

Some use sketching to map out the shape, scale, and color of a finished work. This is very different from the idea I'm proposing. A sketch's relationship to the finished work can, in fact, be oblique. As I show in this book, in some cases the path deviates so that the final artwork seems to have almost no relationship to its origin. It's interesting and worthwhile to see the different tangents the mind takes.

This is different from the Renaissance concept of sketching. Artists then were less tentative and exploratory. For example, when you compare Leonardo da Vinci's sketch of St. Jerome with his finished painting, you'll see that everything implicit in the preliminary drawing has been dutifully realized in the painting. Modernism changed the function of the sketch.

At that juncture, the objective of art was no longer concerned with accurately representing the real world.

The sketch, incidentally, is not necessarily meant to be seen by anyone except the artist. And yet we adore seeing artists' sketches because they reveal how their minds function. Who would not want a sketch by Leonardo? It would essentially be a picture of the brain of one of the greatest geniuses in history.

The fidelity of the sketch varies too. Rough or refined, tight or loose—sometimes you develop a sketch further to see if it's a path worth taking. Many sketches even look like finished works.

This finished effect also tends to happen when you start on a computer. Over-reliance on technology has discouraged people from drawing with their hands. Drawing is useful because it helps you refocus and recalibrate your existing perceptions about something. The loss of that ability has been replaced by the acuity for finding things on the internet. What tends to happen is that you manufacture alternative choices for the same subject and then pick the one that seems to be most effective. Everything seems immediately finite. It prevents an essential mode of thought, which is this journey toward an unknown destination.

& FINISH

This image was inspired by a photograph showing columns and a checkerboard floor. The idea of a reclining nude emerged unconsciously to combine with the image of the photograph. Other elements were added— the landscape, the flowers.

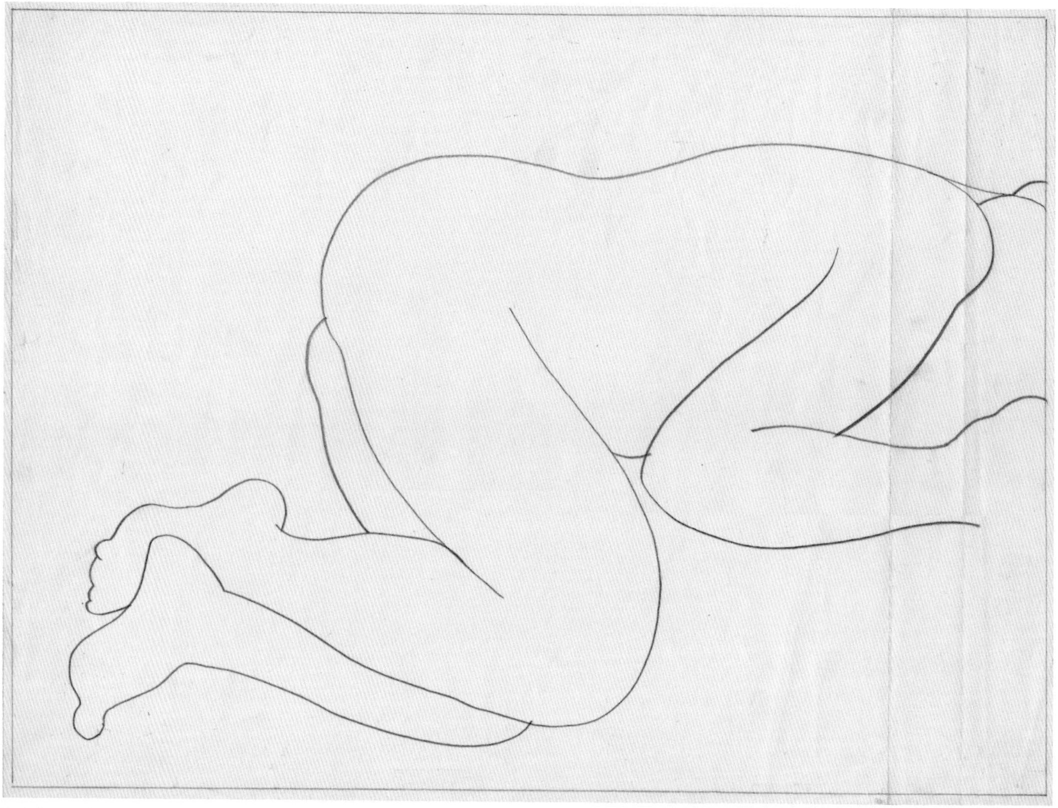

Nude study.

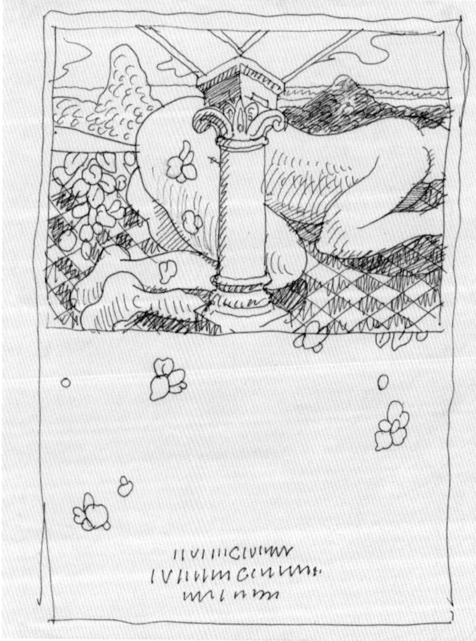

Sketch for poster.

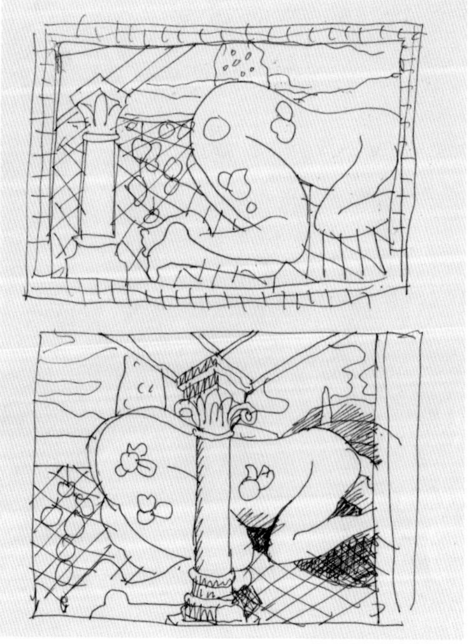

Sketches.

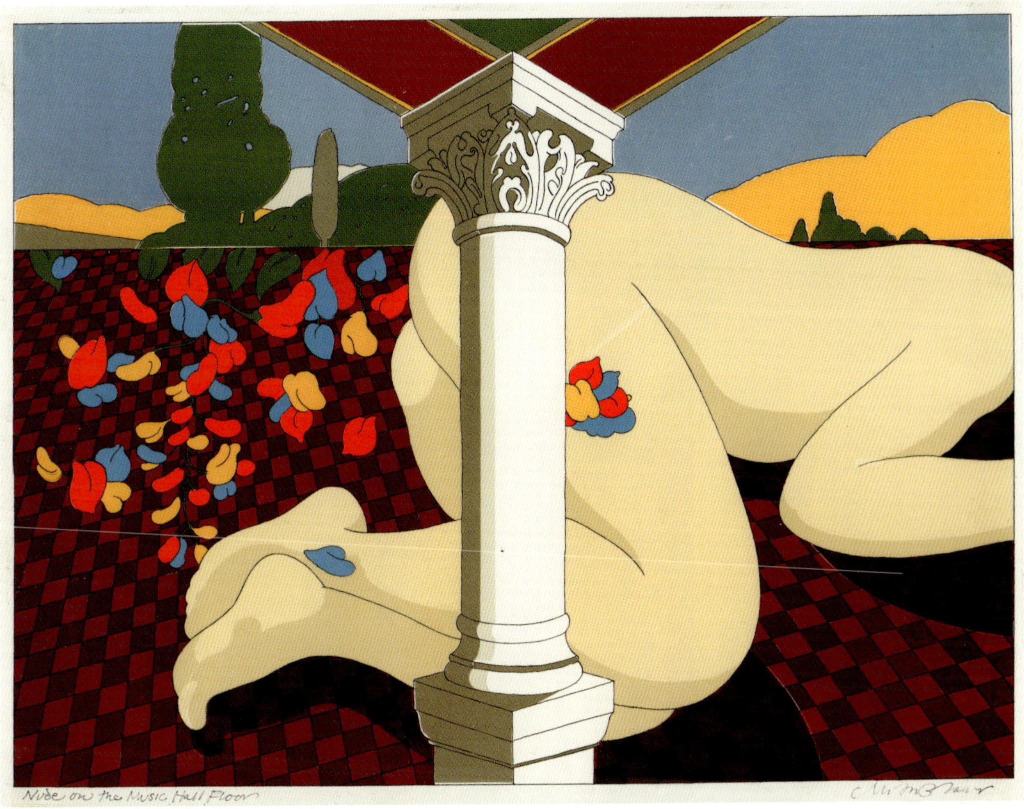

Finished work.

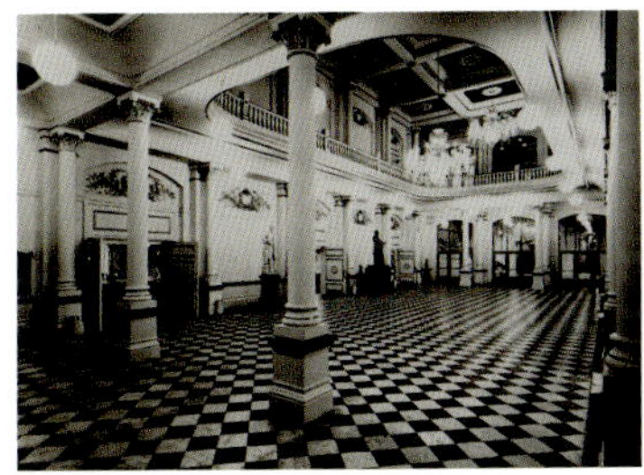

Original reference photo of the dance hall.

The decision to turn the view of a cabinet from frontal to diagonal was the most critical turn in developing the image. The visibility of the object in the cabinet became an issue as color was applied to the black-and-white drawing. Repeating the cabinet as an image on the wall became a kind of internal joke.

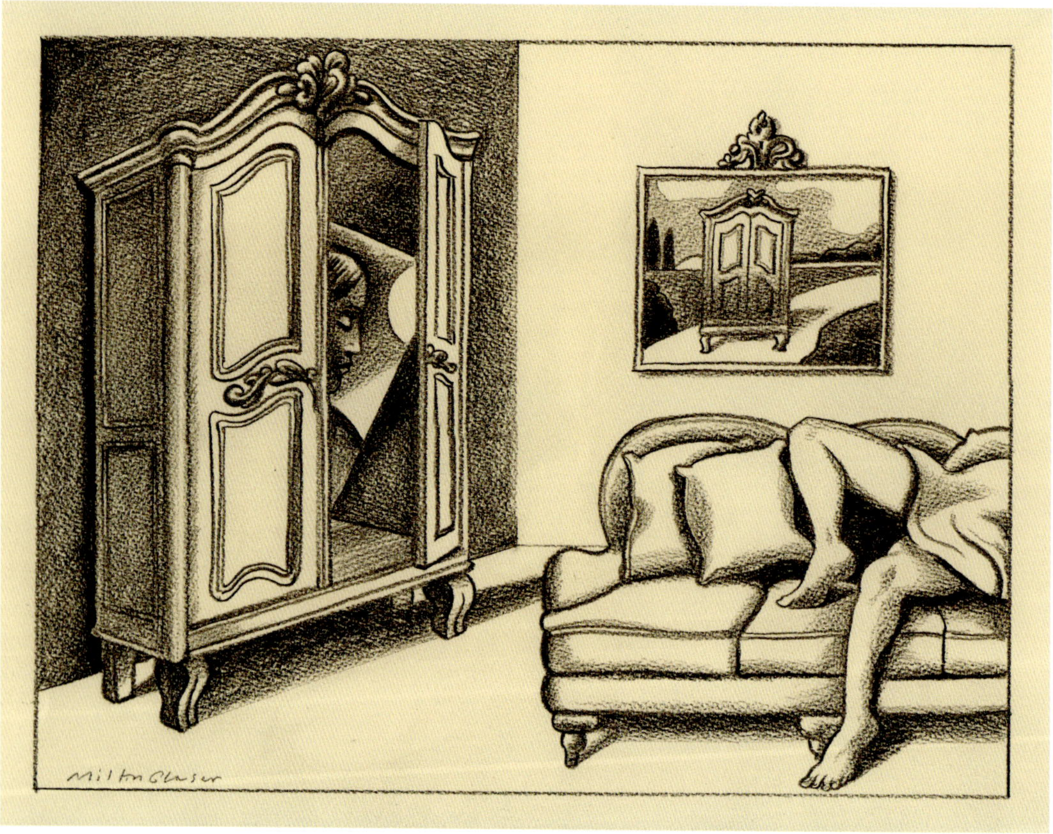

Black and white version.

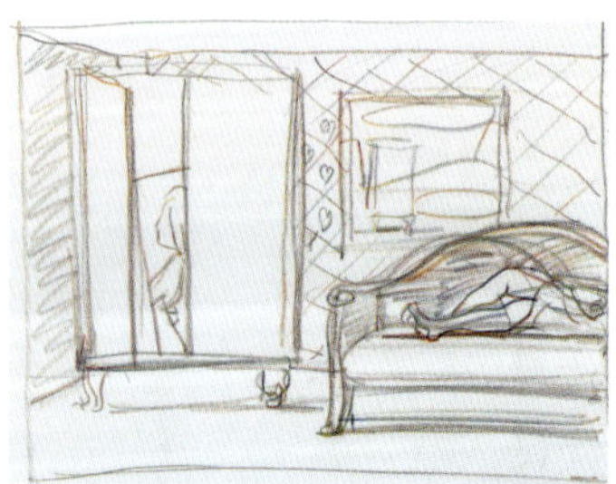

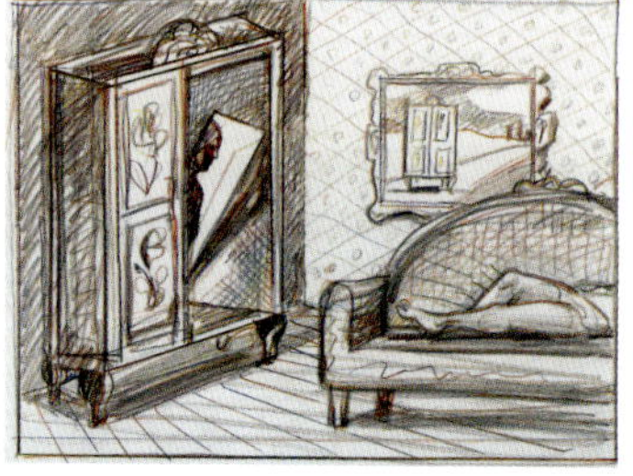

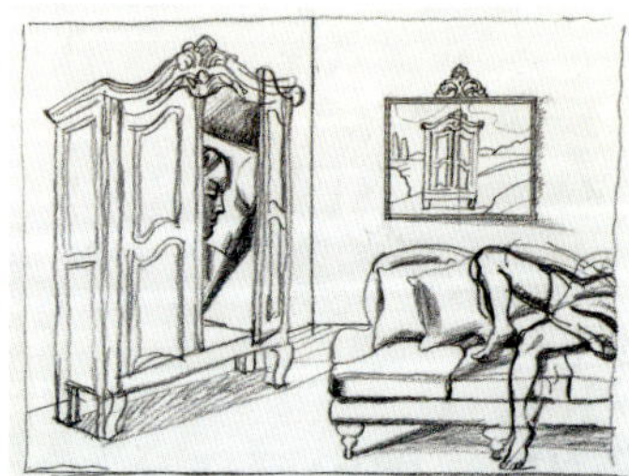

Early sketches.

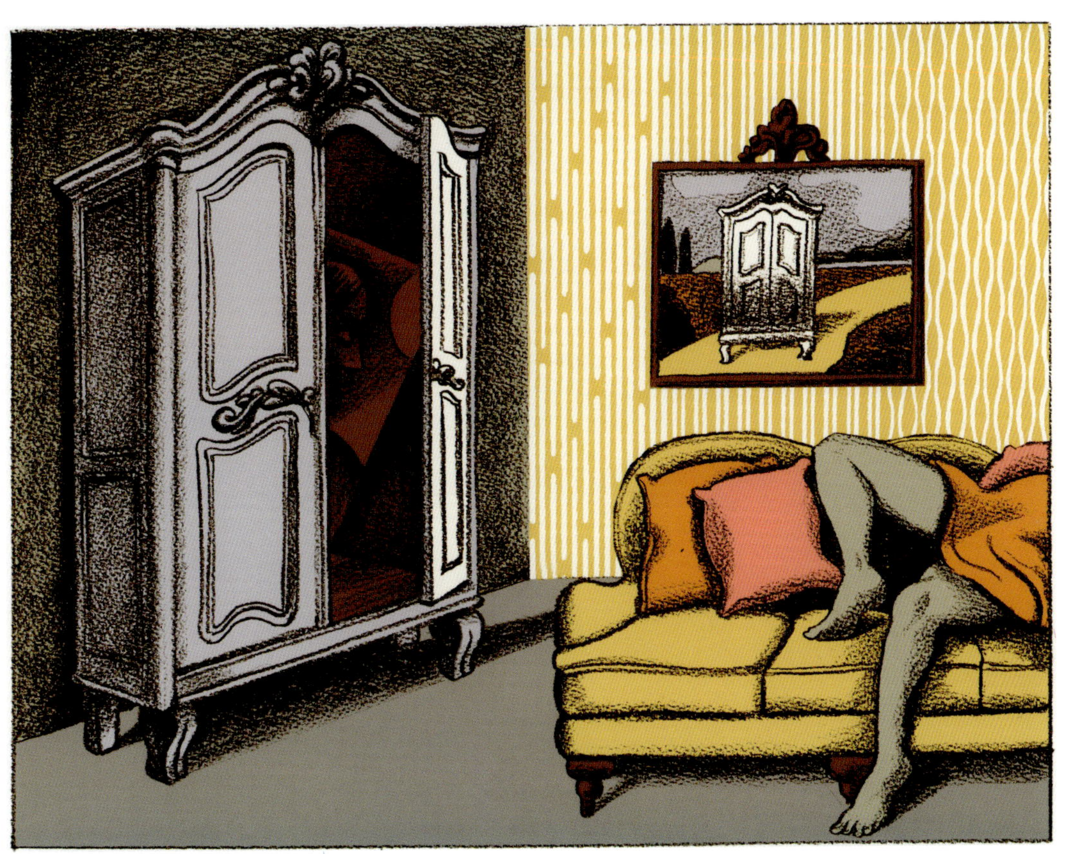

Color version.

This monotype was developed from a tentative drawing that manages to include most of the material except for the submerged portrait and hand, which occurred later, in the printmaking process. When a print is made, the image is reversed.

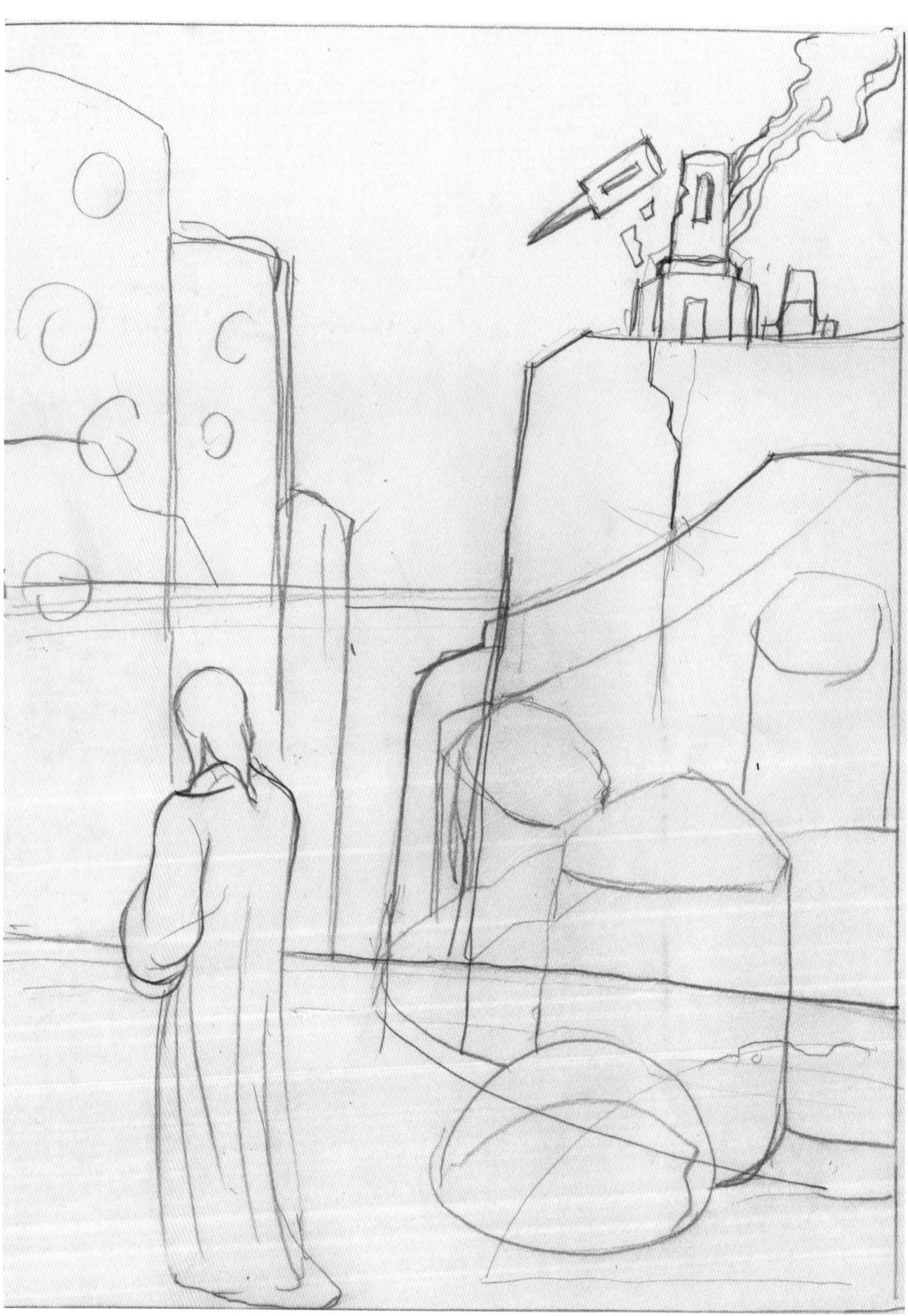

Pencil sketch.

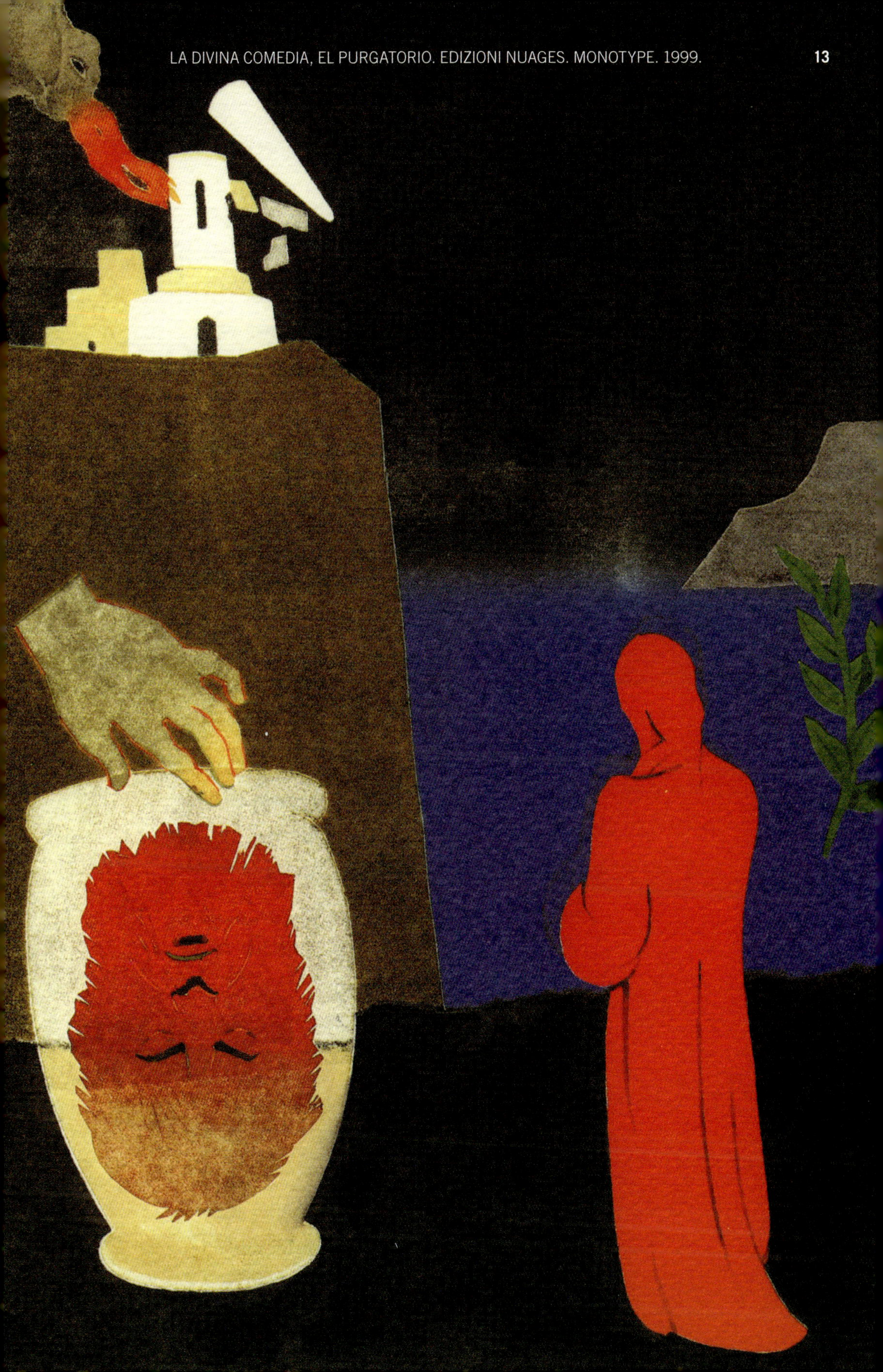

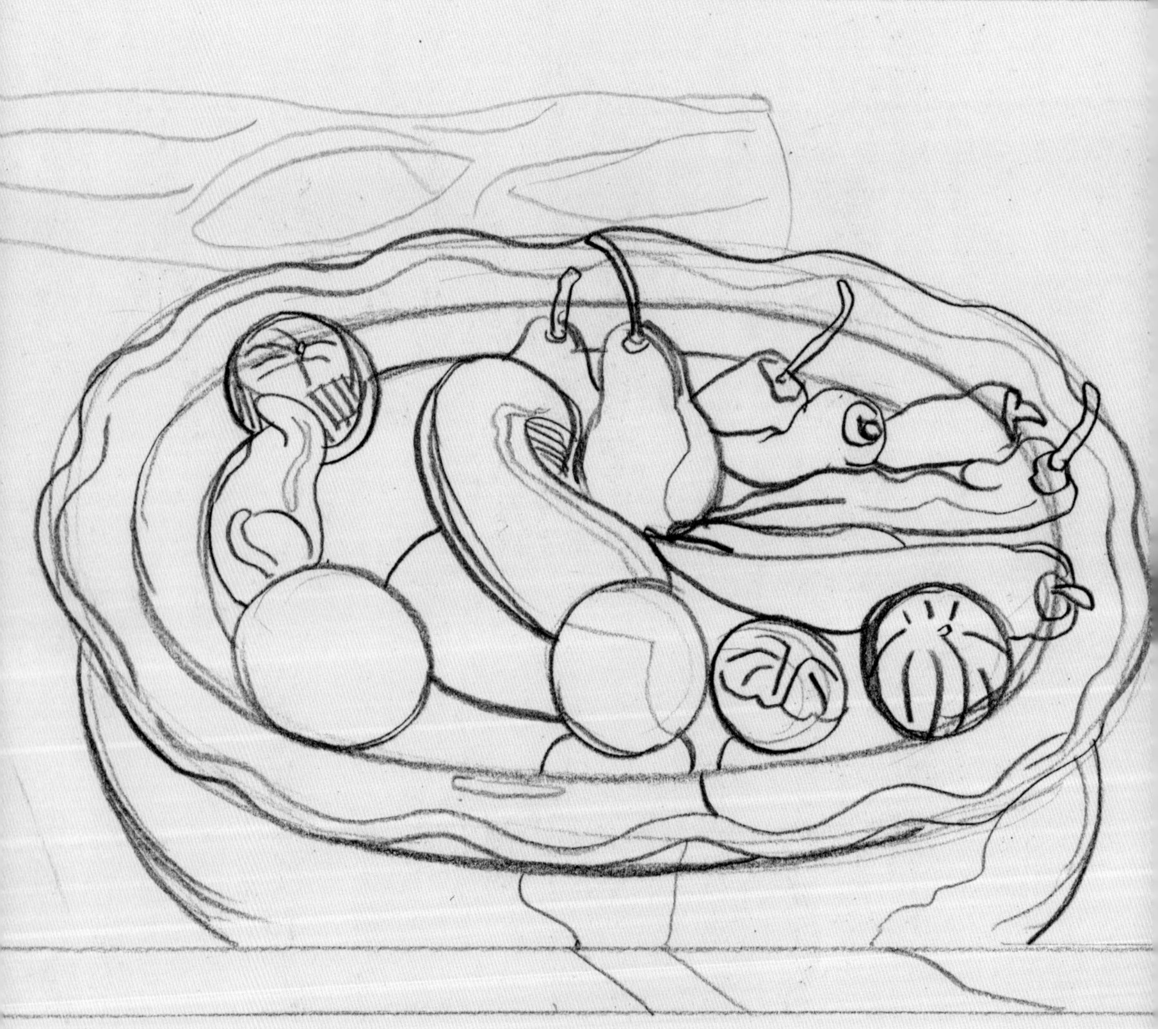

Initial pencil sketch.

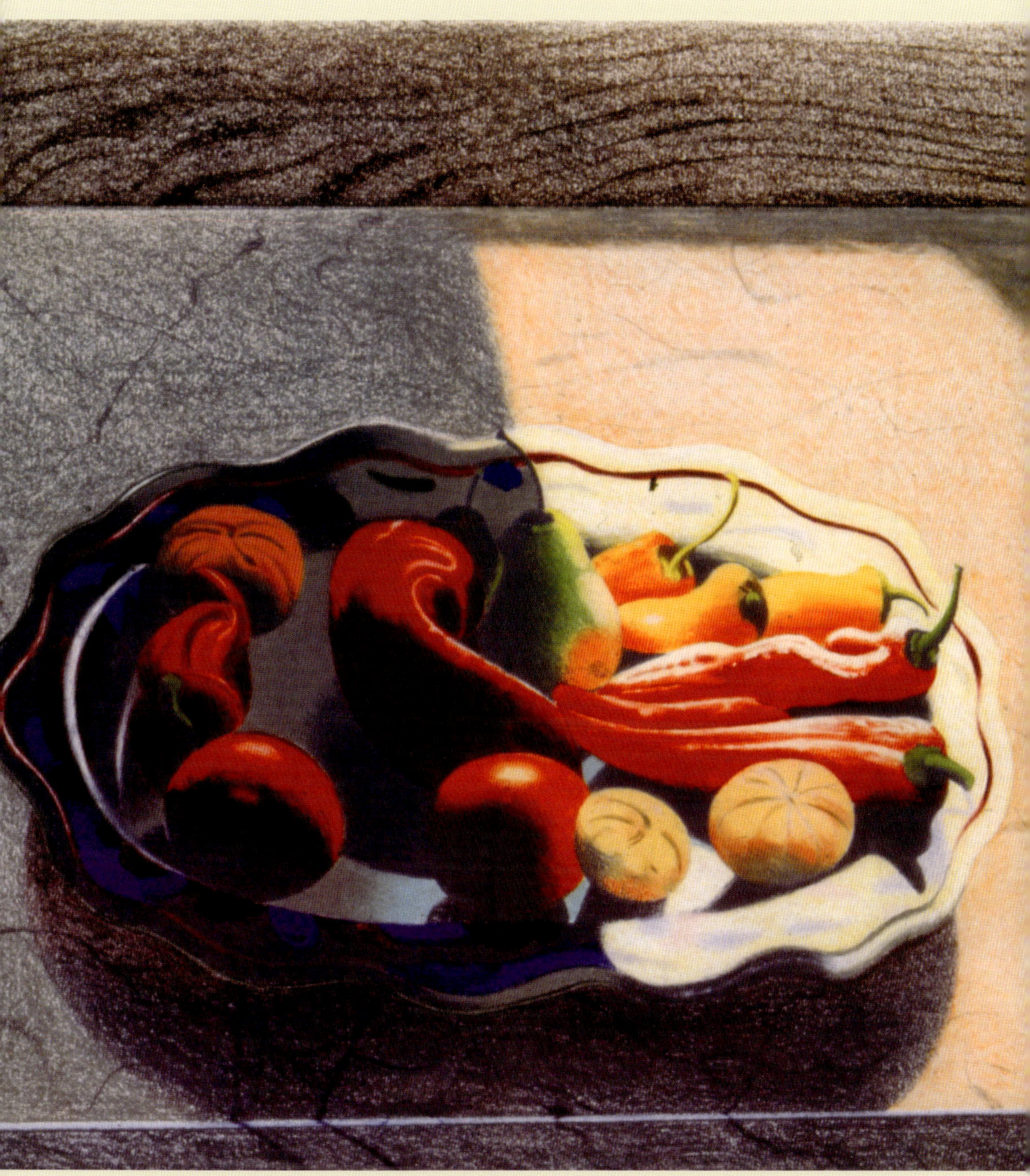

Final image.

For this magazine illustration, the sketch contains all the material needed to develop the complete image. Very little has been changed. I portrayed Sigmund Freud as a source of heavenly authority.

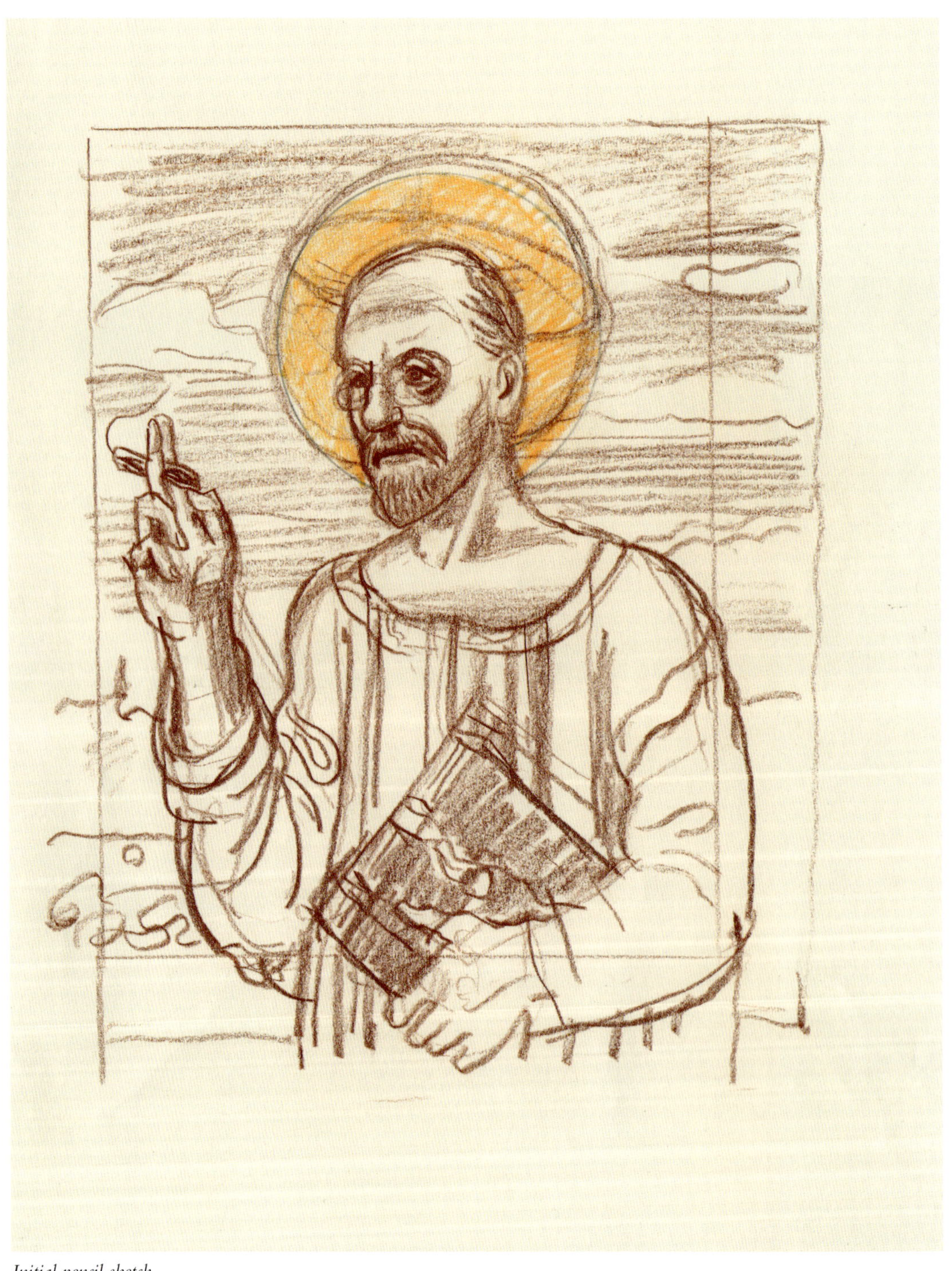

Initial pencil sketch.

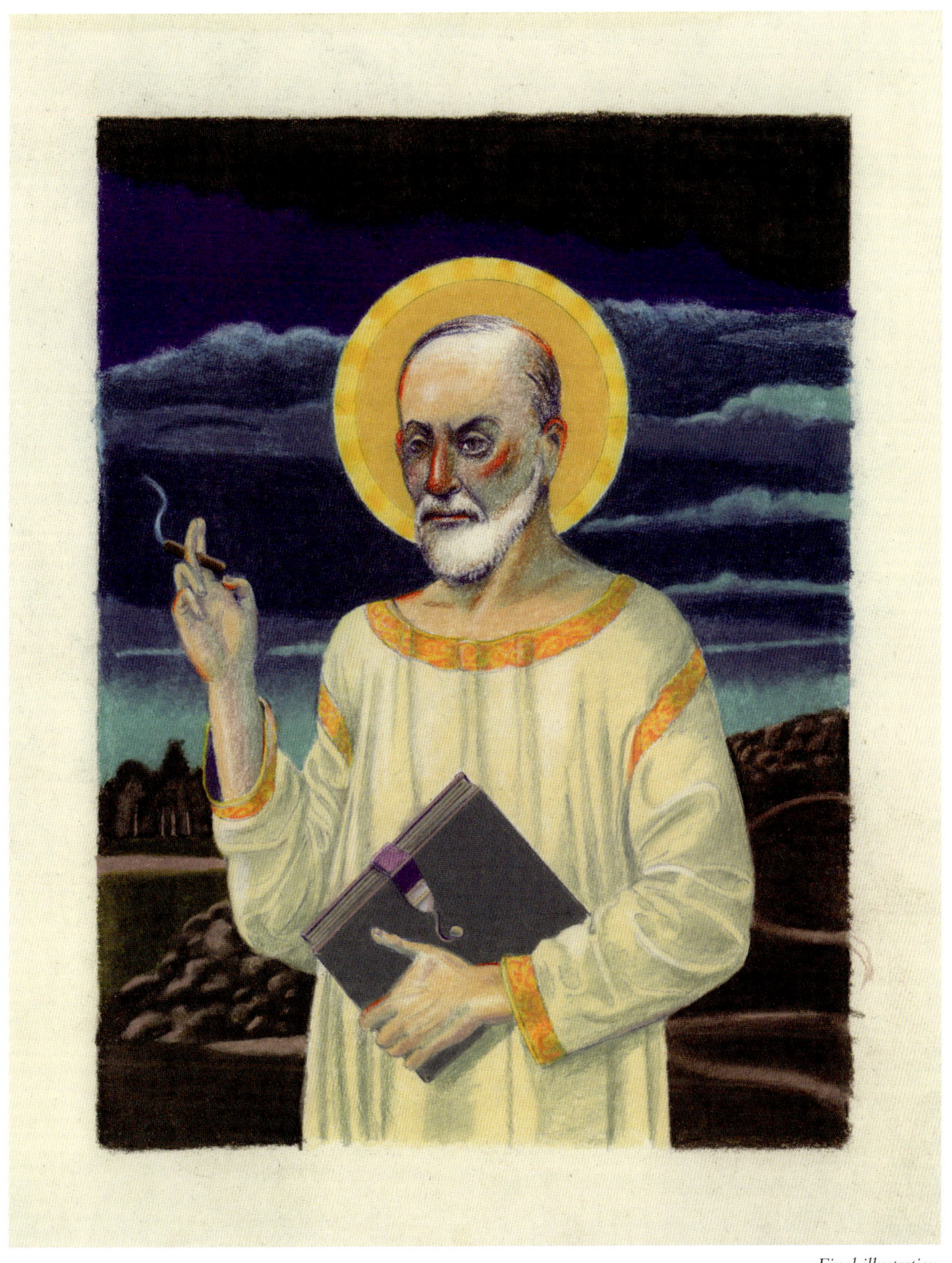

Final illustration.

An early engraving, shown on the bottom of this page was the reference for these drawings of Dante.
It was then turned into a mezzotint in color. Mezzotint is a manner of engraving on copper or steel by
scraping or burnishing a roughened surface to produce light and shade.

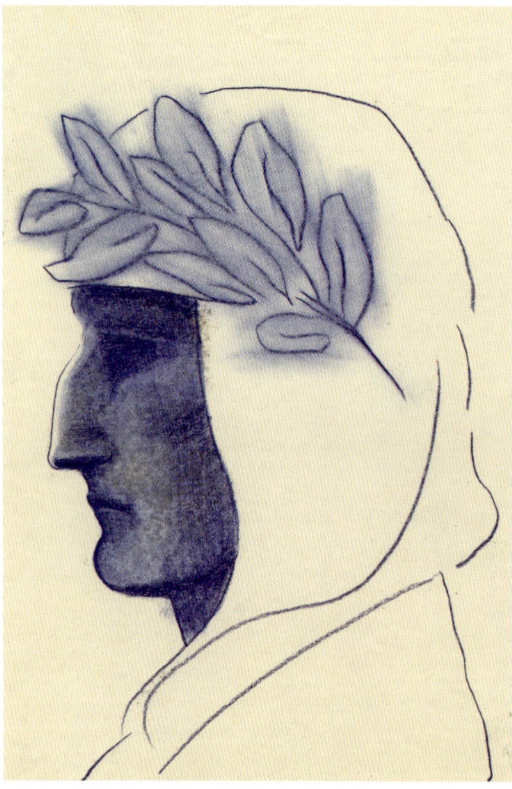

Early colored pencil sketch.

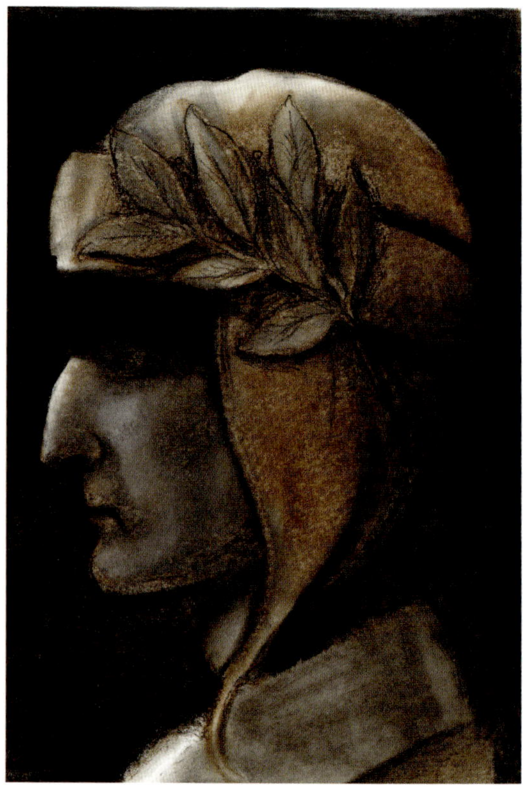

Further pen study.

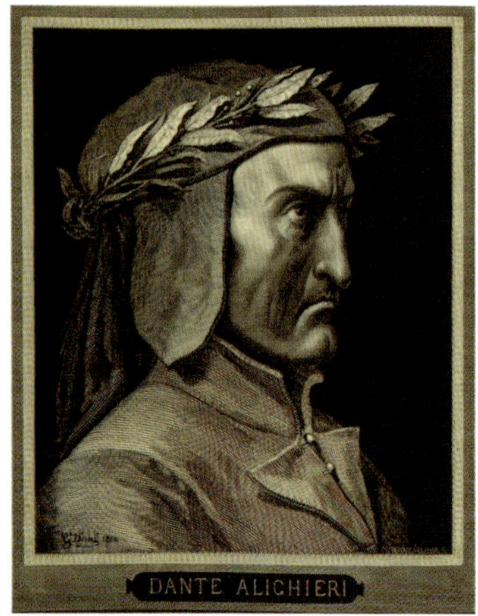

*Portrait of Dante Alighieri
engraved by Gustave Doré.*

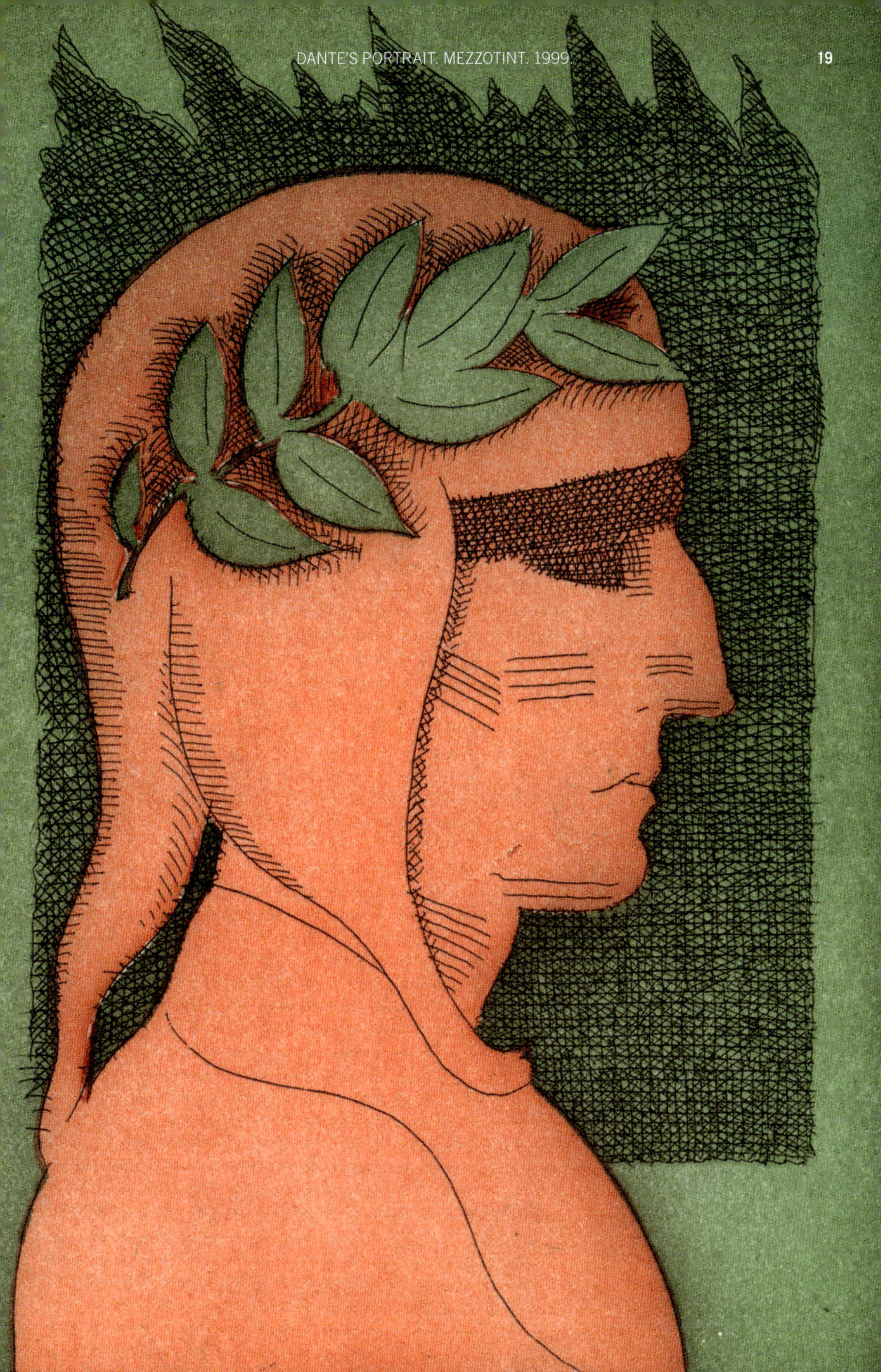

In this study for a Rhode Island tourism campaign, the issue was finding commercially available fonts to get close to the initial sketch.

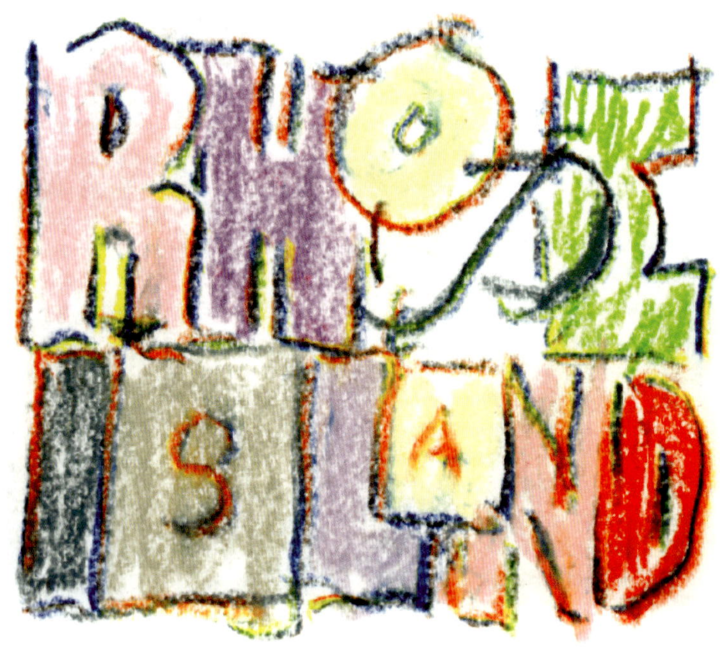

Initial color pencil sketch.

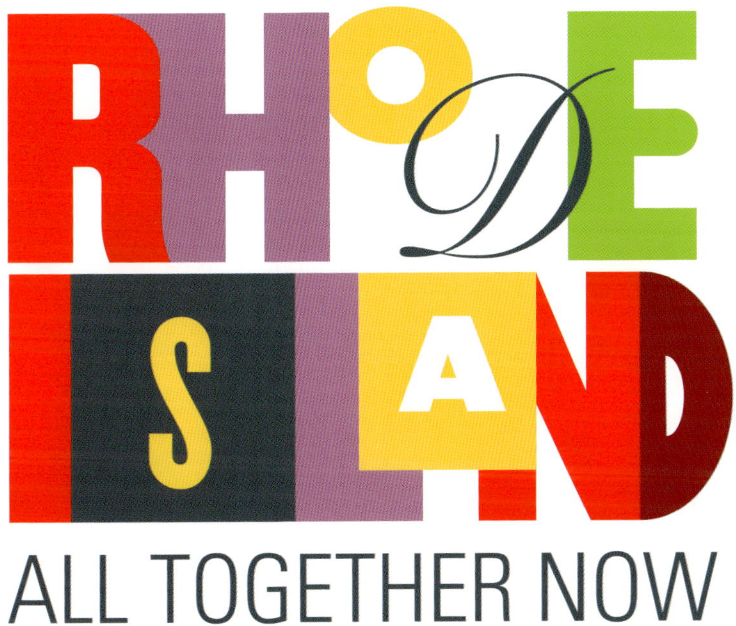

One of the iterations made with the computer.

The original drawing here was quite tentative but manages to include all the elements of the finished work.

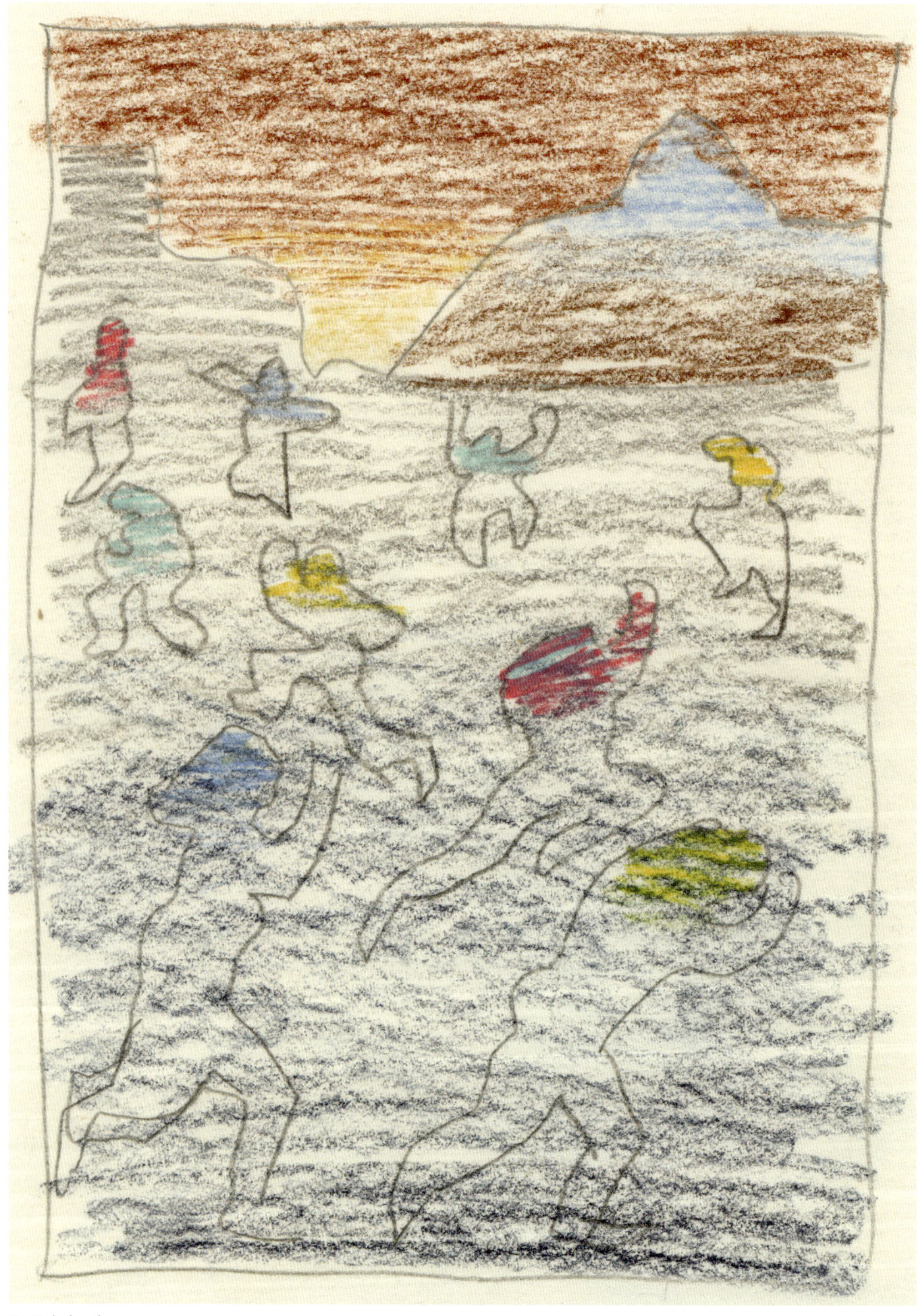

Initial sketch.

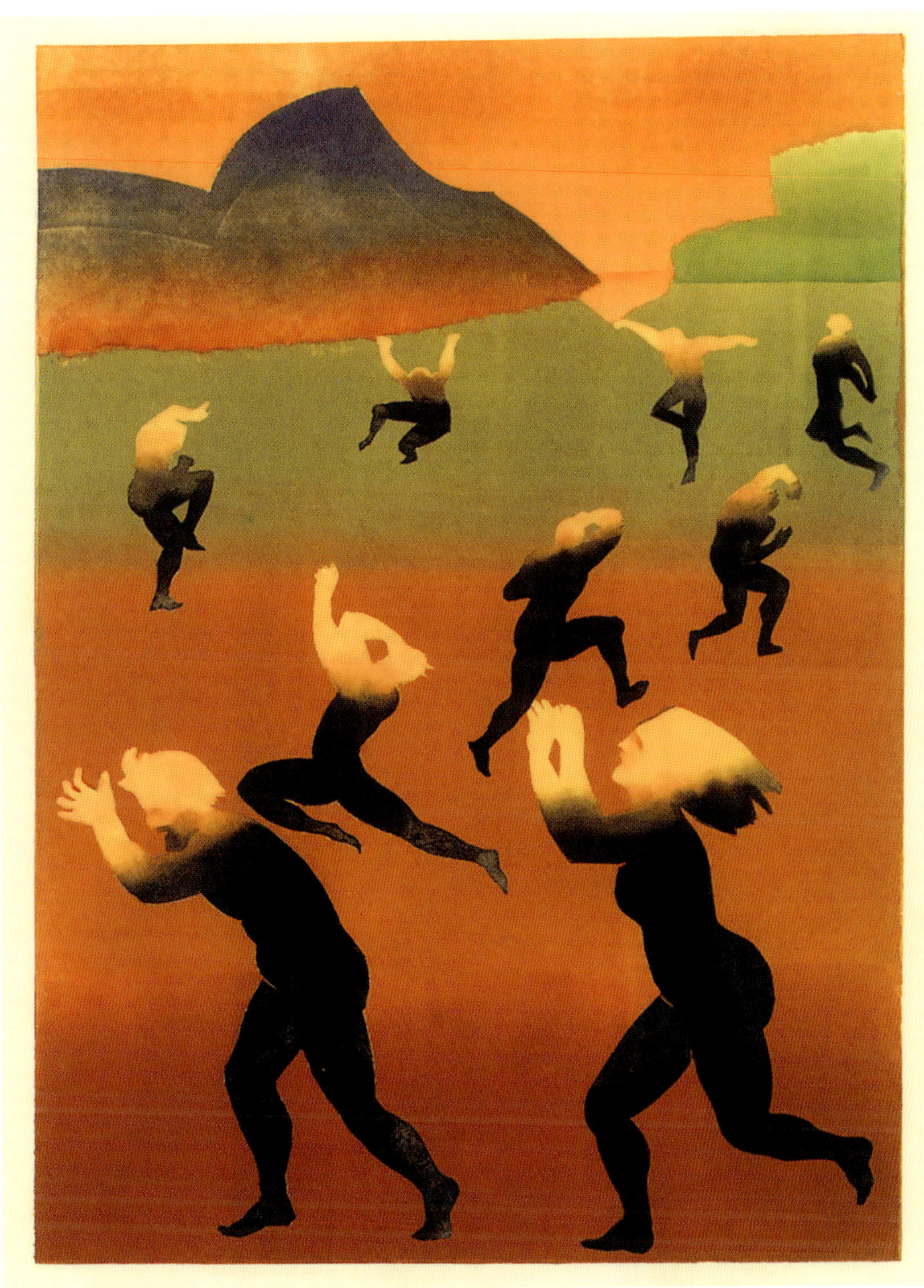

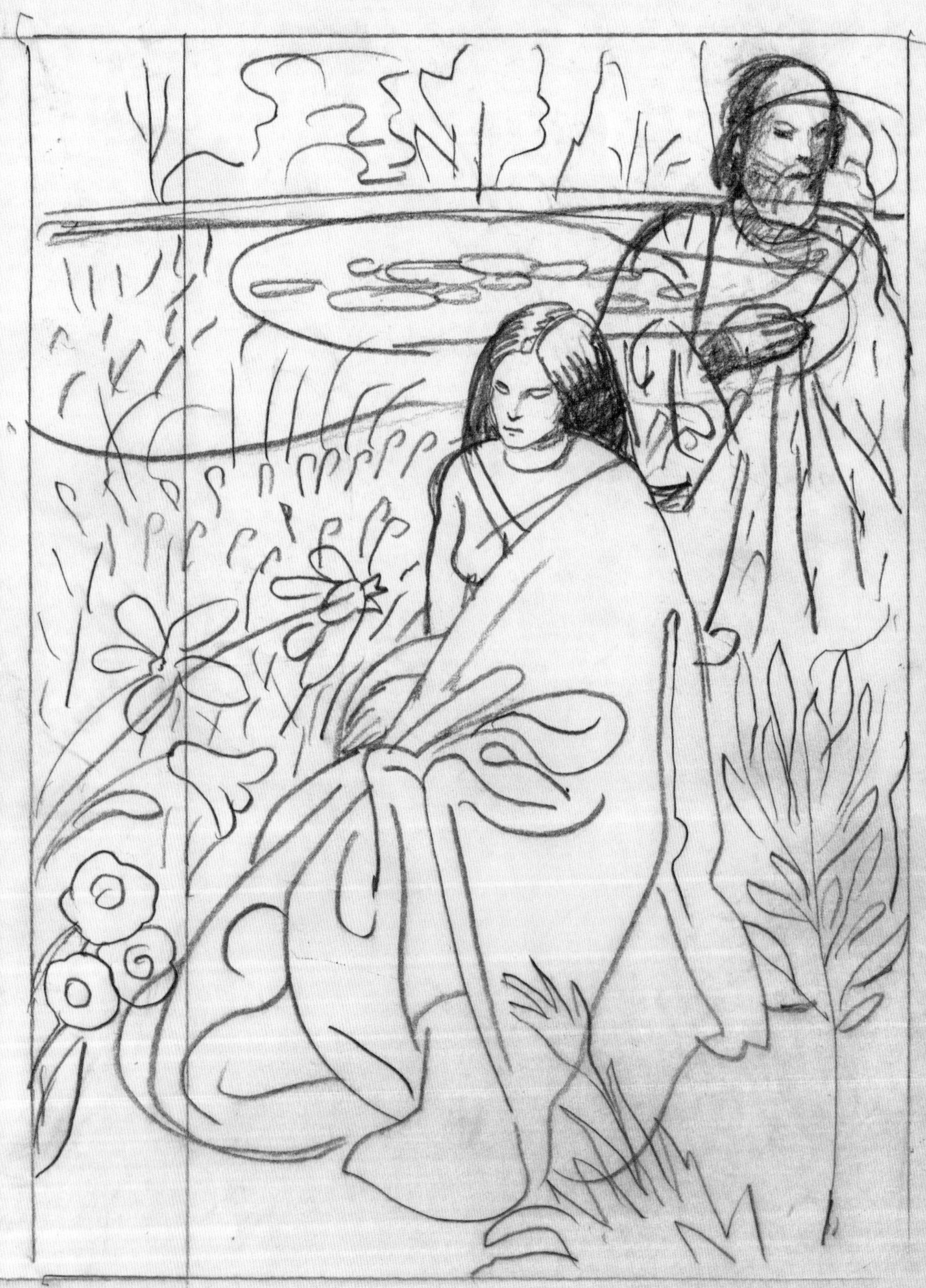

Pencil study.

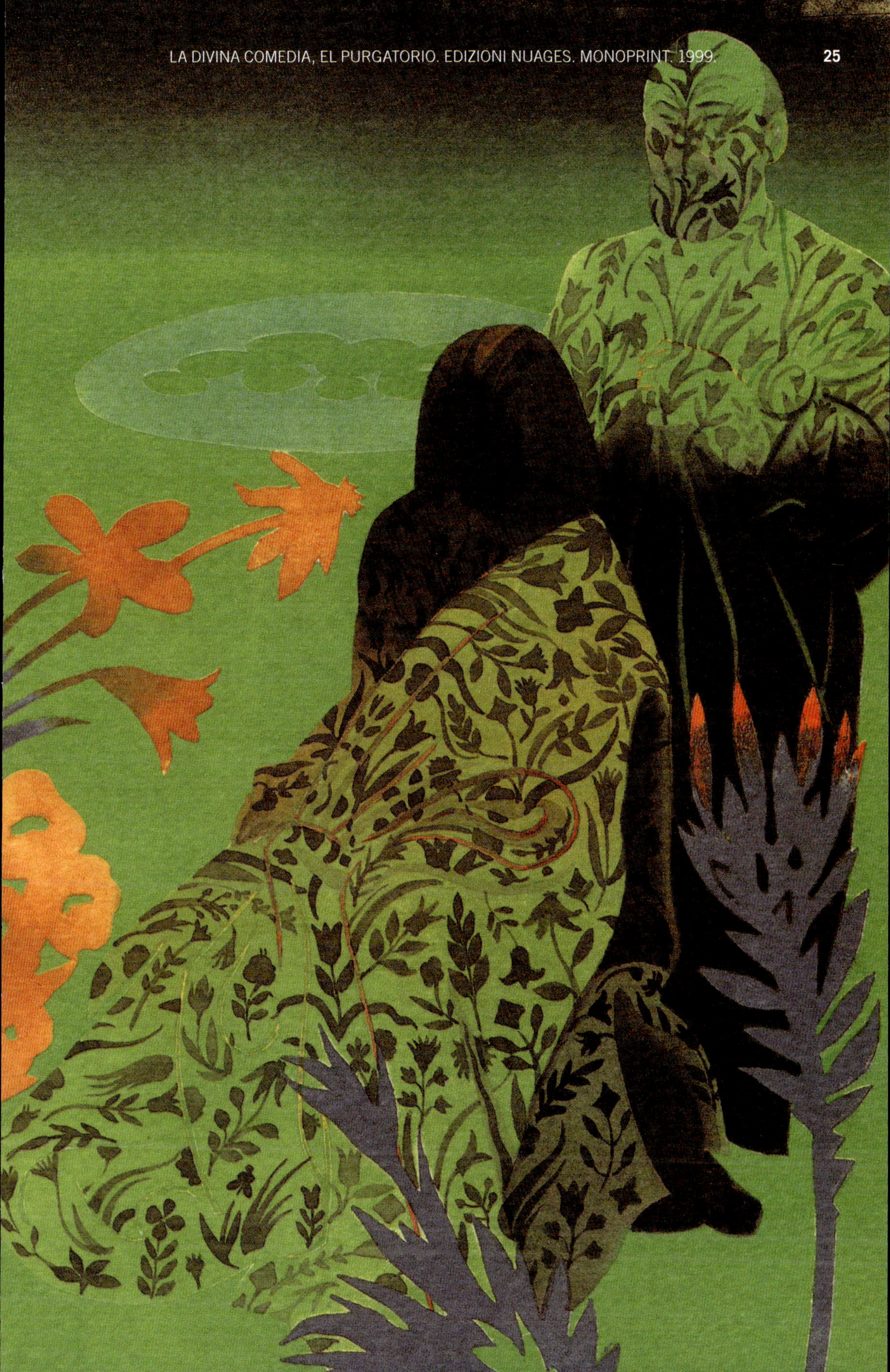

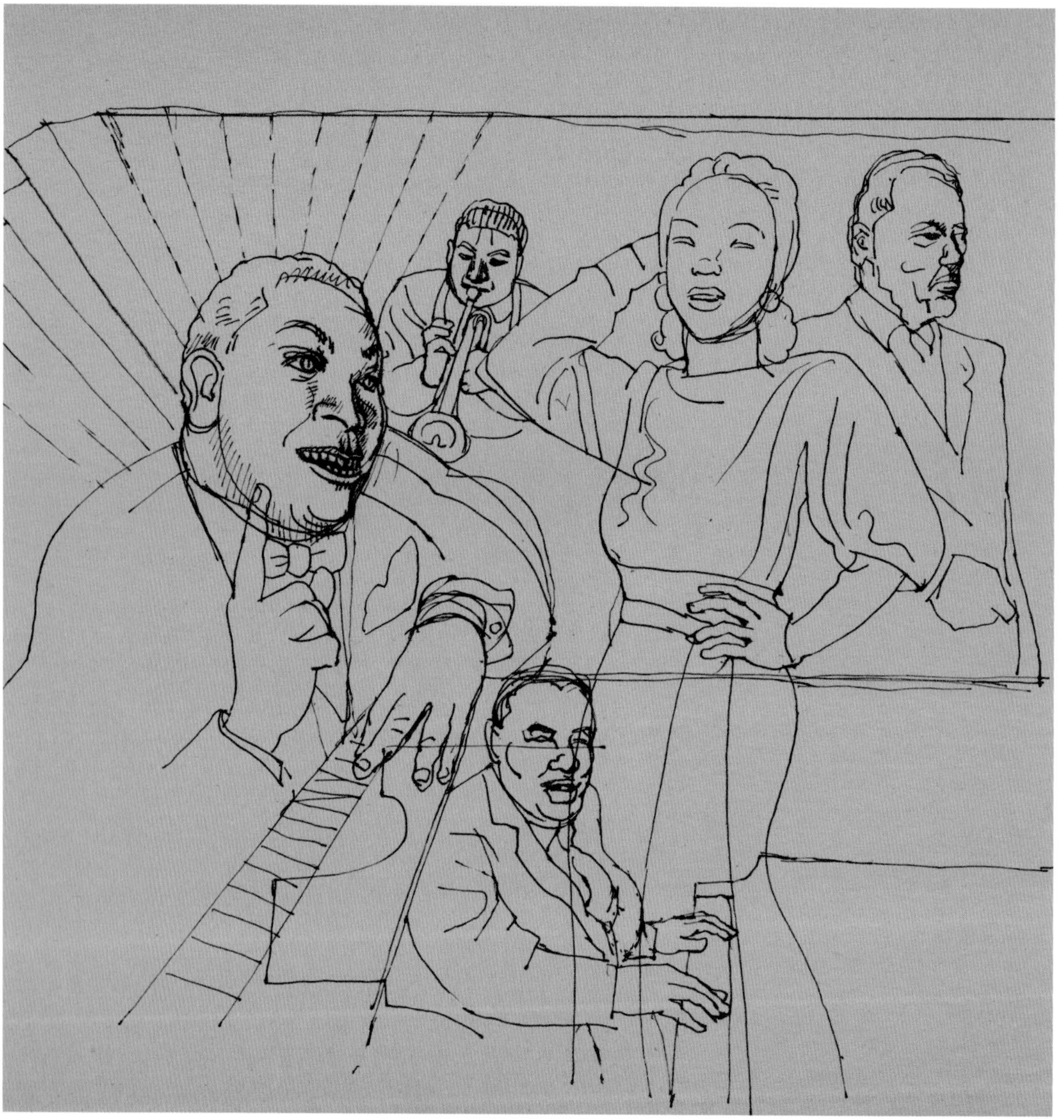

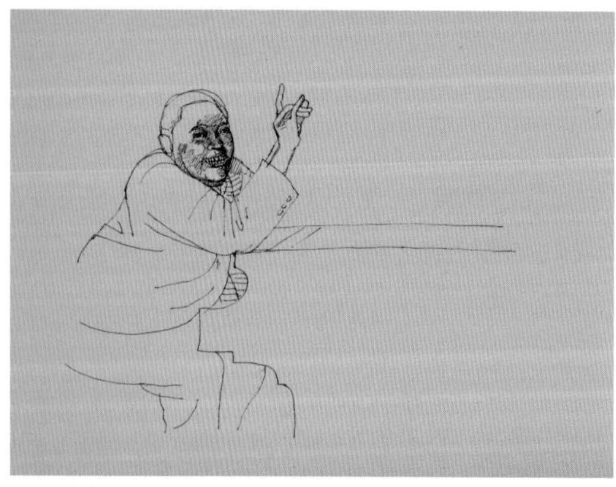

Pencil sketch.

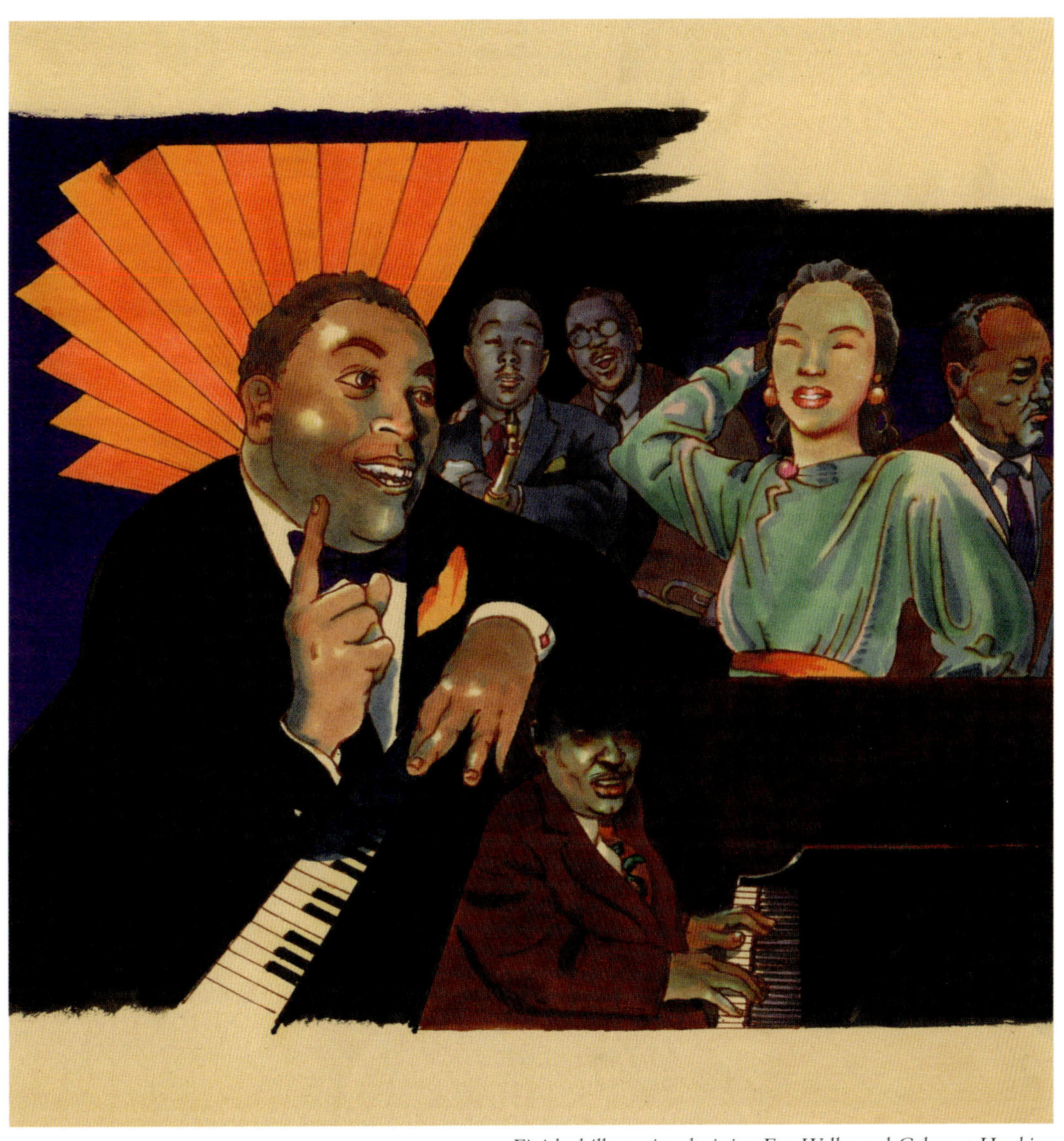

Finished illustration depicting Fats Waller and Coleman Hawkins.

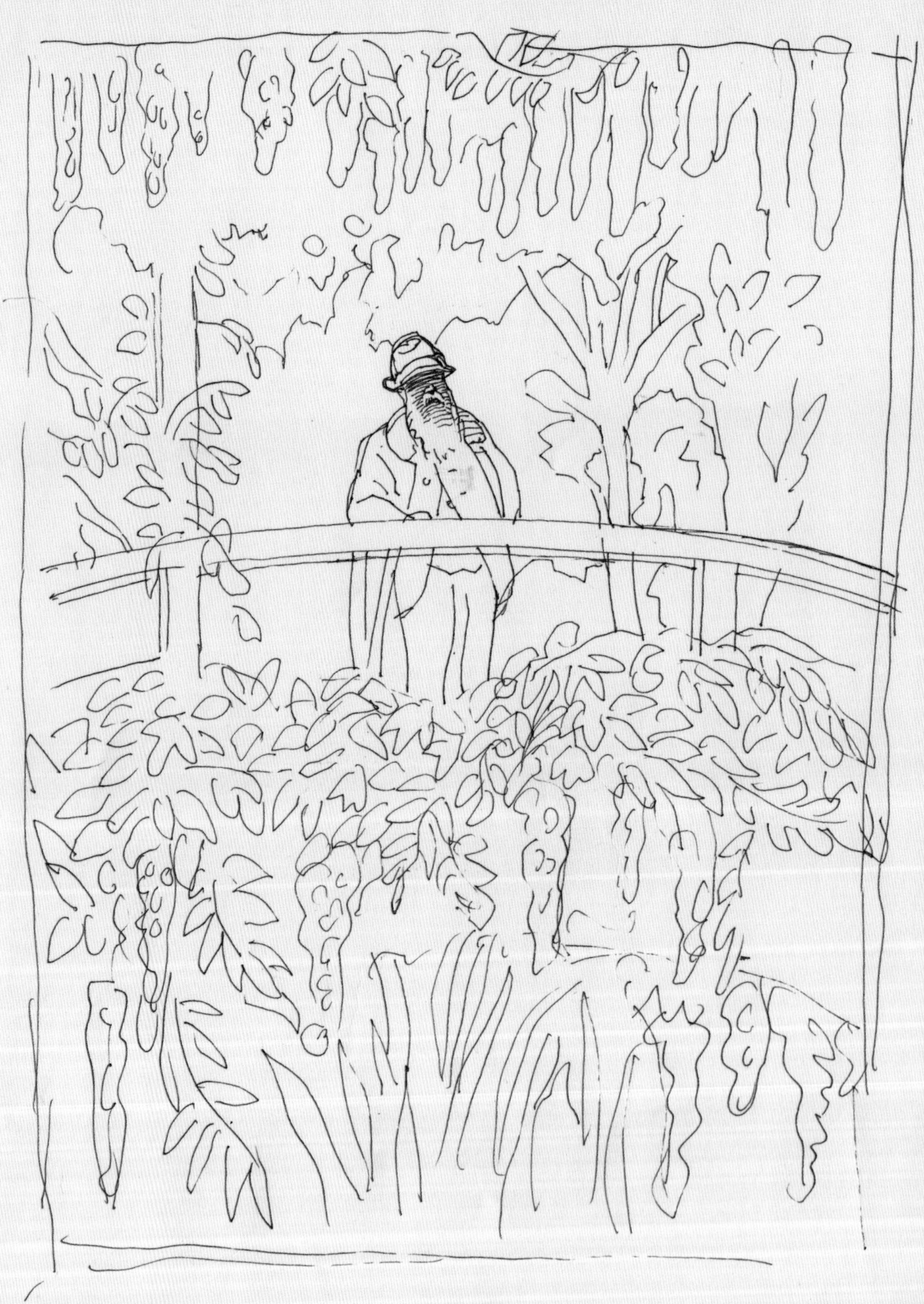

Pen and ink drawing.

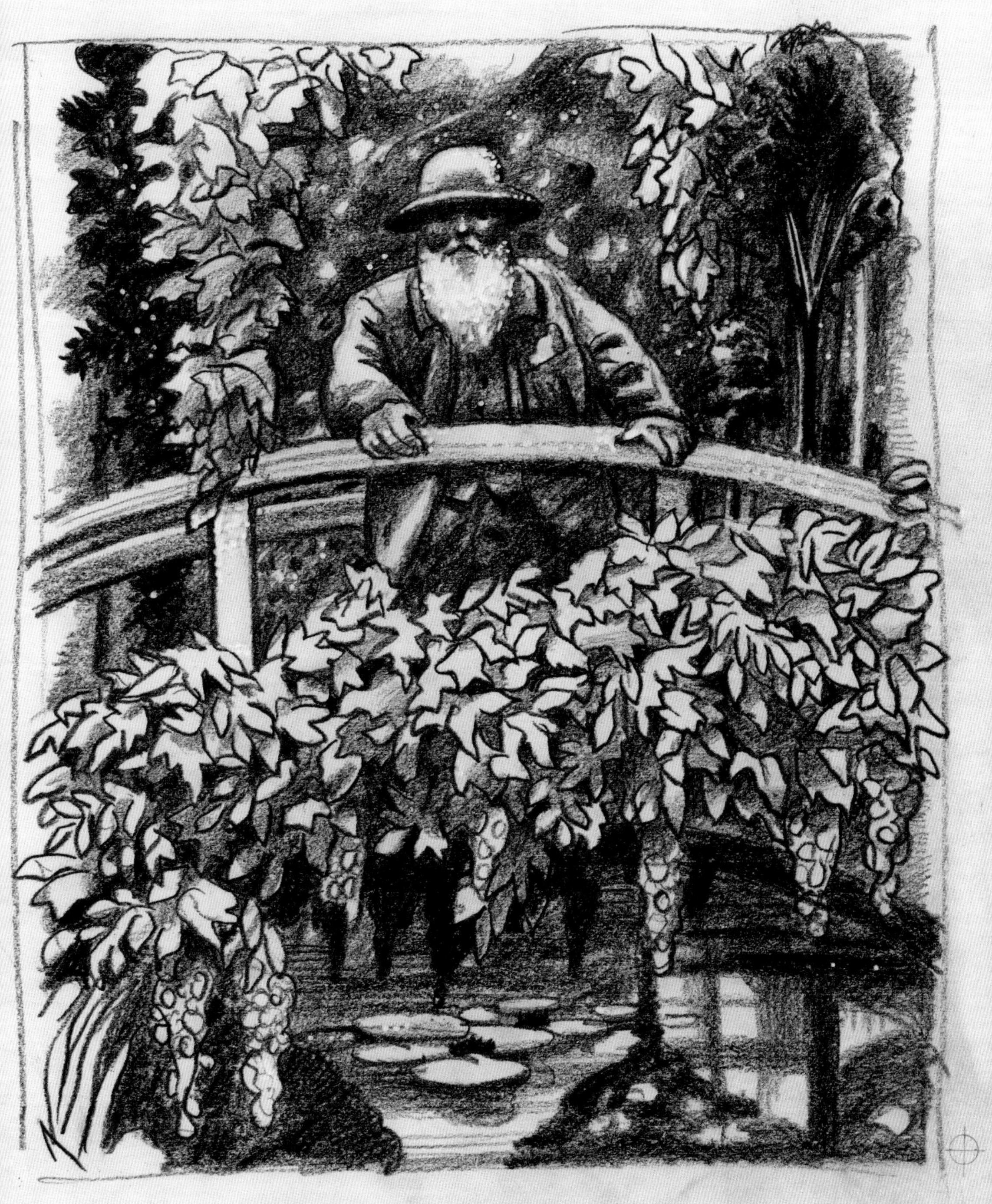

Final lithograph.

A series of palette drawings led to one version showing paint stretched across a torn palette, which was chosen for the cover of Graphis magazine. The typography on the cover echoes the illustration's central idea of being torn apart. The image is an homage to Bruno Zimm, a painter who owned the house my wife and I bought in Woodstock.

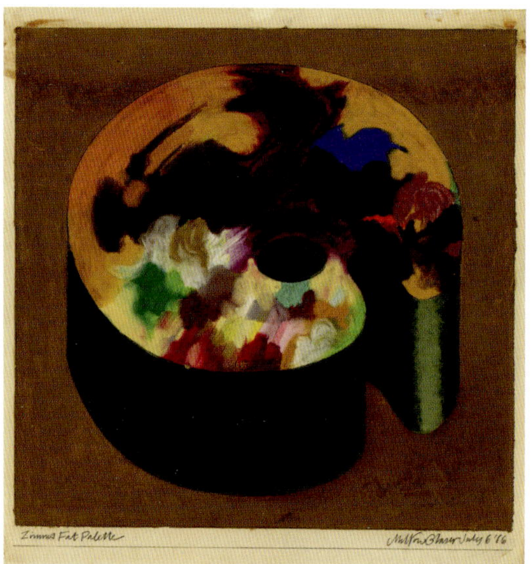

Zimm's fat palette.

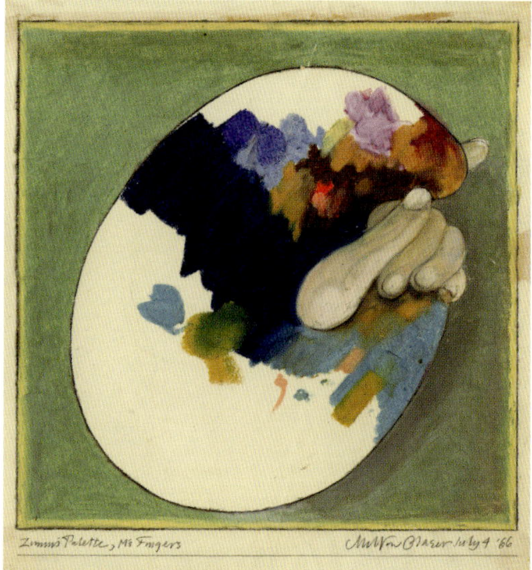

Zimm's palette, Milton's fingers.

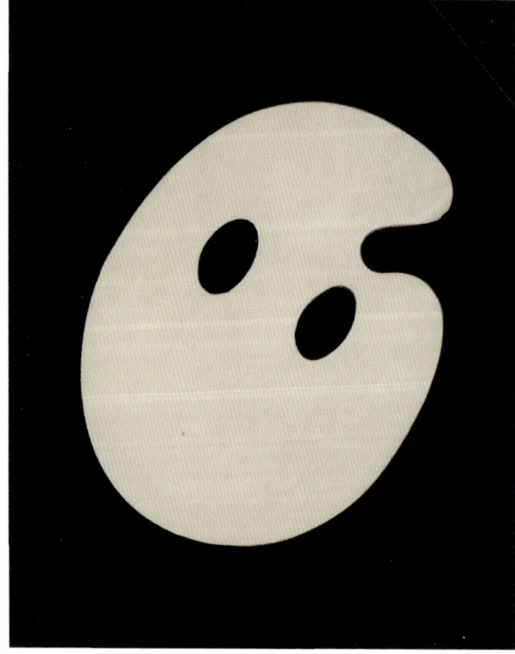

Zimm's black palette.

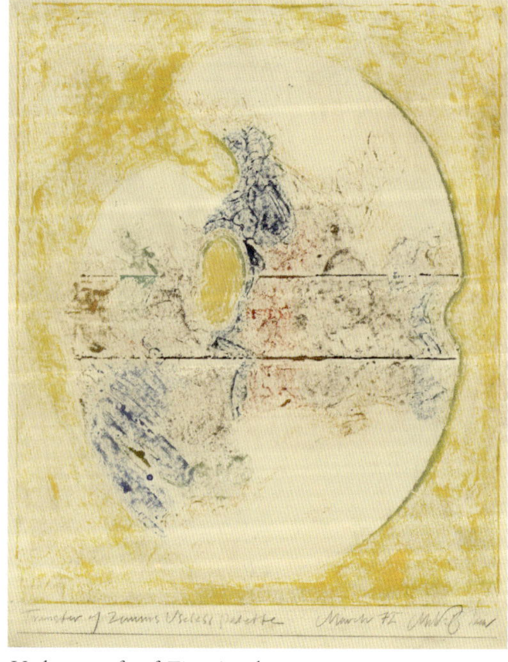

Useless transfer of Zimm's palette.

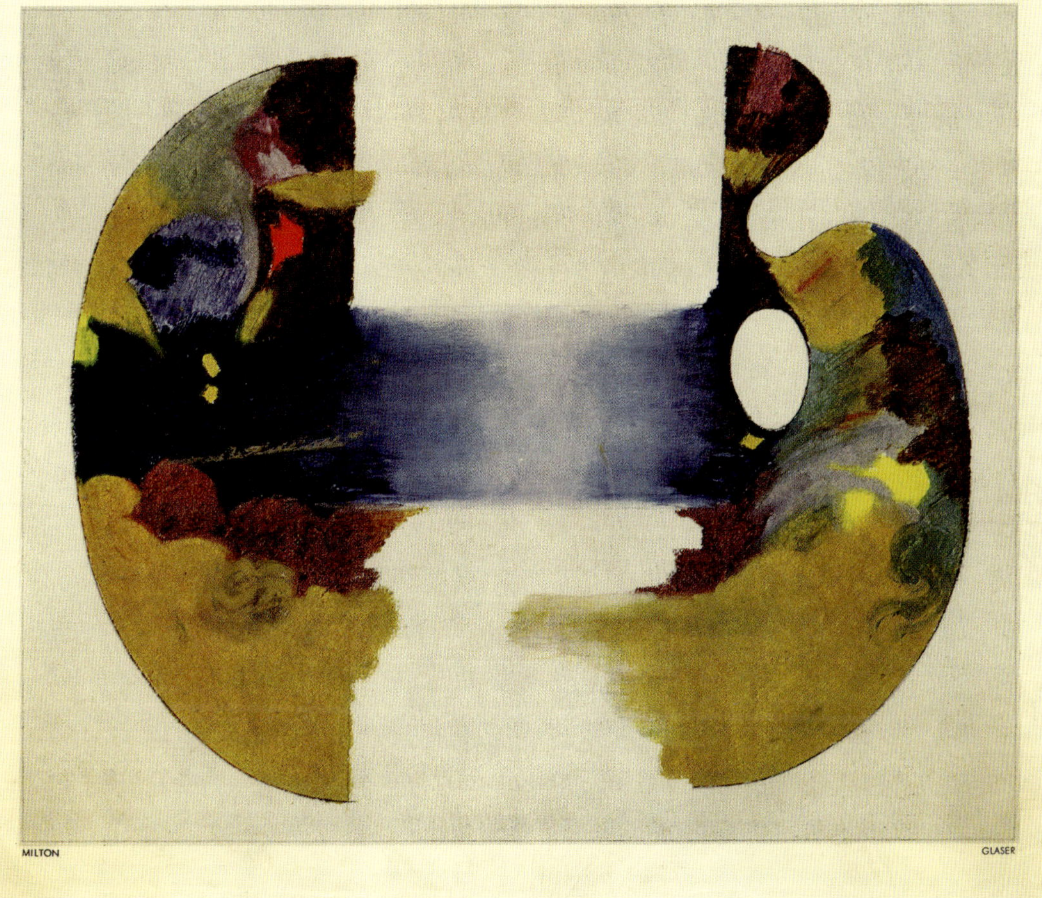

Graphis *cover.*

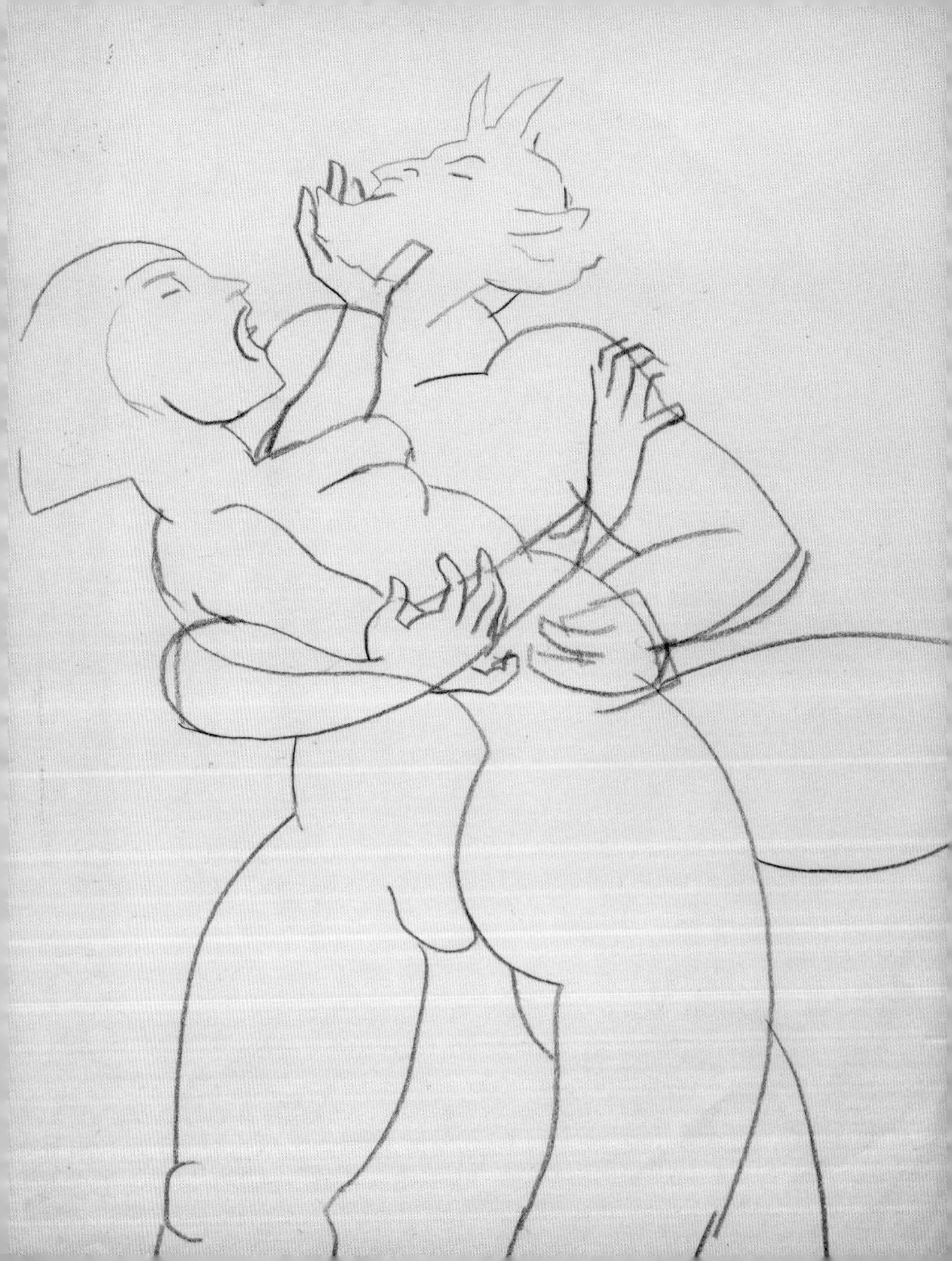

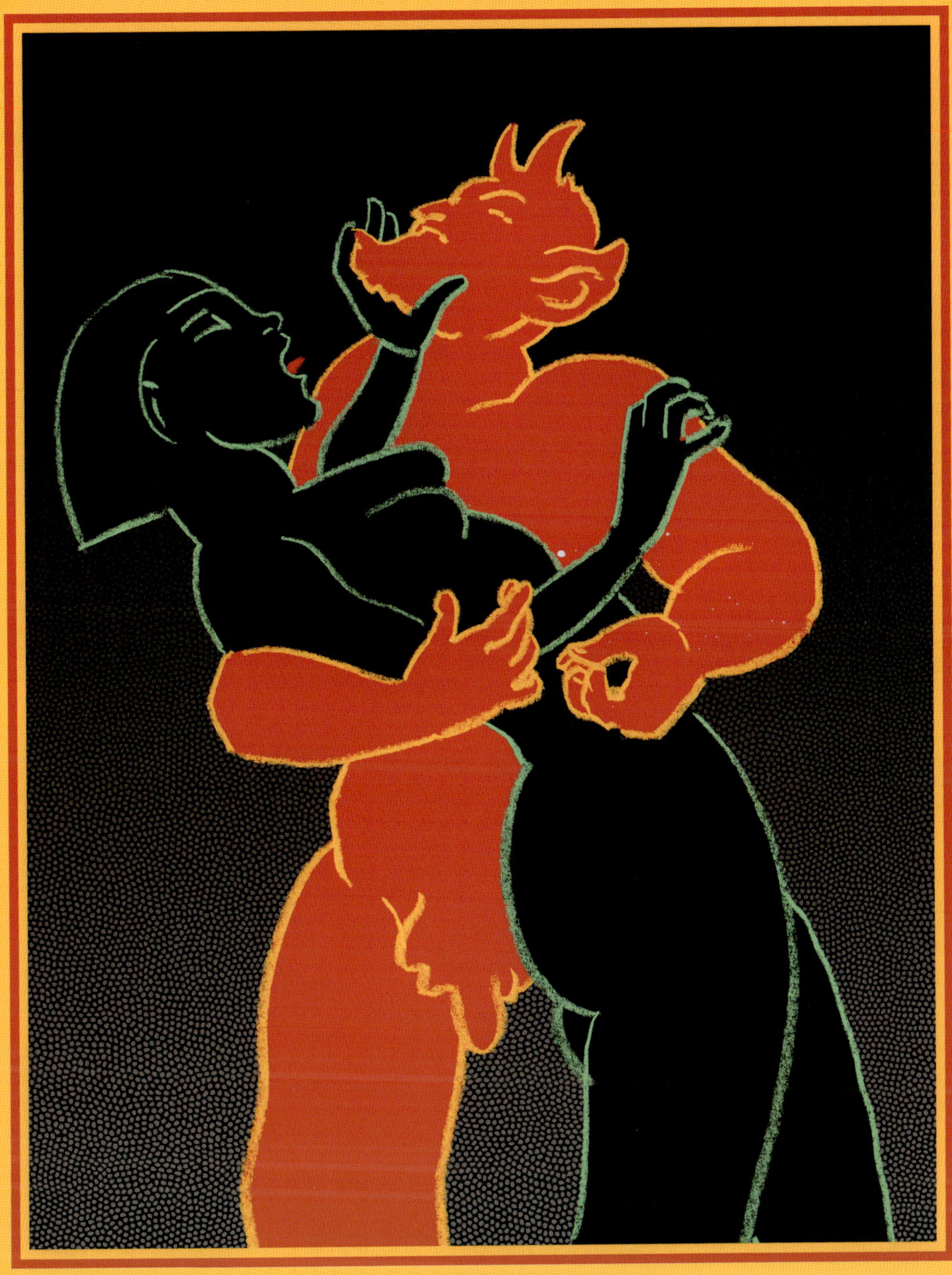

The idea for I Love NY came to me in a cab days after New York State accepted a typographic mark
I came up with. I was doodling on the way to a client meeting and another idea suggested itself. Somehow,
I managed to convince Bill Doyle, the assistant commissioner of commerce, to consider the new design
and get it approved. This little item that almost didn't come into being has become my most frequently
reproduced work.

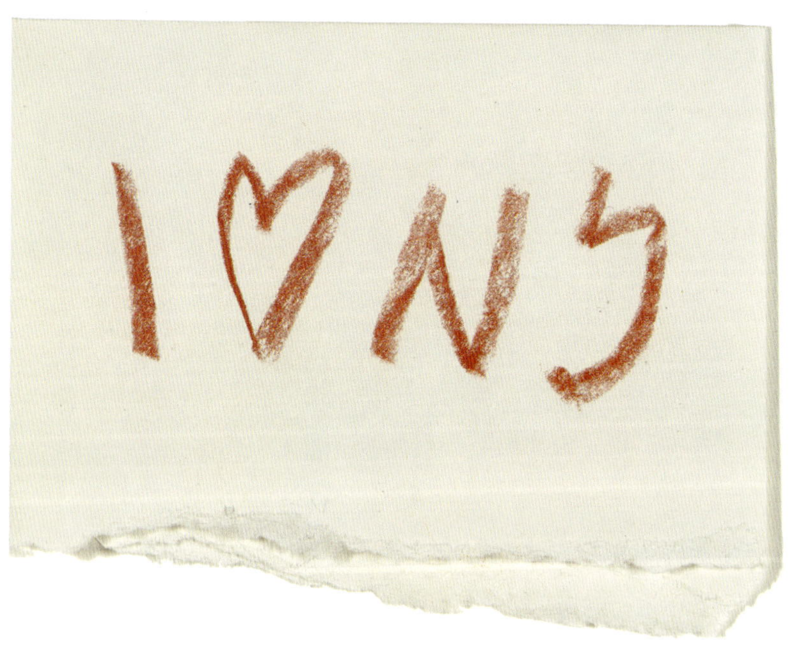

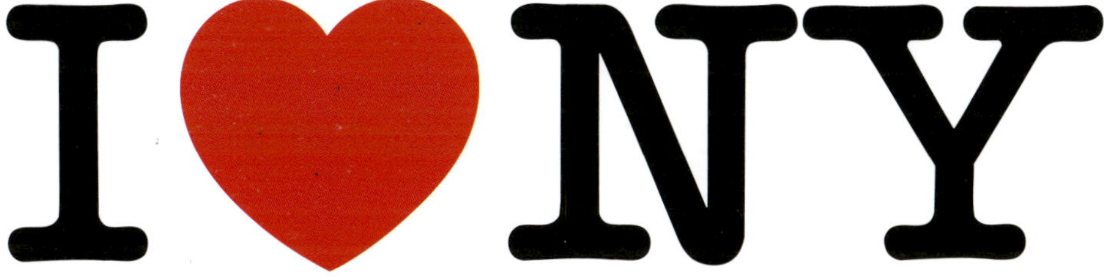

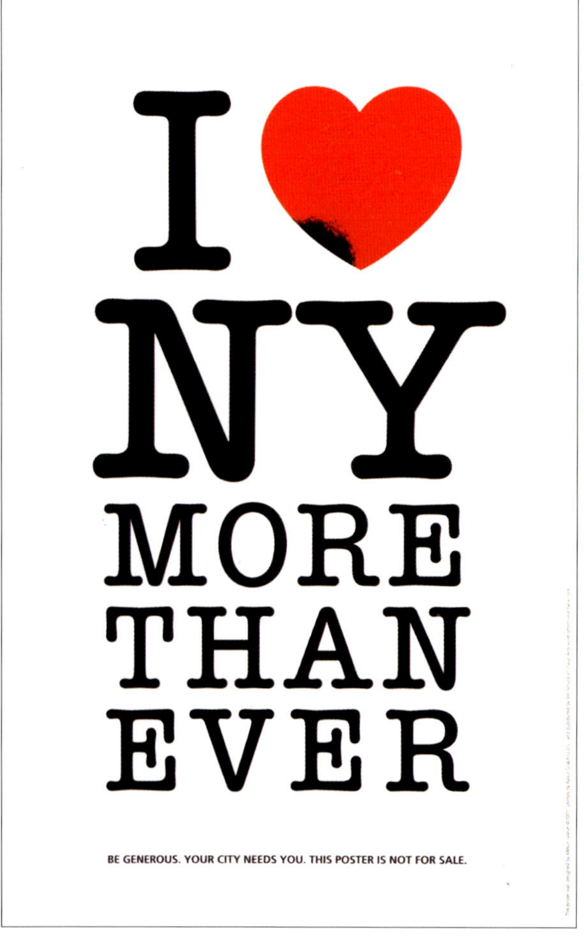

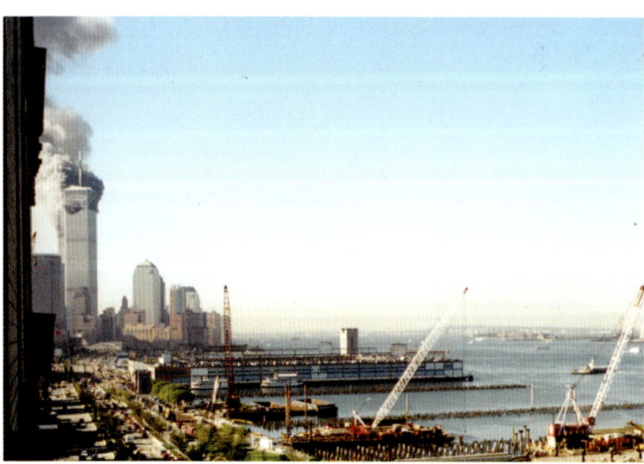

Photo by Cosmos.

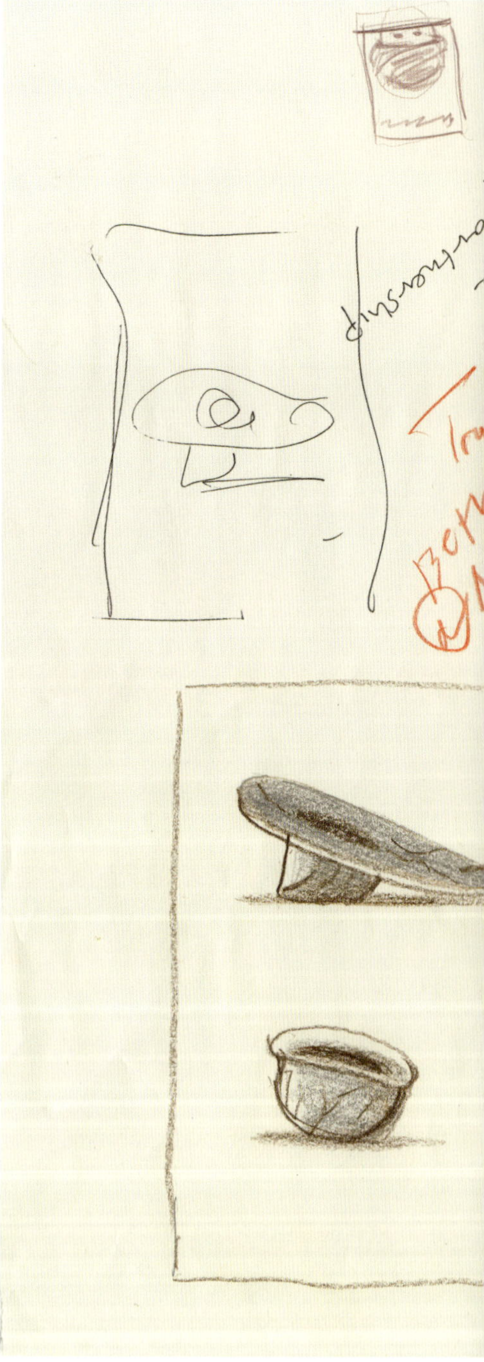

HEARTWORK
WINDOW
POSTERS
DECALS
BUTTONS
ART 4 NY
ALL TOGETHER NOW!
WE WILL NEVER FORGET
KOSNER
HAMIL
SILAS
MARTYL
HUEY
MOVE OUT? NEVER! ♡ NY
I ♥ NY MORE THAN EVER
ART AGAINST TERROR
I ♥ NY MORE THAN EVER
I ♥ NY MORE THAN EVER
I ♥ NY MORE THEN EVER, MOVE OUT? NEVER!
I ♥ NY MORE THEN EVER
I ♥ NY MORE THAN EVER
YOUR NEIGHBOR IS NOT THE ENEMY
OUR

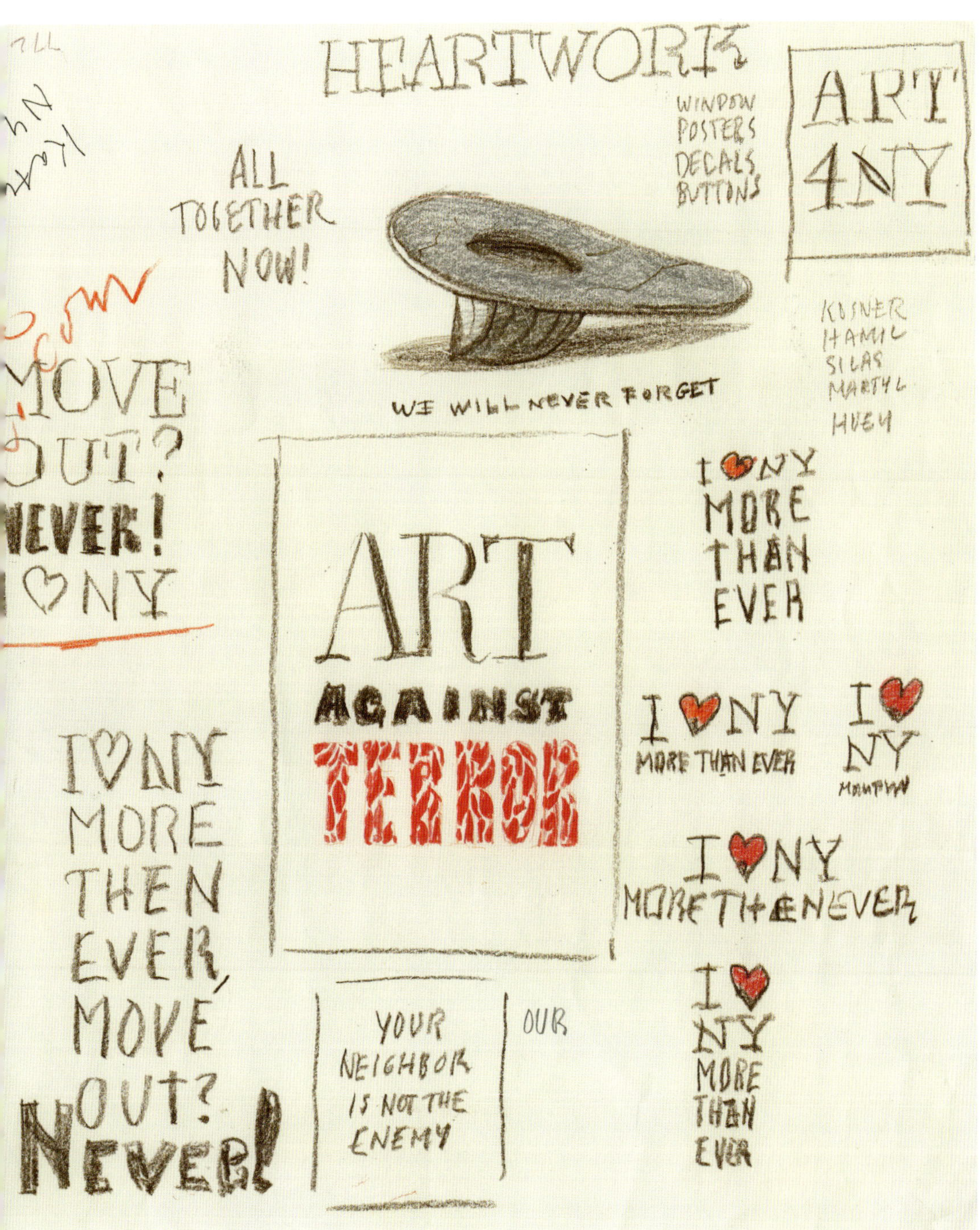

Sketches.

A series of preliminary studies in watercolor yielded the poster solution in two colors, red and green, which overlap in printing to produce black.

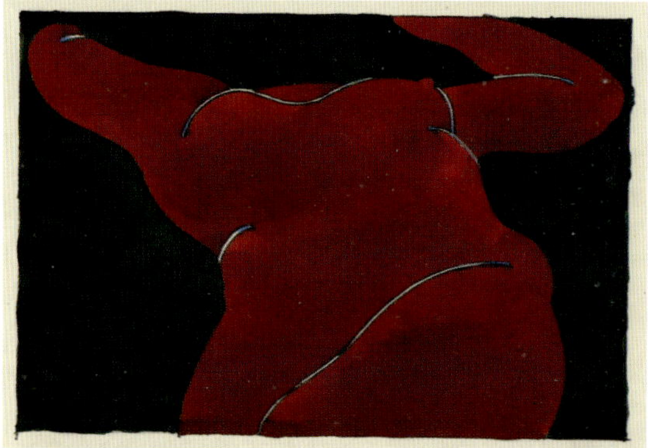

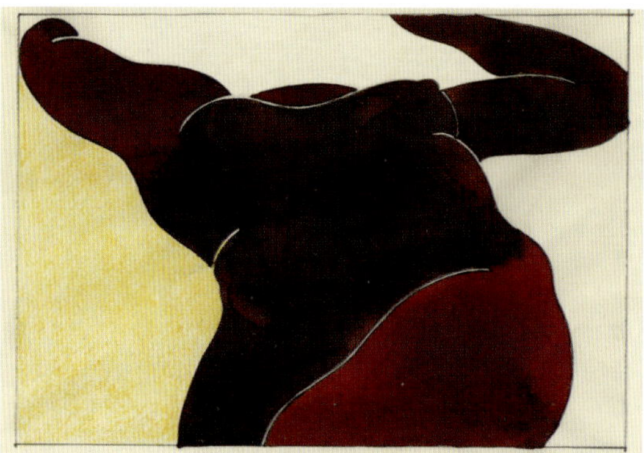

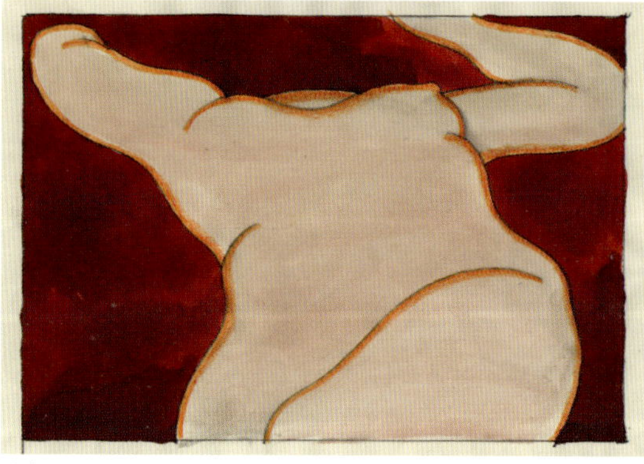

Color variations.

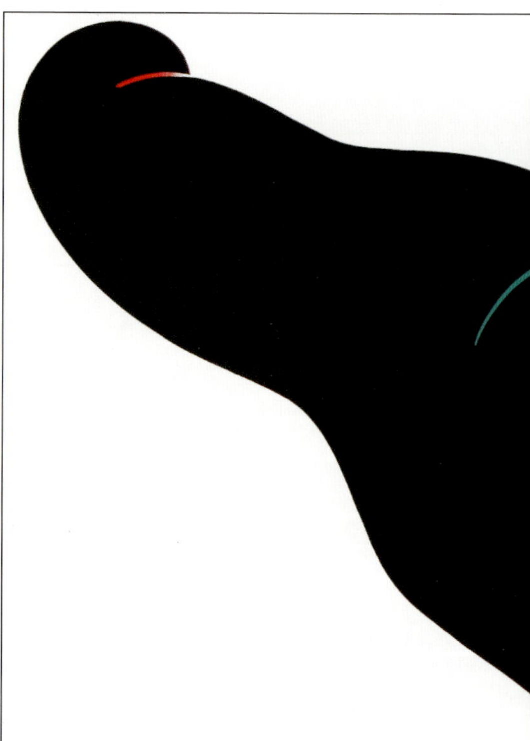

Final poster.

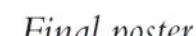

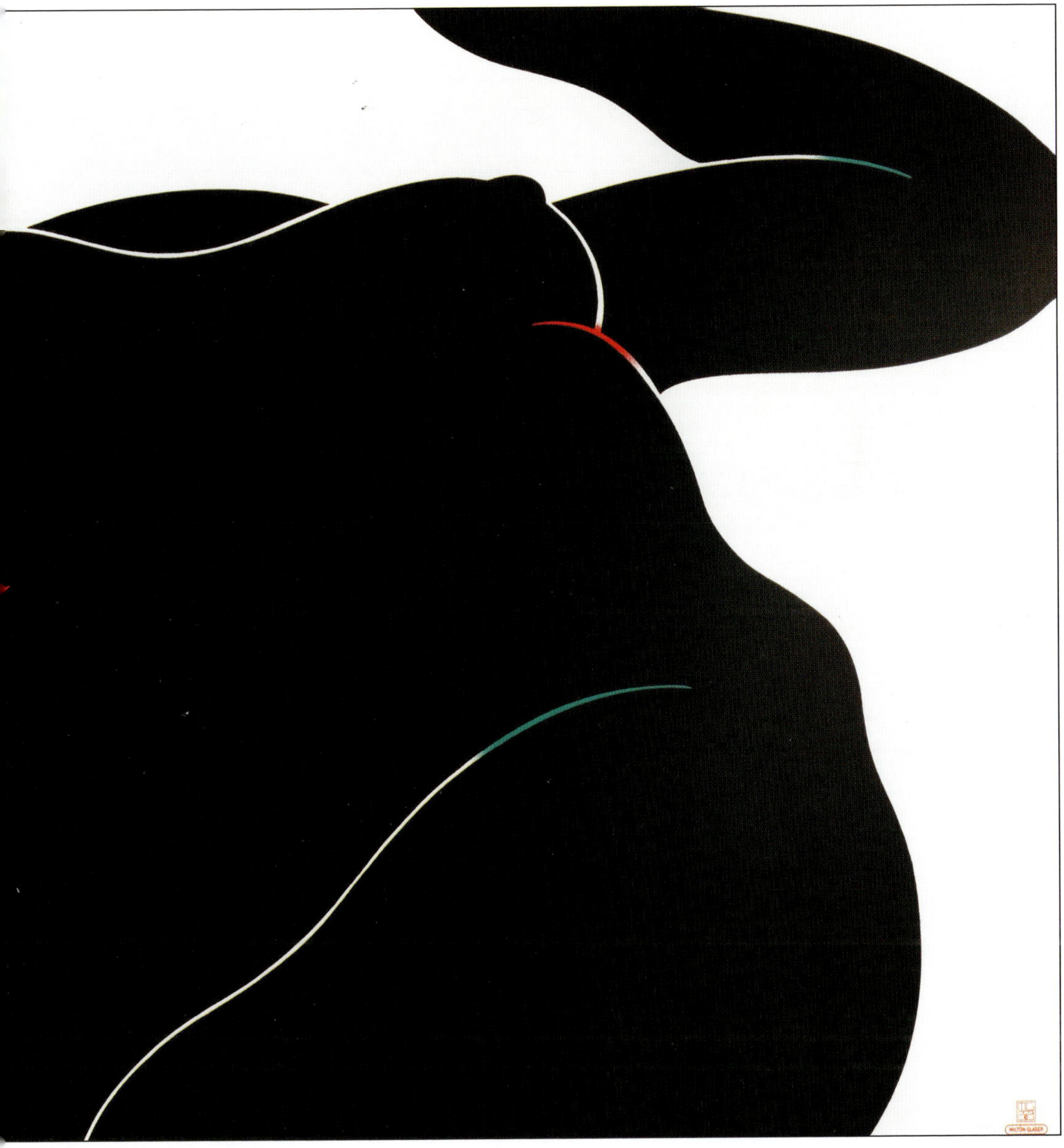

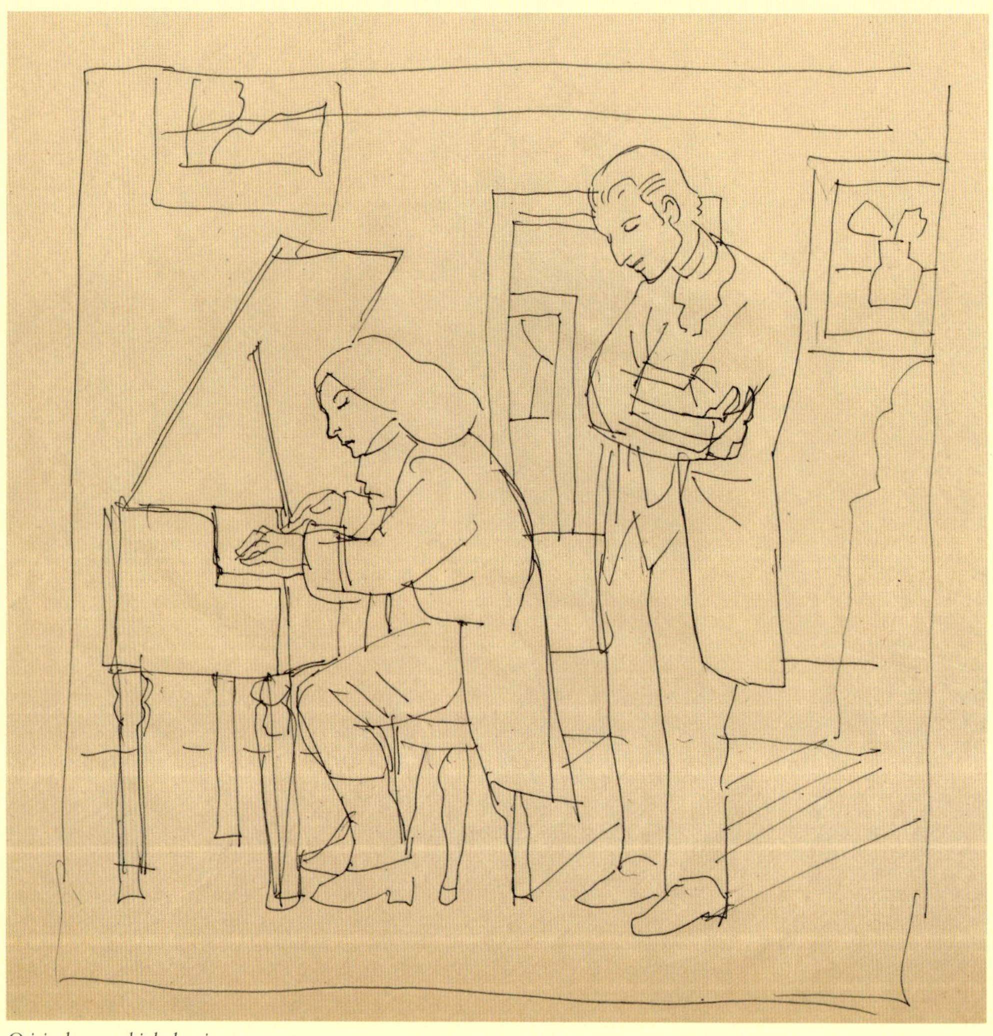

Original pen and ink drawing.

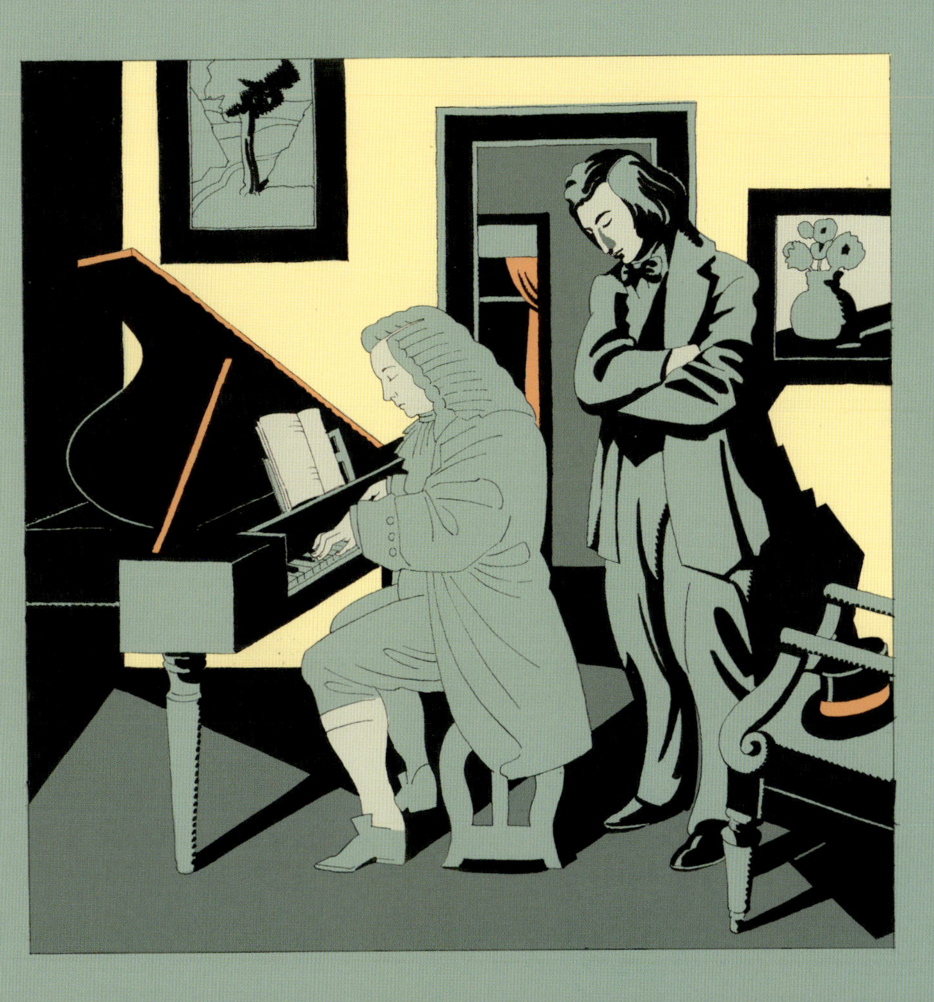

Final print.

This portrait of a soldier for a book of Guillaume Apollinaire stories was transformed in execution, imposing a vase of flowers on the original version of the illustration.

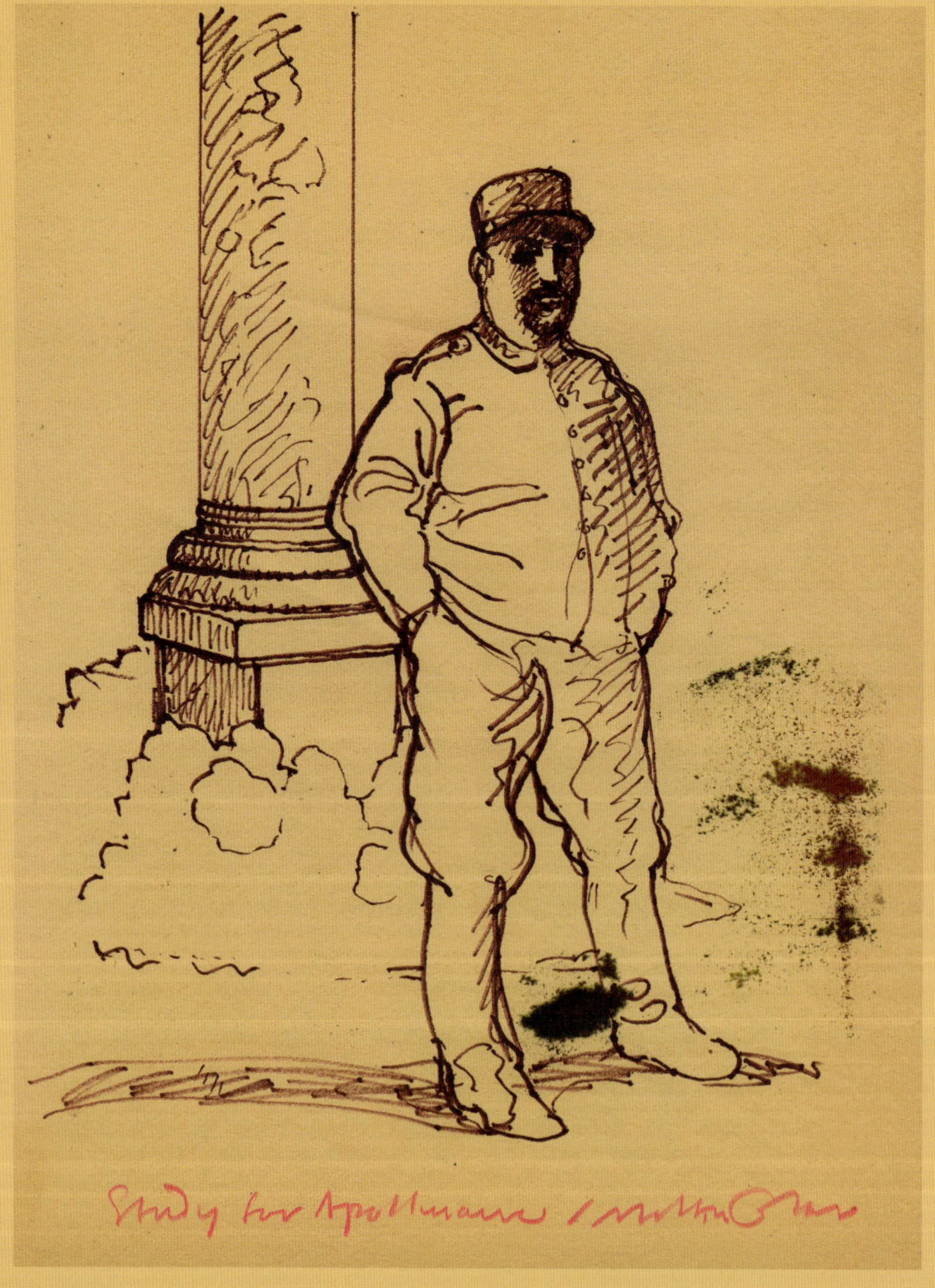

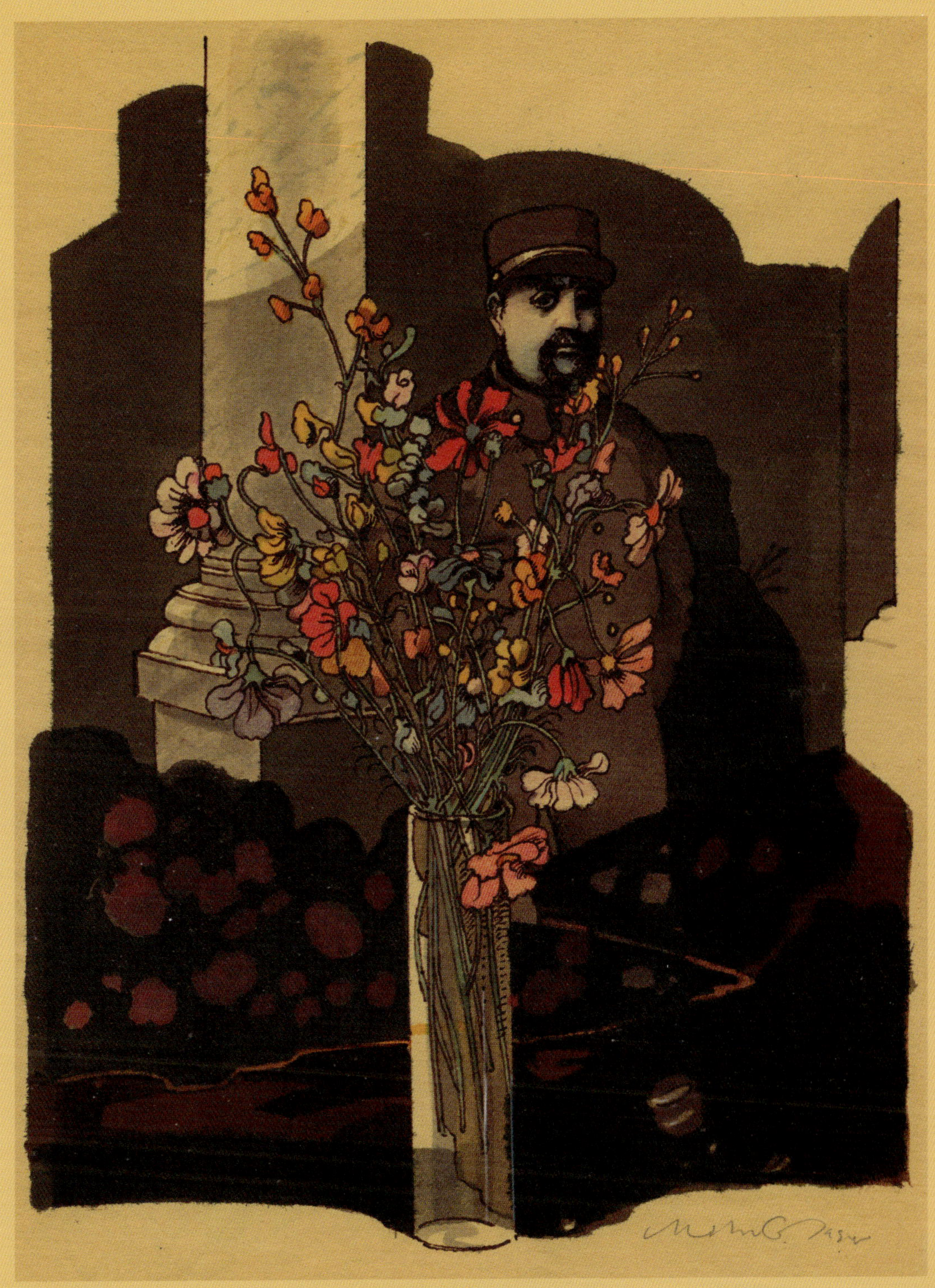

This drawing of Pan listening to music starts fuzzy and becomes increasingly sharp, although the earlier sketches seem more emotional and poetic than the final version.

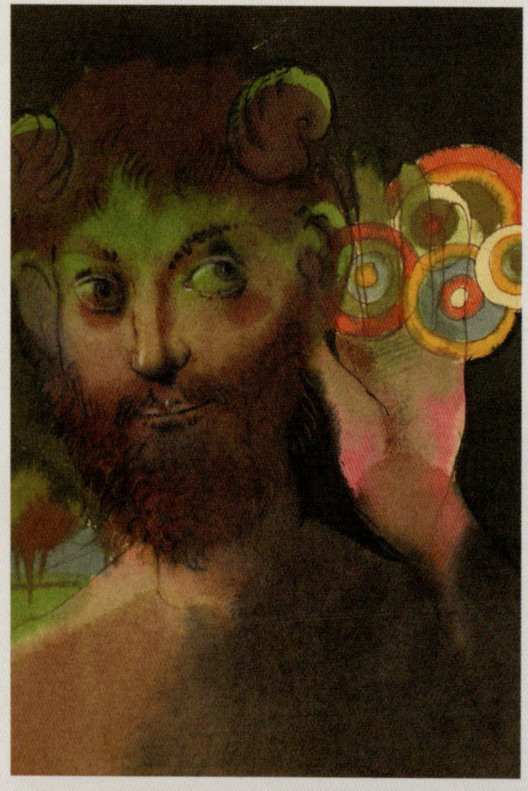

Preliminary sketches.

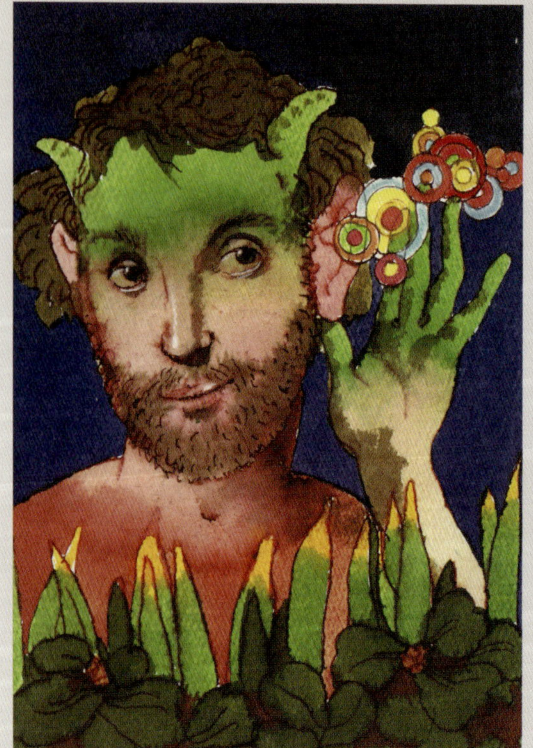

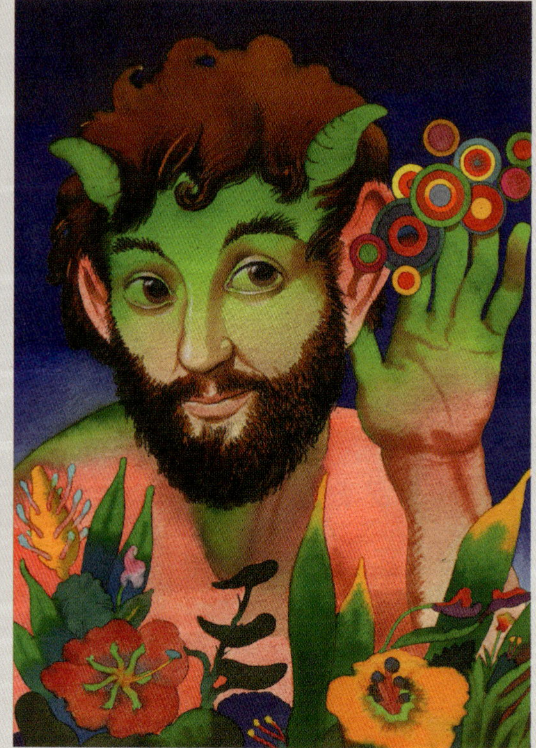

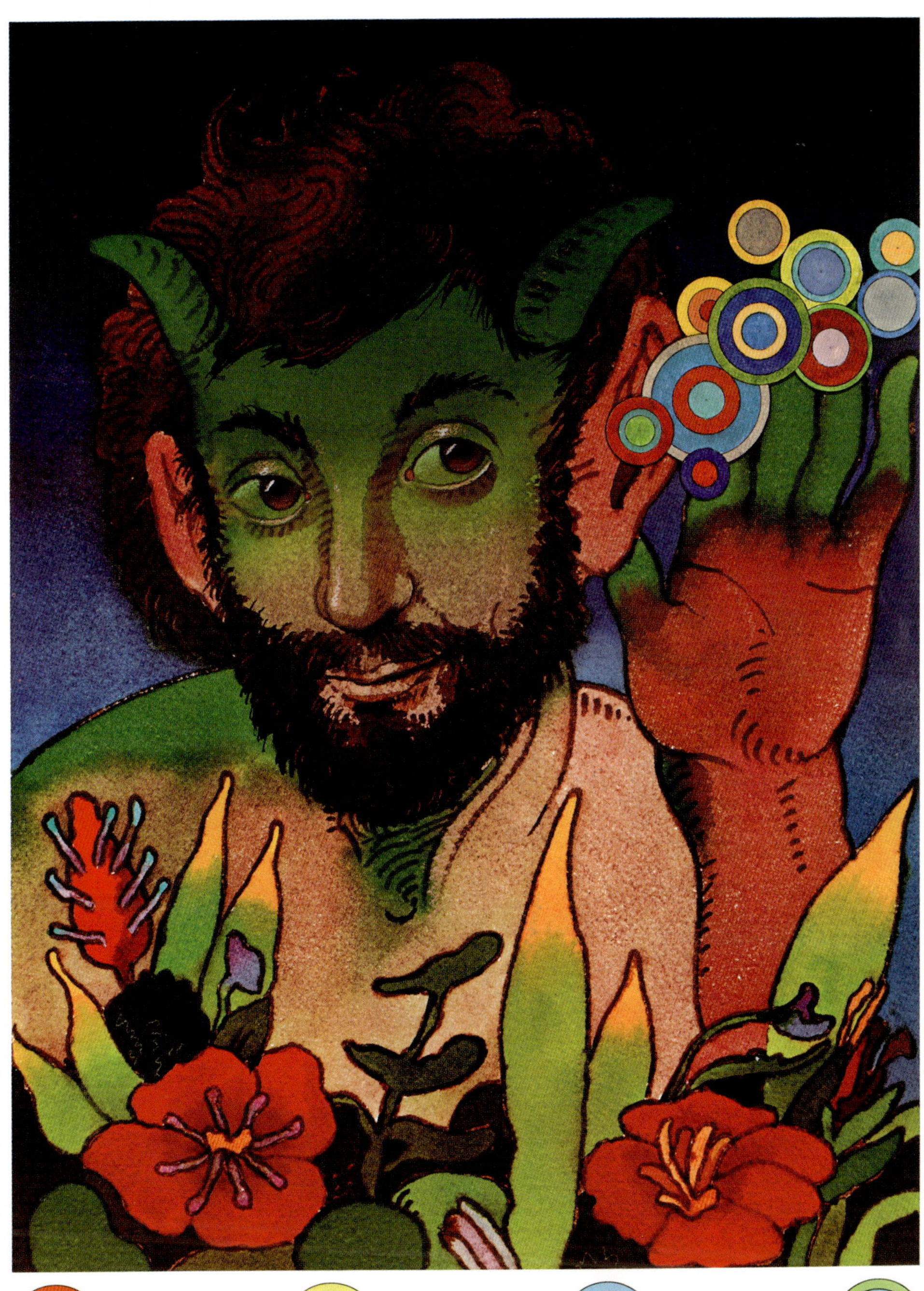
Saratoga Performing Arts Center, Saratoga Springs, New York
S P A C
Saratoga Performing Arts Center, Saratoga Springs, New York
MILTON GLASER

The progression from sketch to finish is dependent on the blue diagonal form, contrasting with the red of the rest of the painting. The sketch describes the subject and the scale. In the execution, the blue diagonal form contrasting with the red becomes the most important element.

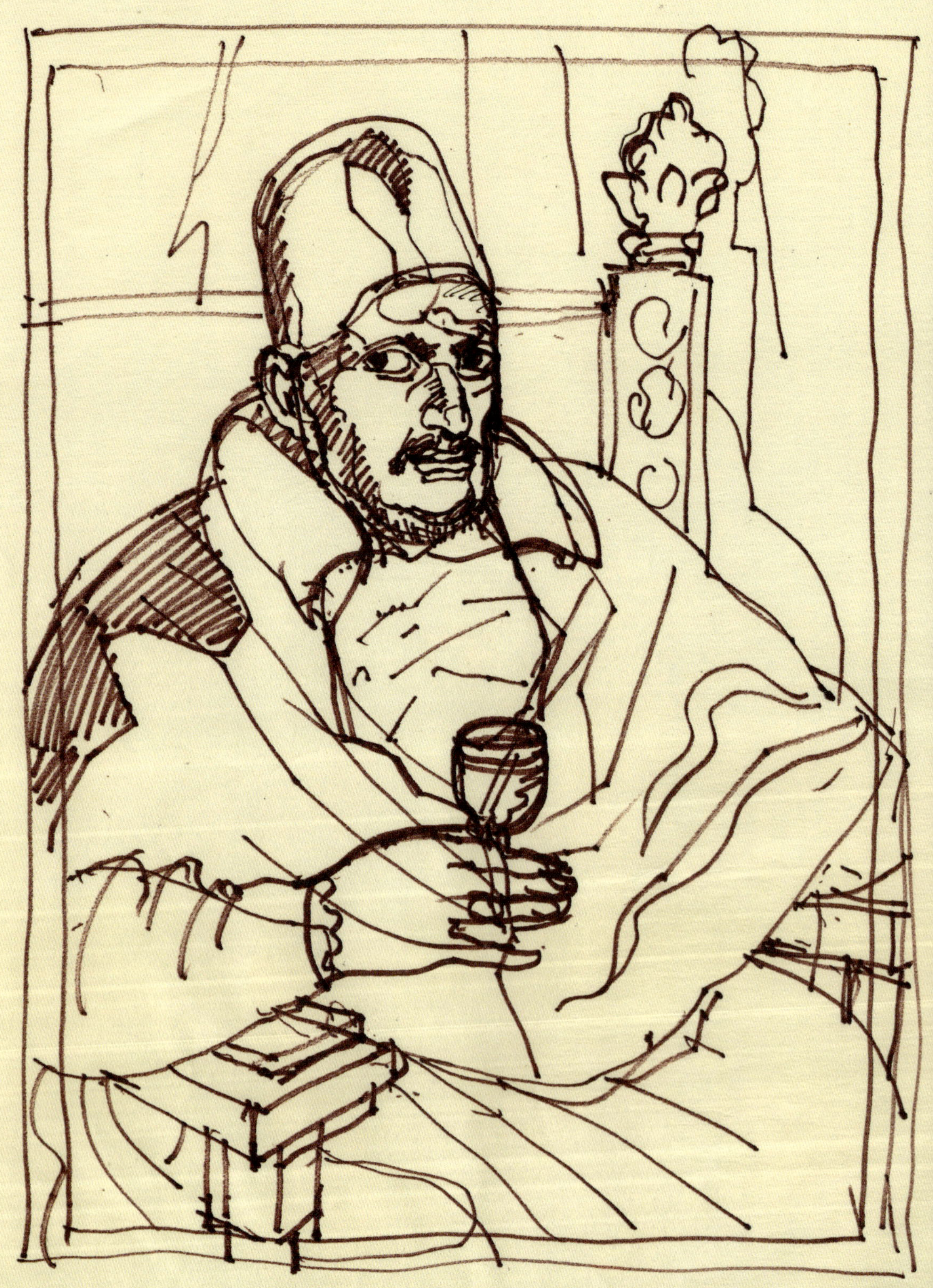

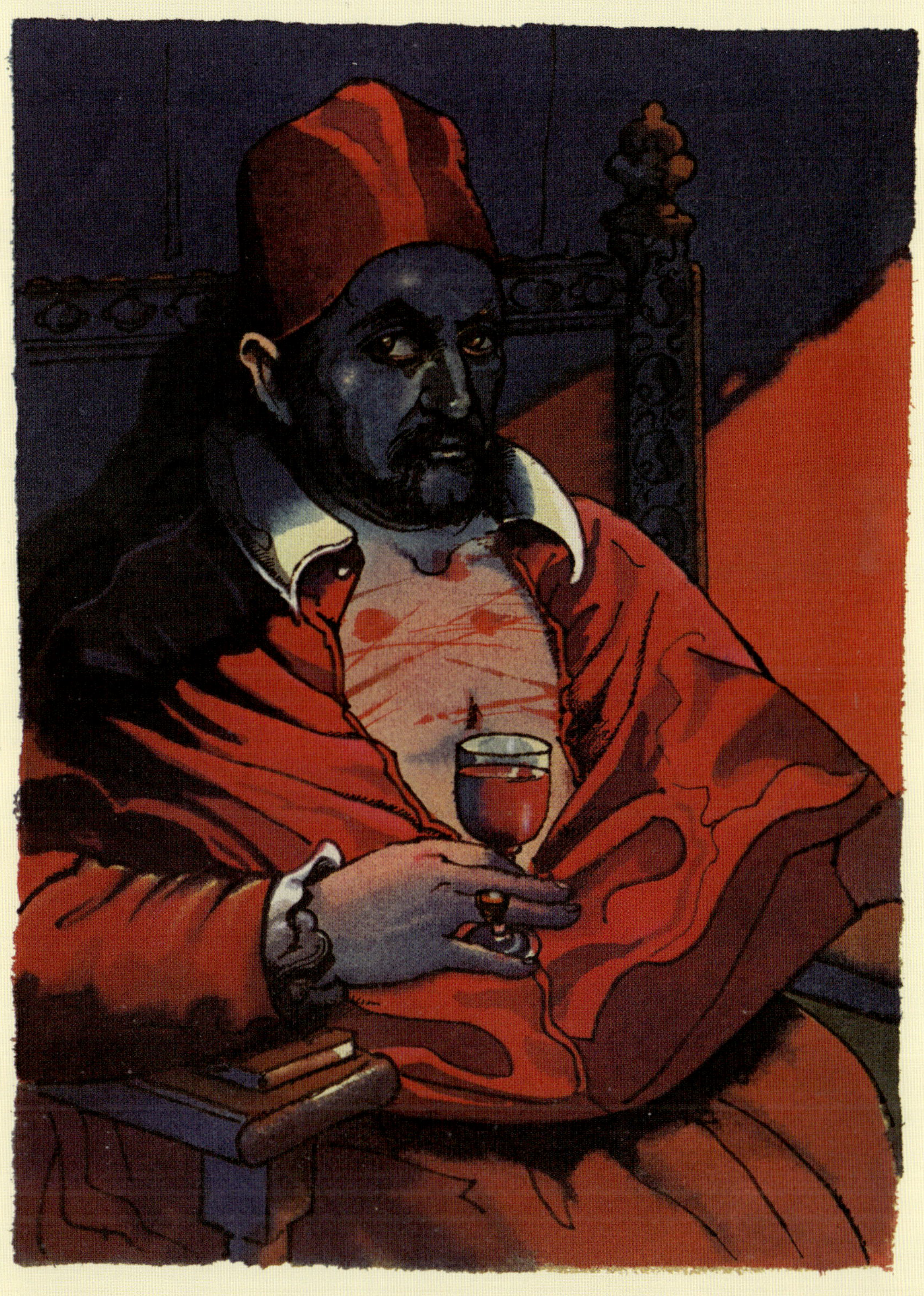

I always loved this painting, *Bath of Psyche* by Bernardino Luini, a disciple of Leonardo da Vinci. I decided to use it as the basis for a print. I changed the proportions to make it more conventional, rescaled the figures, and imposed a new color sensibility. The idea of using old masters as subject matter is a manifestation of modernism. After *Guernica*, Pablo Picasso almost never created new subject matter and used historical references as his content.

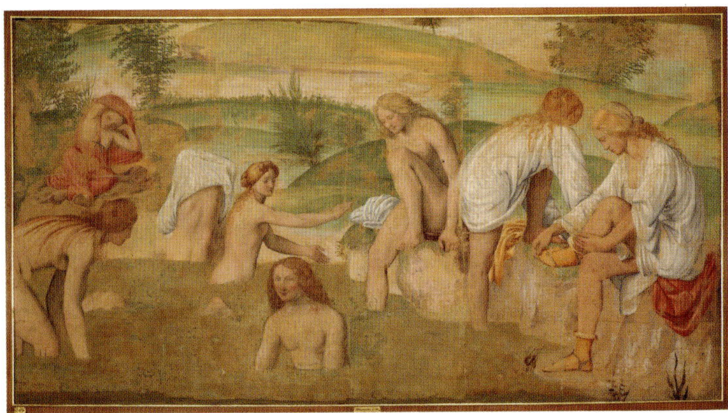

Original painting by Bernardino Luini.

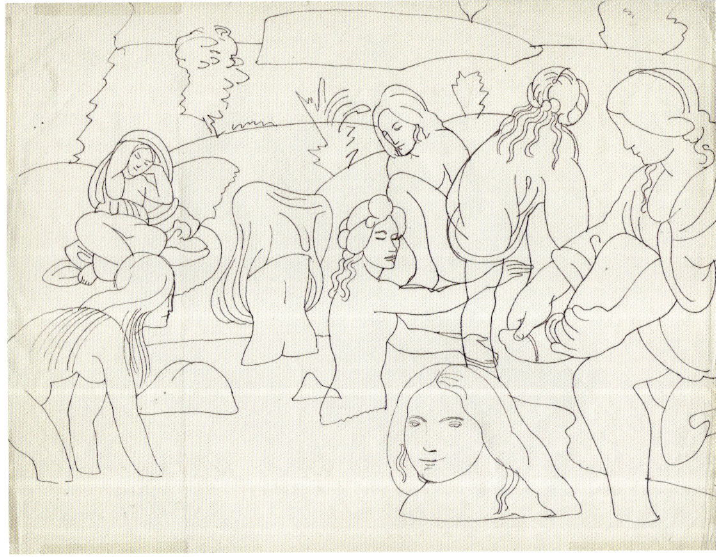

Pencil sketch showing change of scale and proportion.

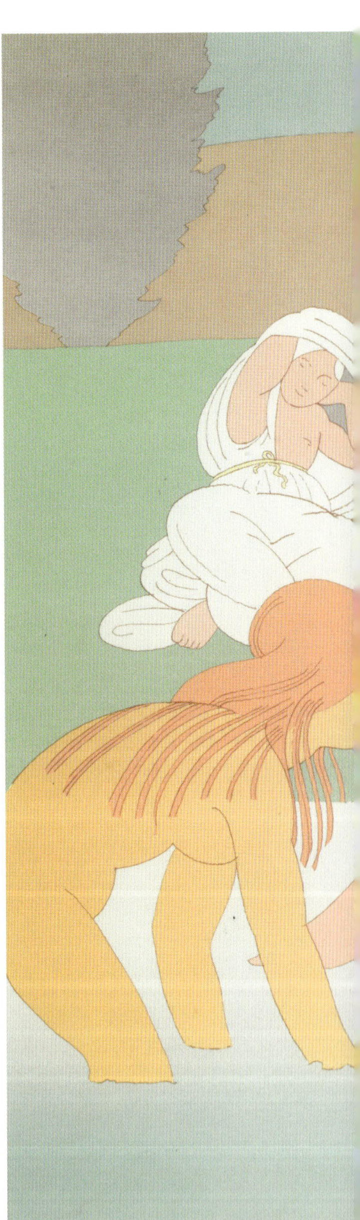

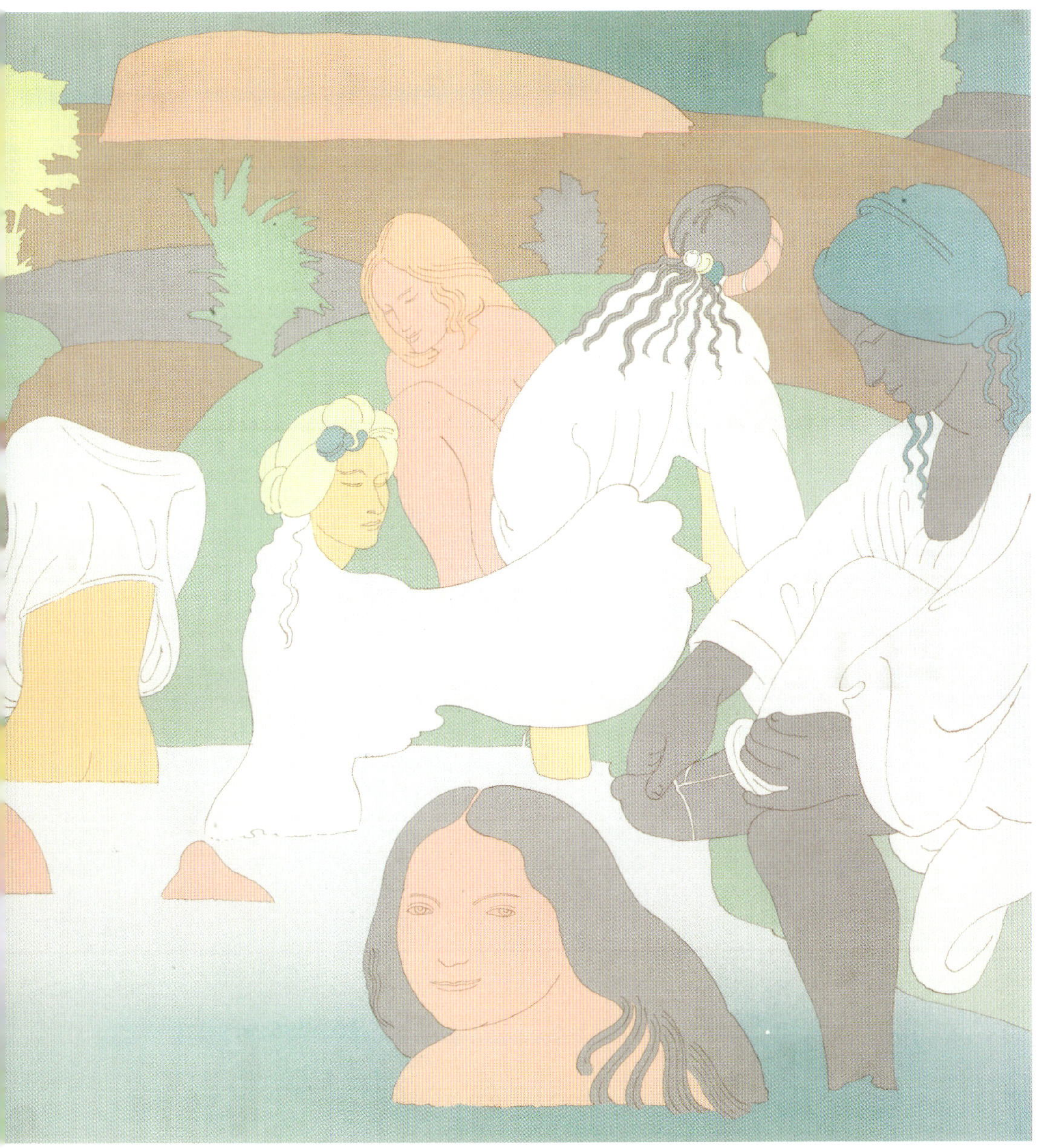

Final print.

Alessi, a great client who manufactures metal kitchenware among other products, decided to go into the wood objects business. It recommended the use of a forest creature named Twergi as a way of identifying a new company with references to forest mythology. My early sketches began with pine-tree shapes and triangular forms to create a movable toy that served as a trademark.

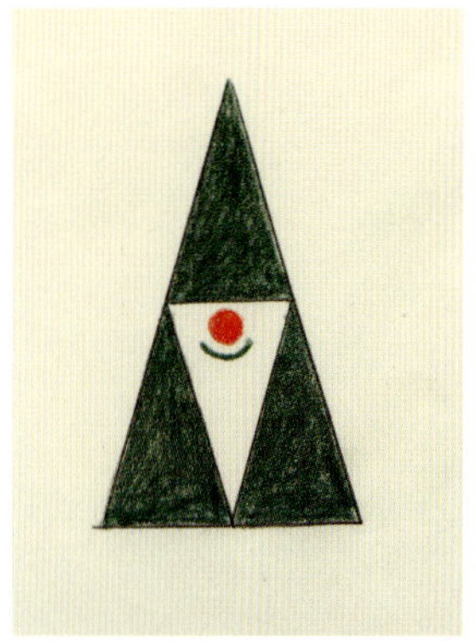

Color study.

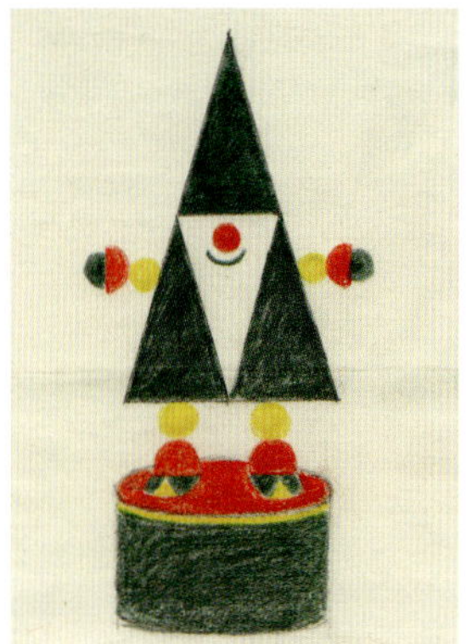

Form and color study.

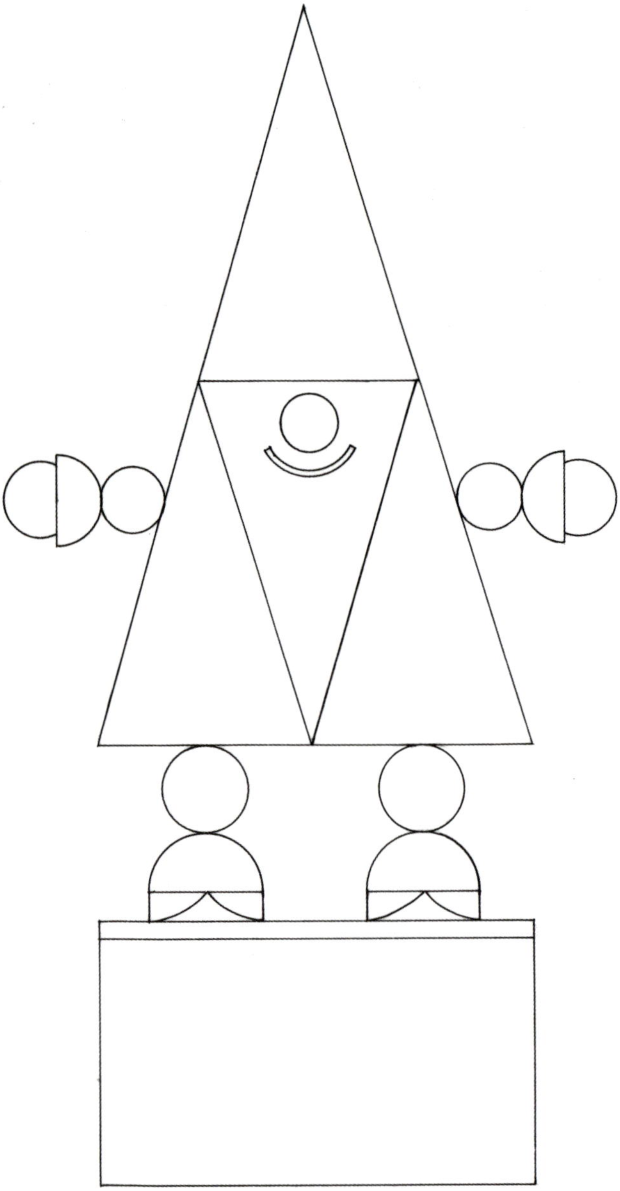

Original drawing showing triangular forms.

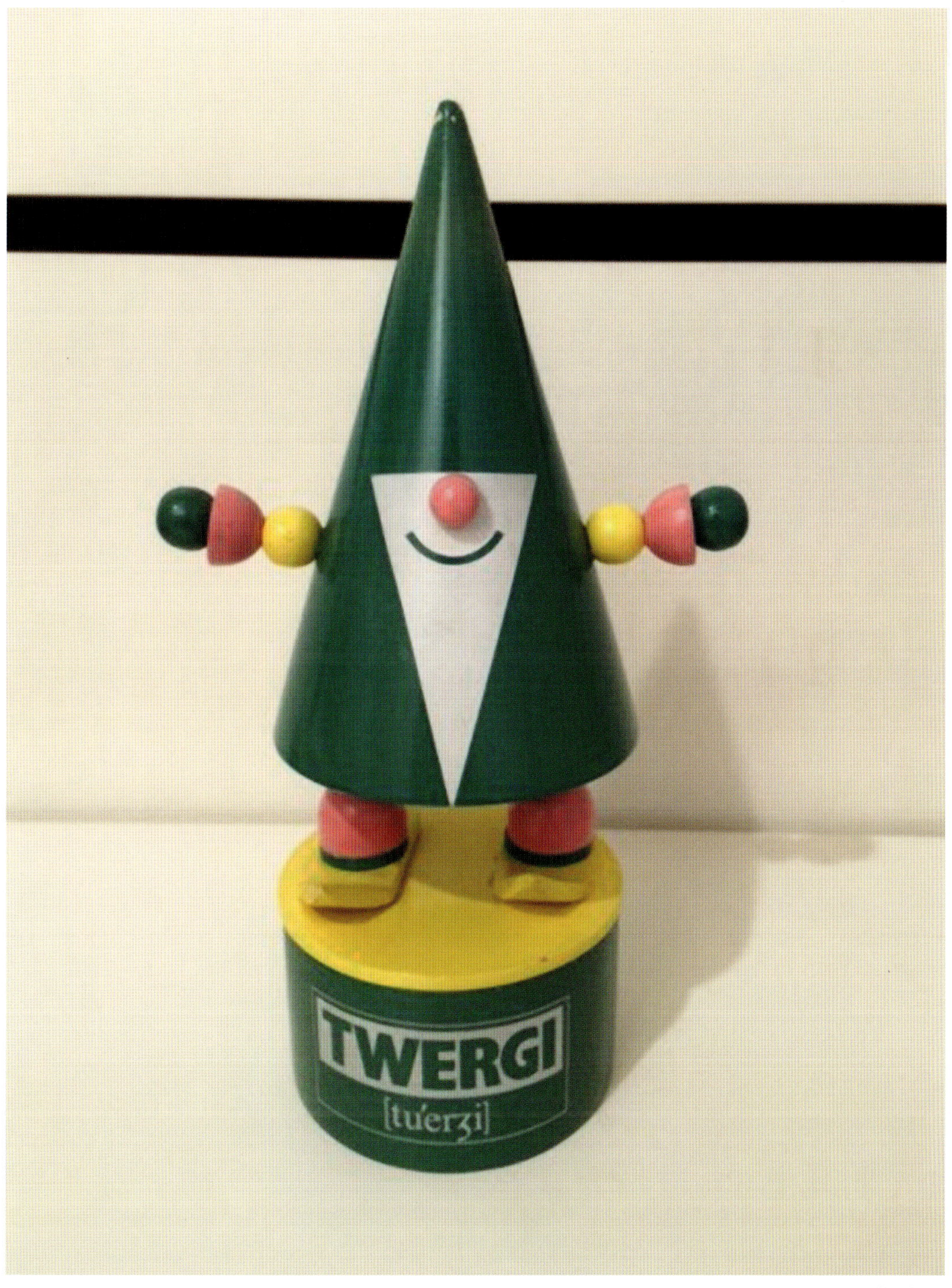

Final sculpture.

The fundamental idea of a new record company breaking through the resistance of the old guard is what we wanted to convey here in this poster for Poppy Records.

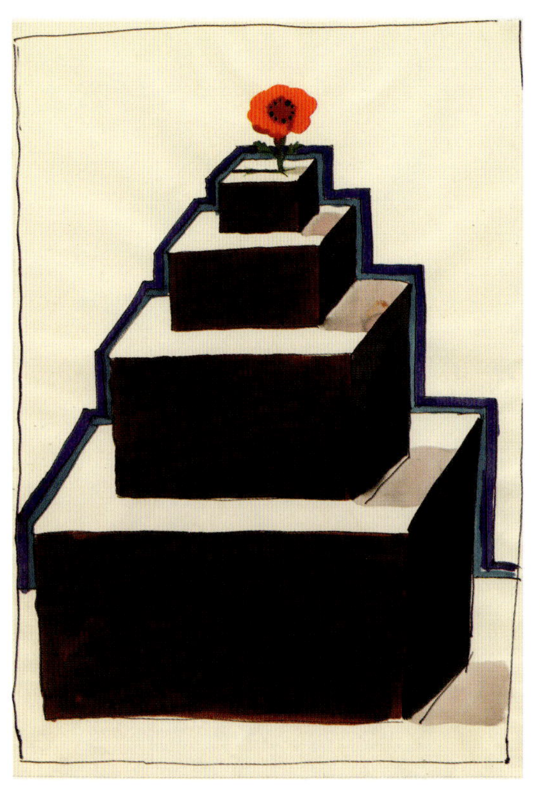

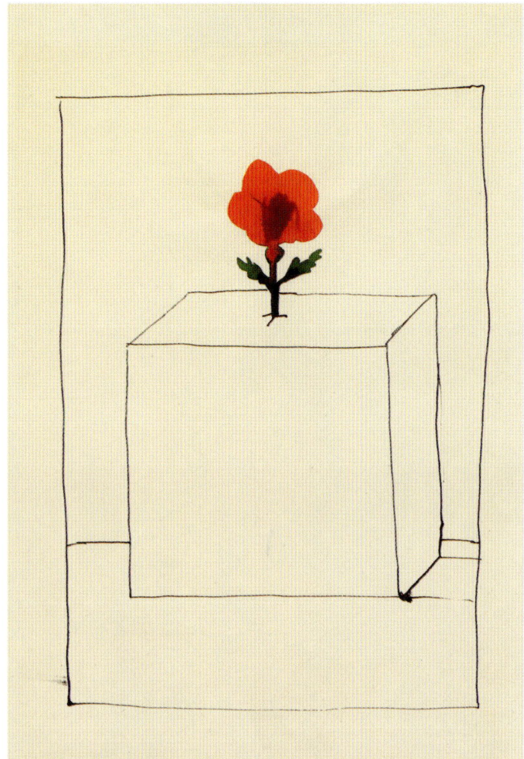

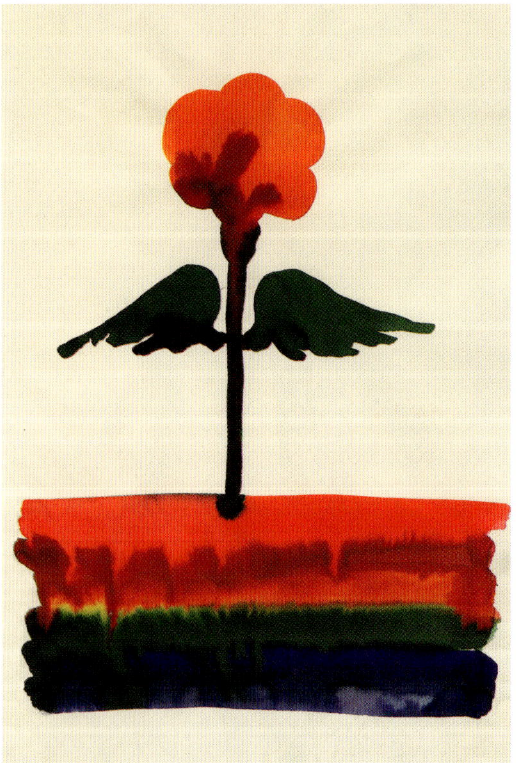

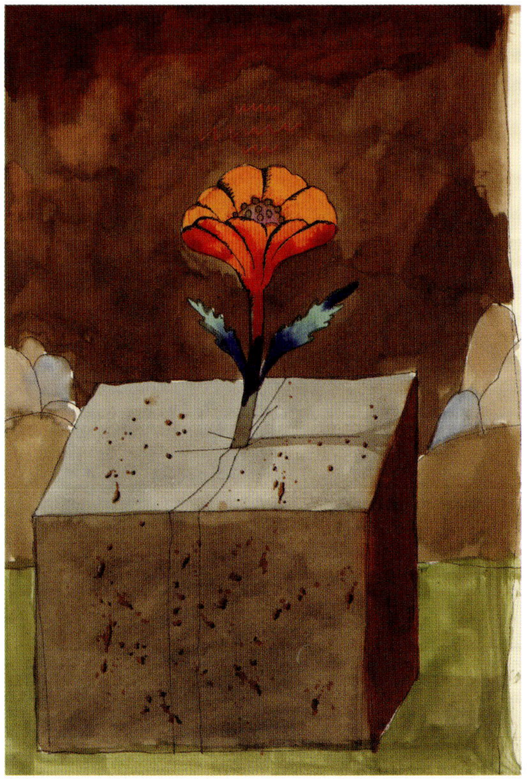

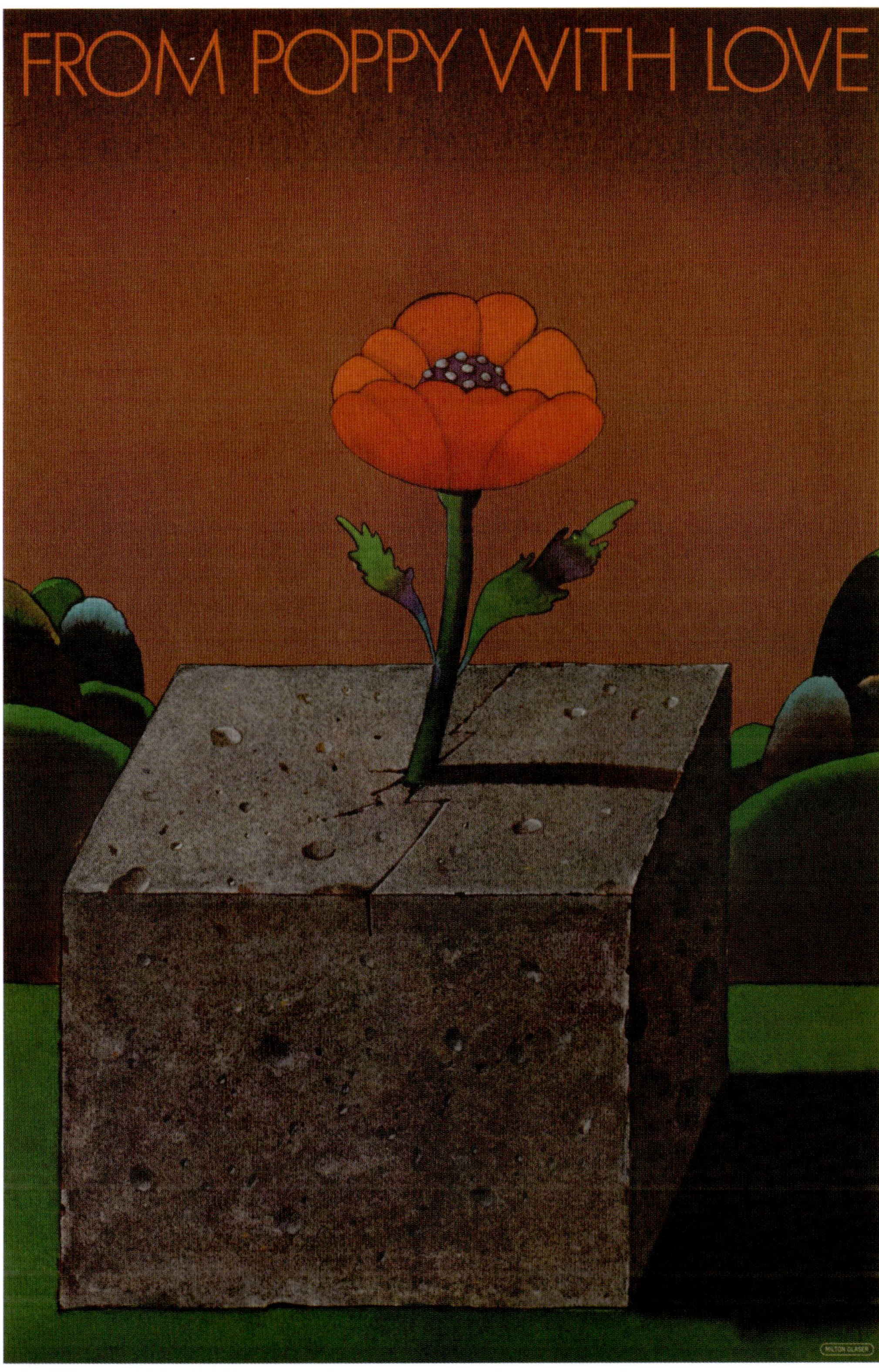
FROM POPPY WITH LOVE
MILTON GLASER

This children's book establishes a space for individual characters to enter and perform. The sequence shows them encountering one another and becomes chaotic as each letterform expresses its identity. Finally they discover they have a larger purpose that depends on cooperation: the creation of words.

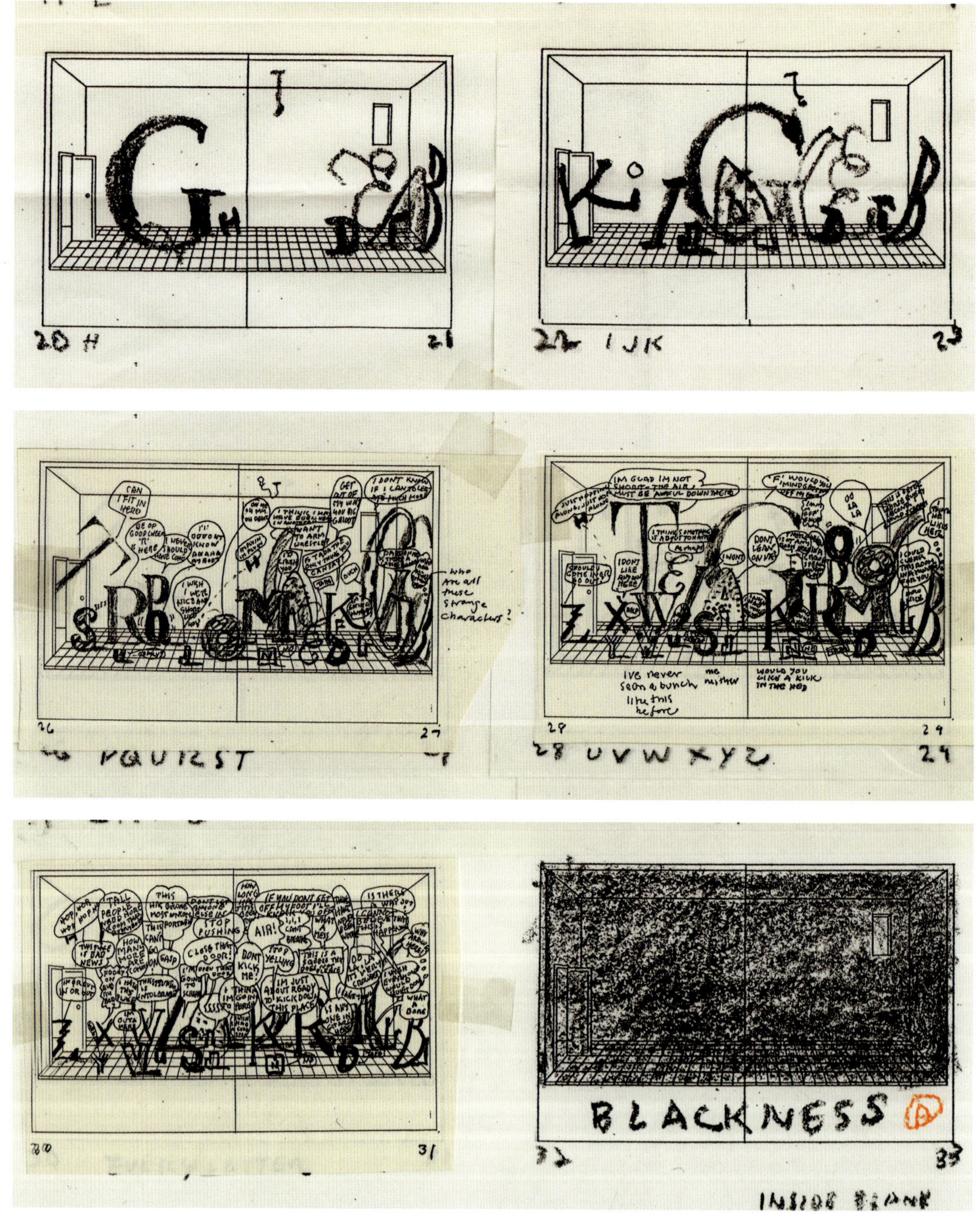

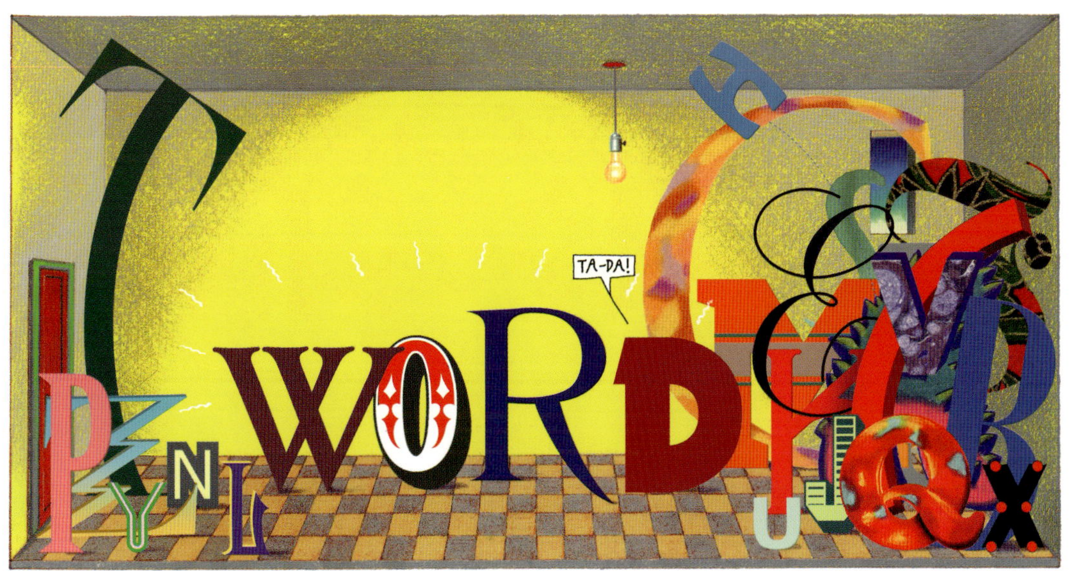
TA-DA!

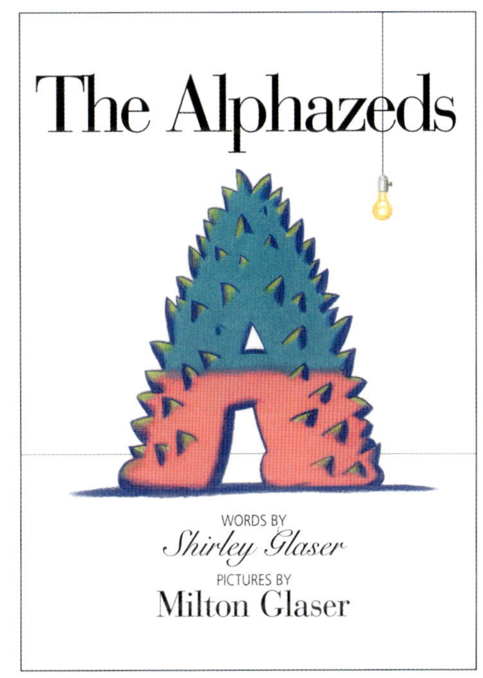
The Alphazeds
WORDS BY
Shirley Glaser
PICTURES BY
Milton Glaser

The sketch for this piece went in another direction than the finish and included the sky, a vase of flowers, and a dimensional ladder casting a shadow. Probably it was more interesting than the final result, which suggests a Joan Miró painting but is less complex than the original idea.

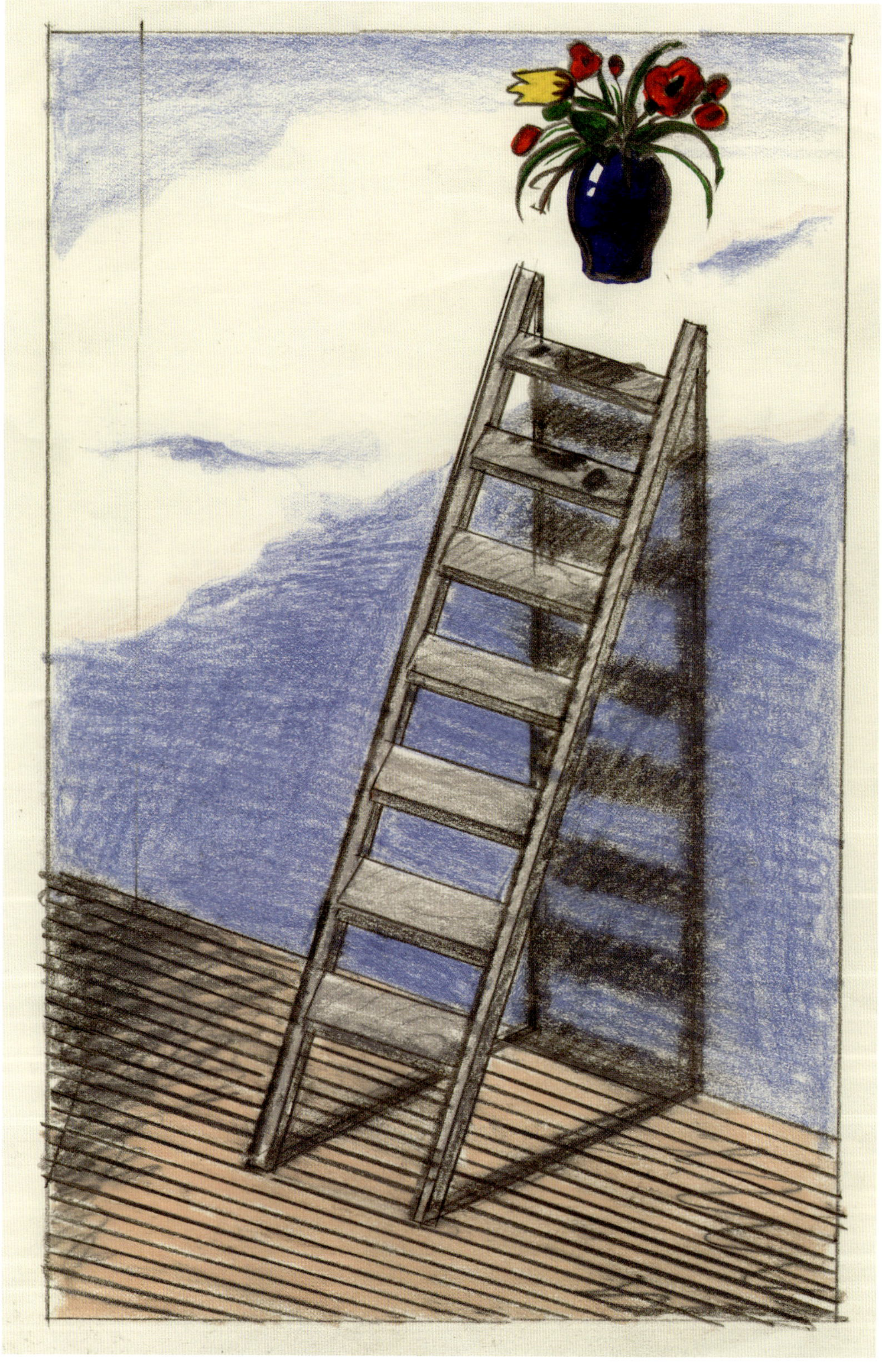

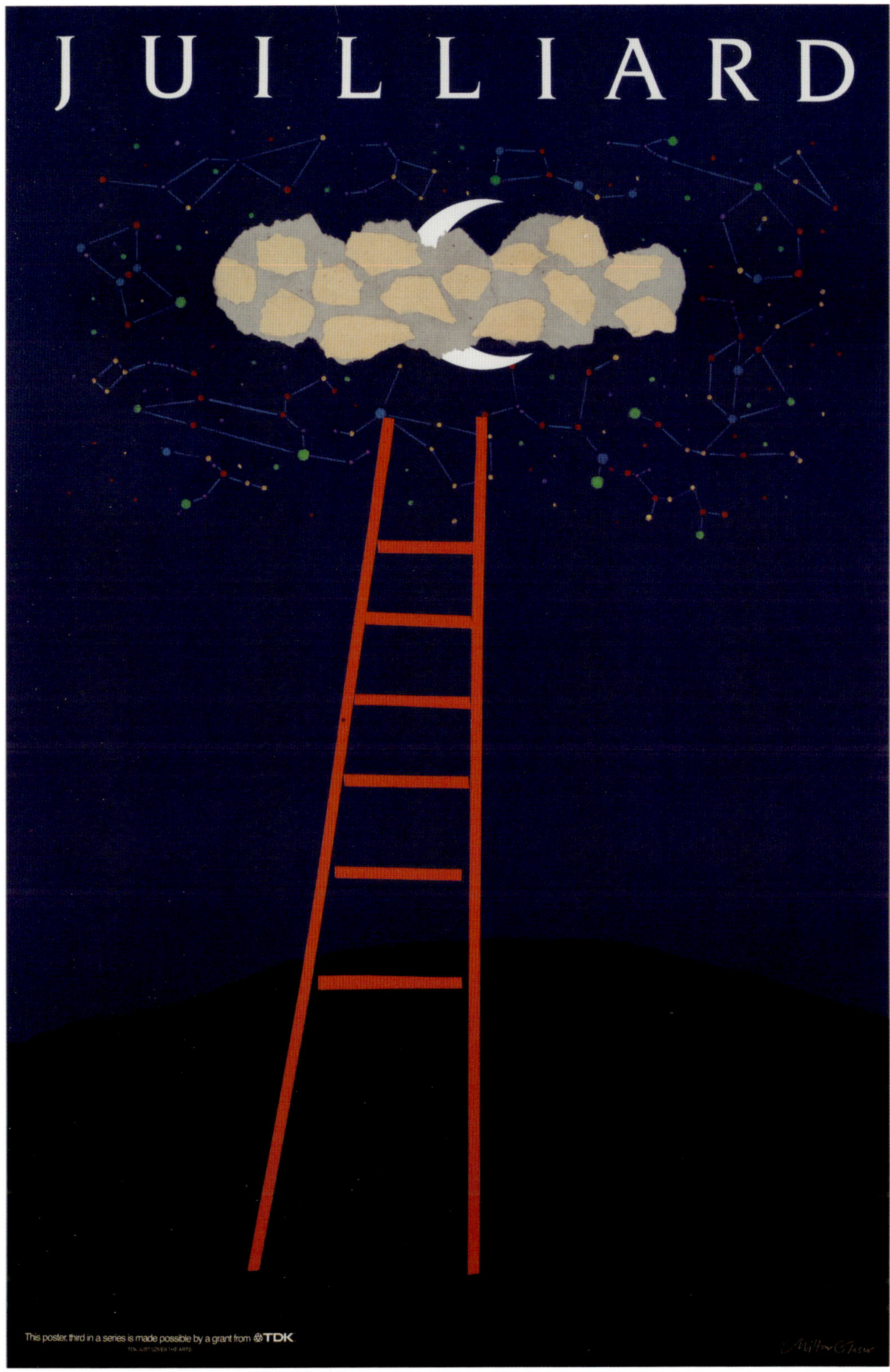
JUILLIARD
This poster, third in a series is made possible by a grant from TDK
TDK JUST LOVES THE ARTS

After beginning with a more naturalistic approach, a stylized version influenced by Felix Vallotton seemed appropriate. The imposition of a grid of dots adds richness to the surface.

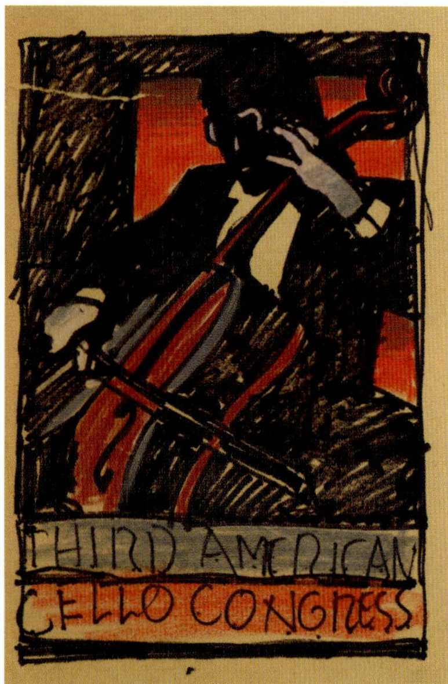
THIRD AMERICAN
CELLO CONGRESS

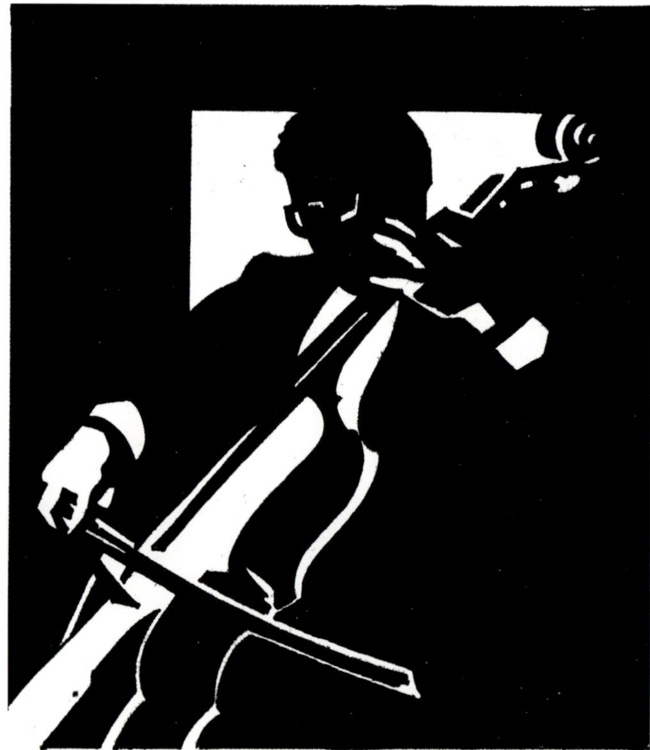

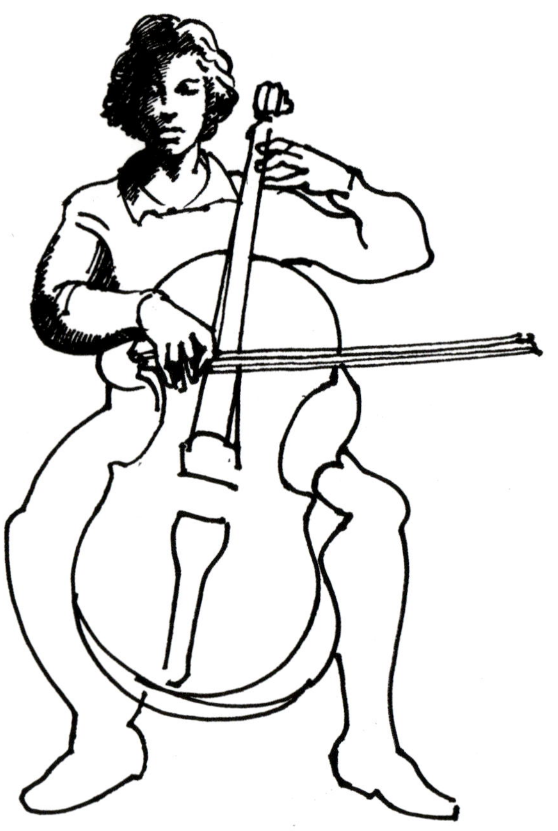

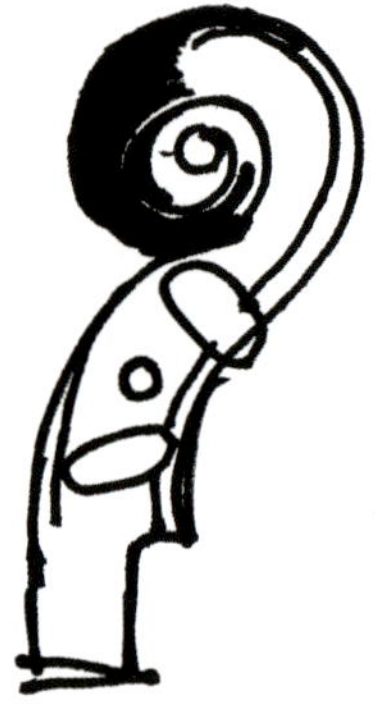

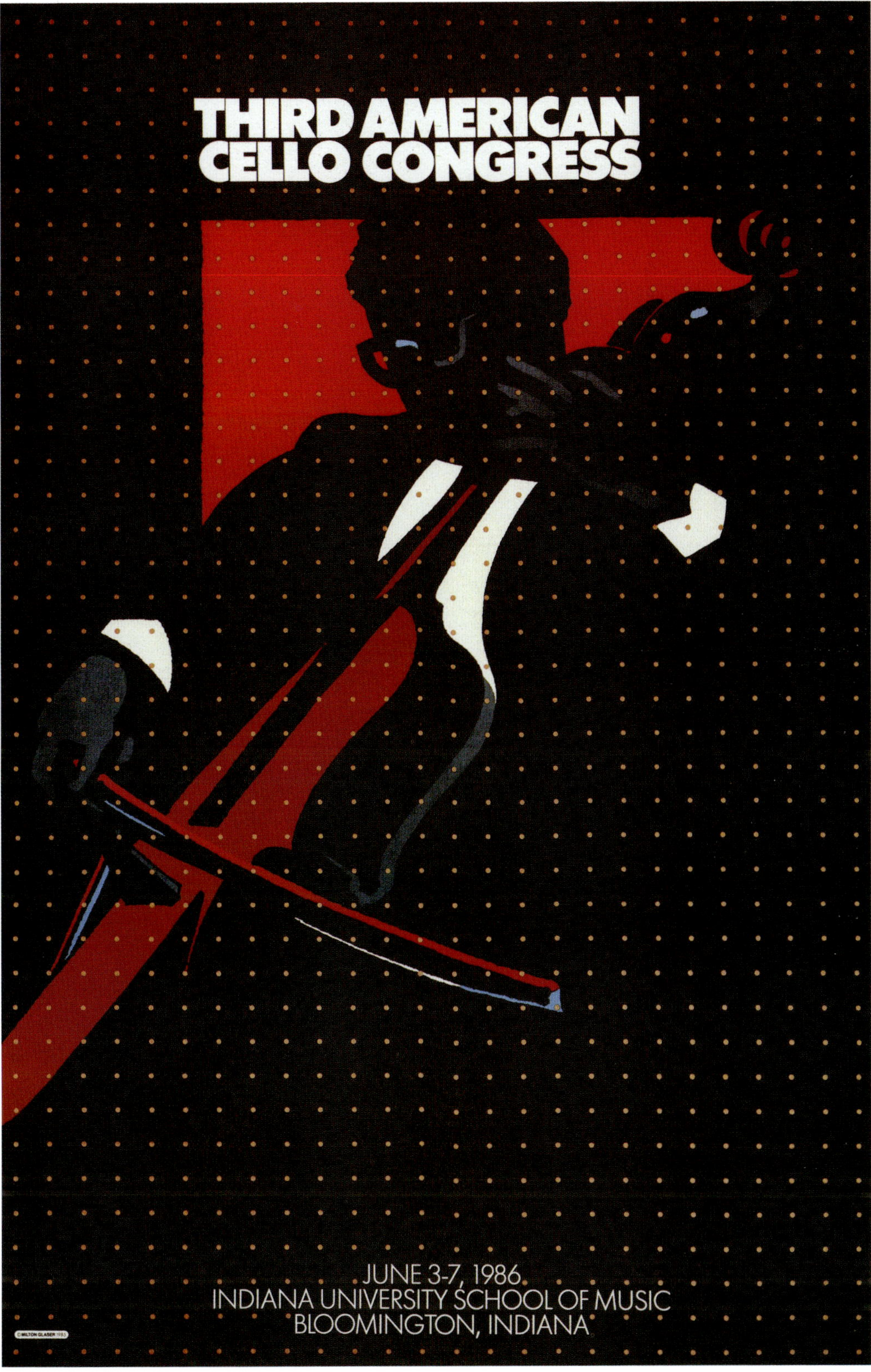
THIRD AMERICAN
CELLO CONGRESS
JUNE 3-7, 1986
INDIANA UNIVERSITY SCHOOL OF MUSIC
BLOOMINGTON, INDIANA

The original idea was about rejuvenation or rebirth. That idea seemed less significant as the work developed.
It ultimately became a division between modernism on the left and romanticism on the right.

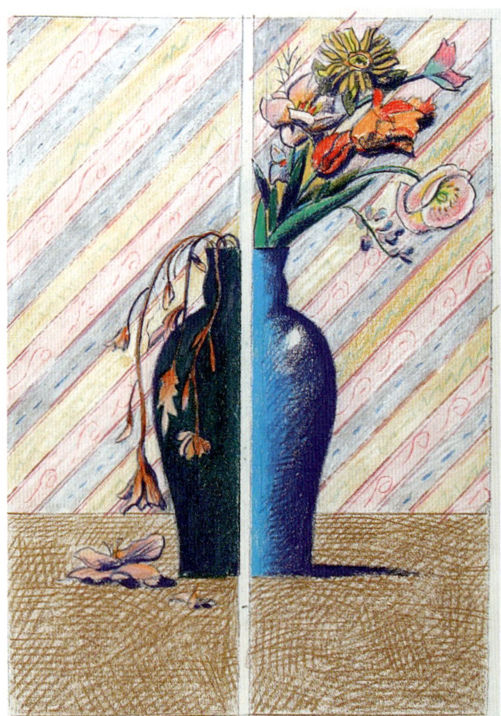

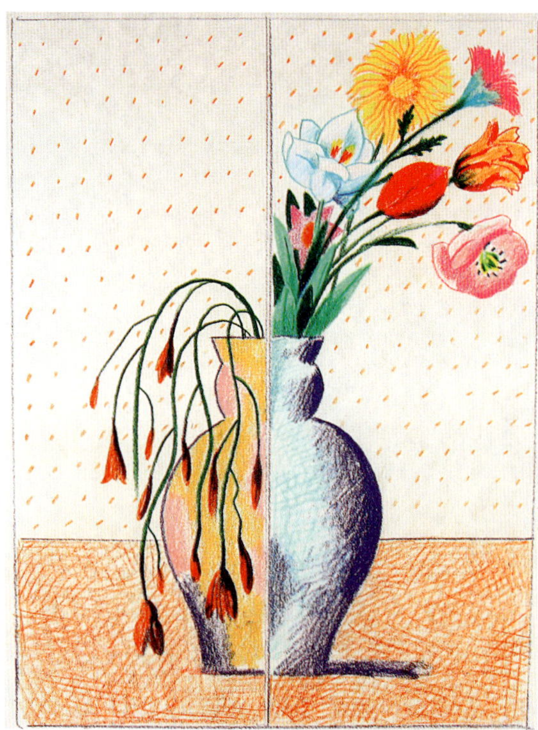

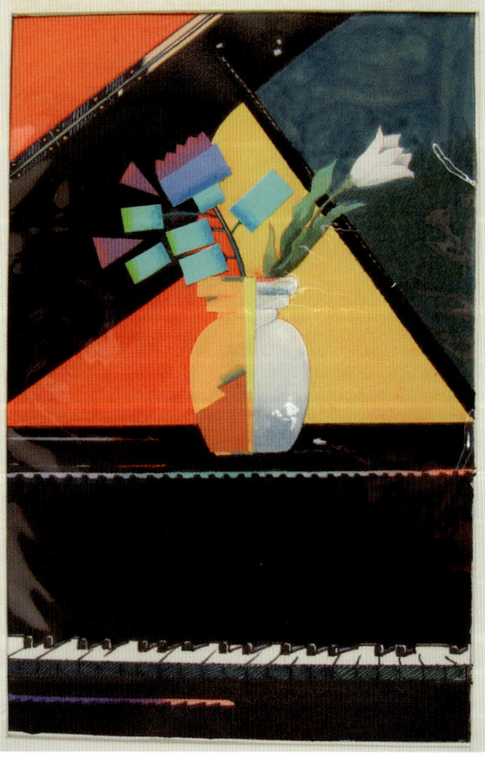

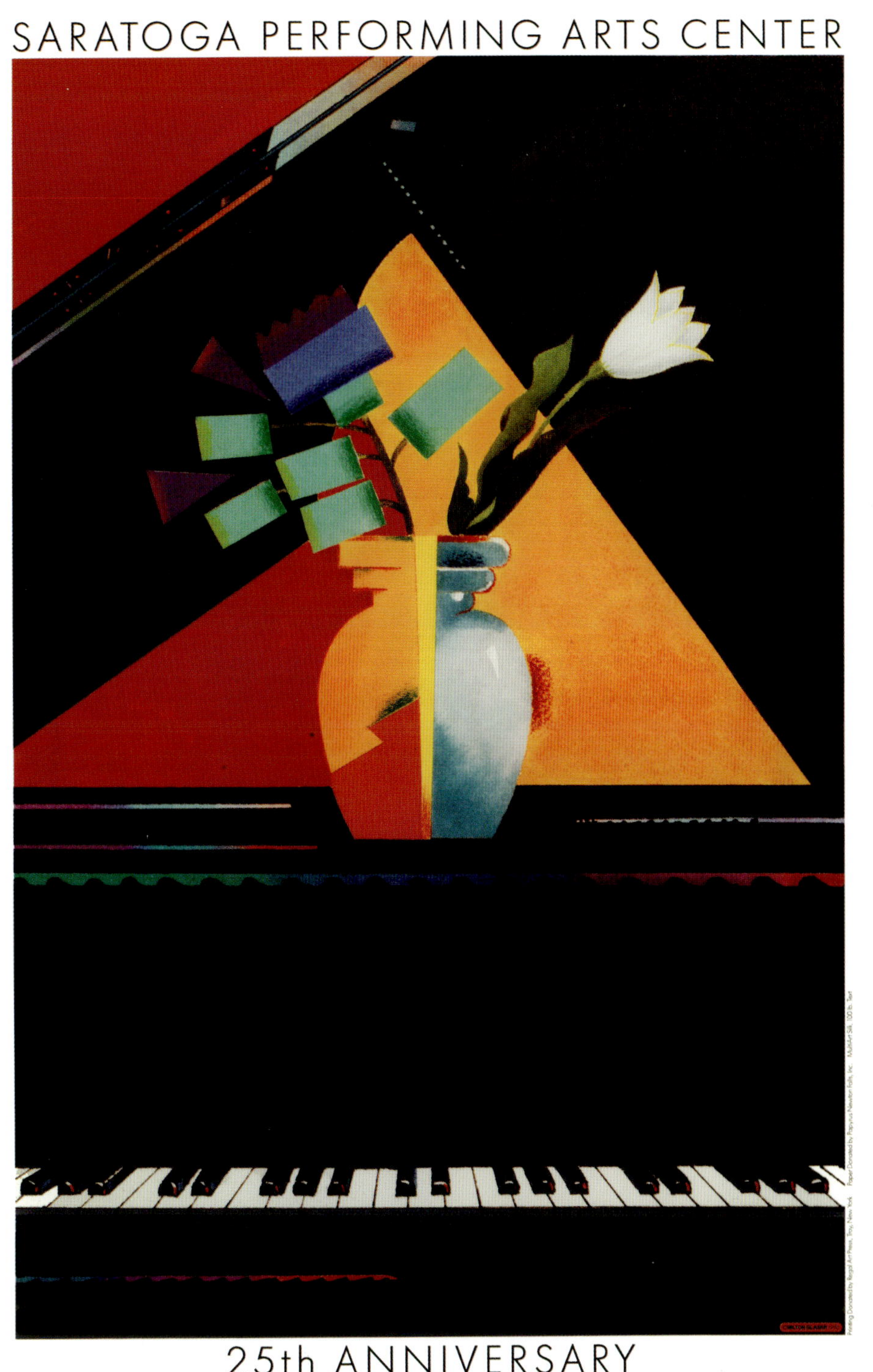
SARATOGA PERFORMING ARTS CENTER
25th ANNIVERSARY

A change in technology (using a pencil versus using a pen) produces a significantly different effect.
The pencil drawing is more ambiguous and poetic than the final drawing in pen and ink. At this moment
I think I prefer the pencil version.

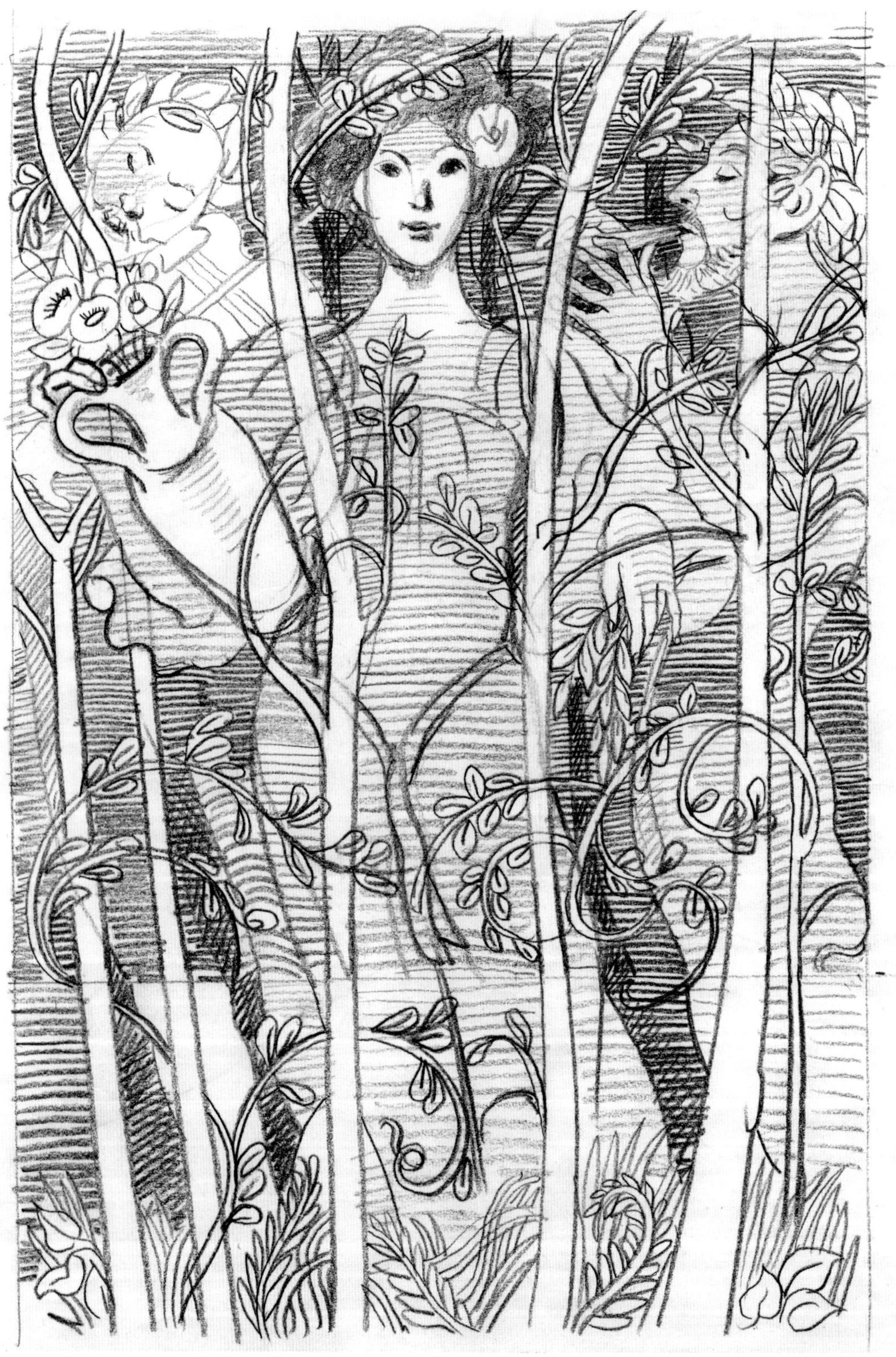

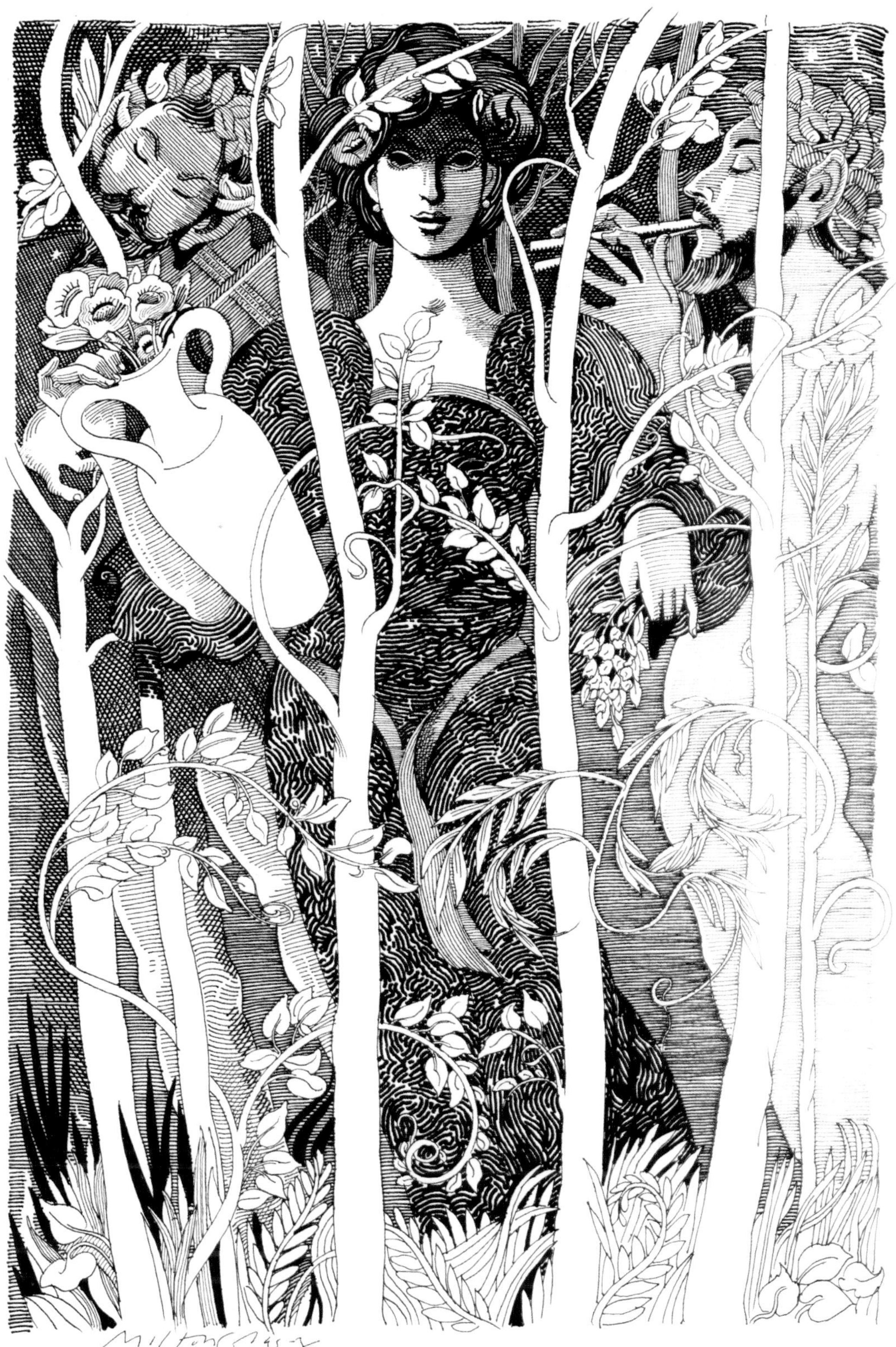

Although the line drawing was quite specific, it needed to be redrawn before washes could be added to create a more convincing composition.

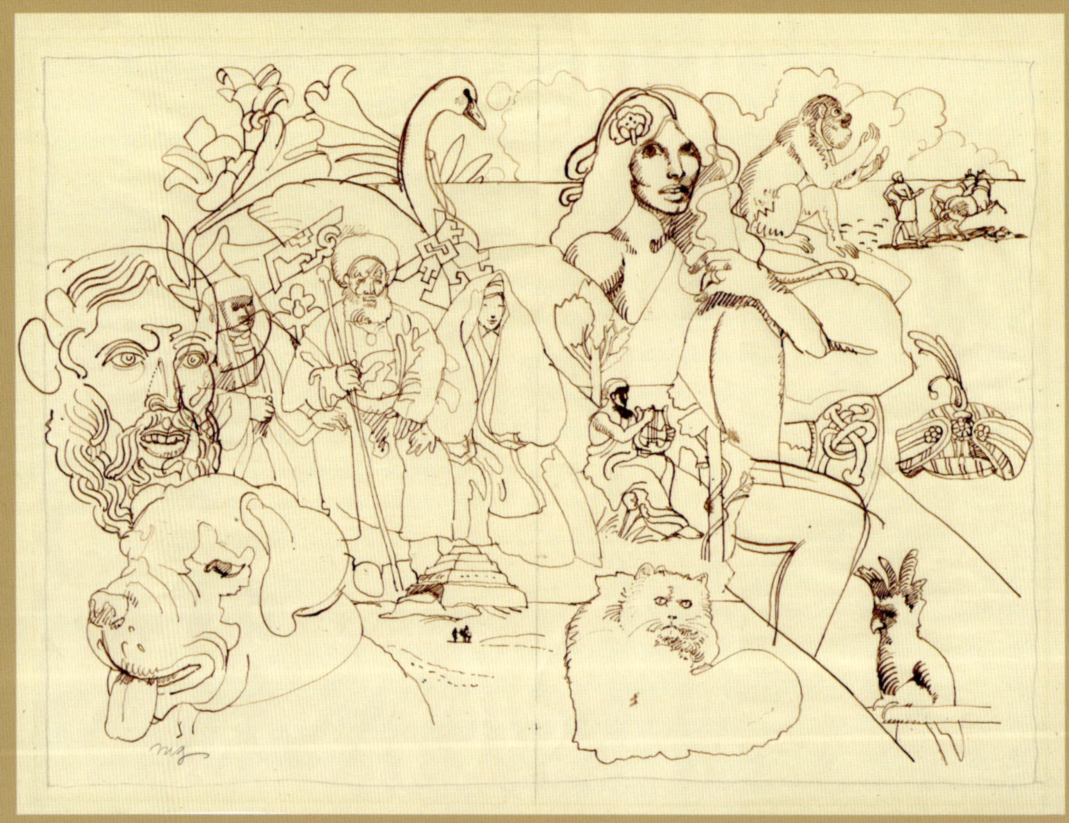

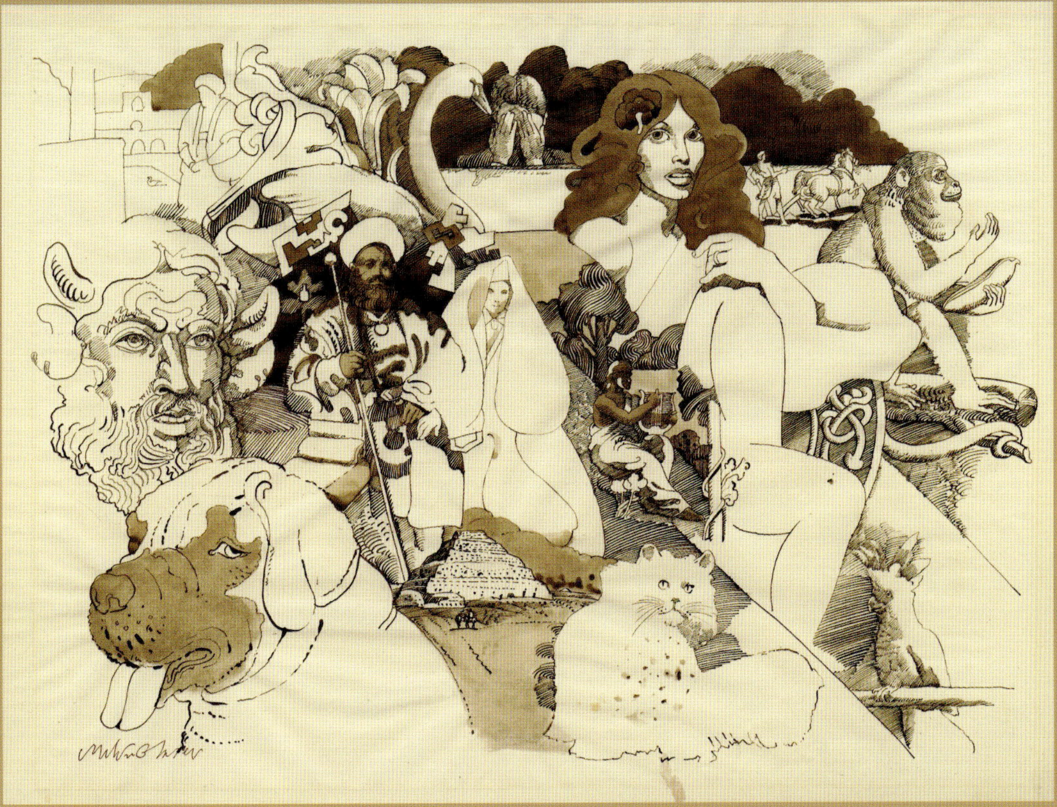

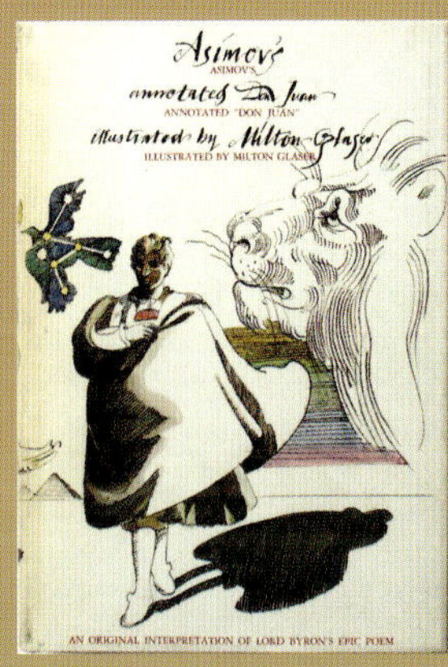

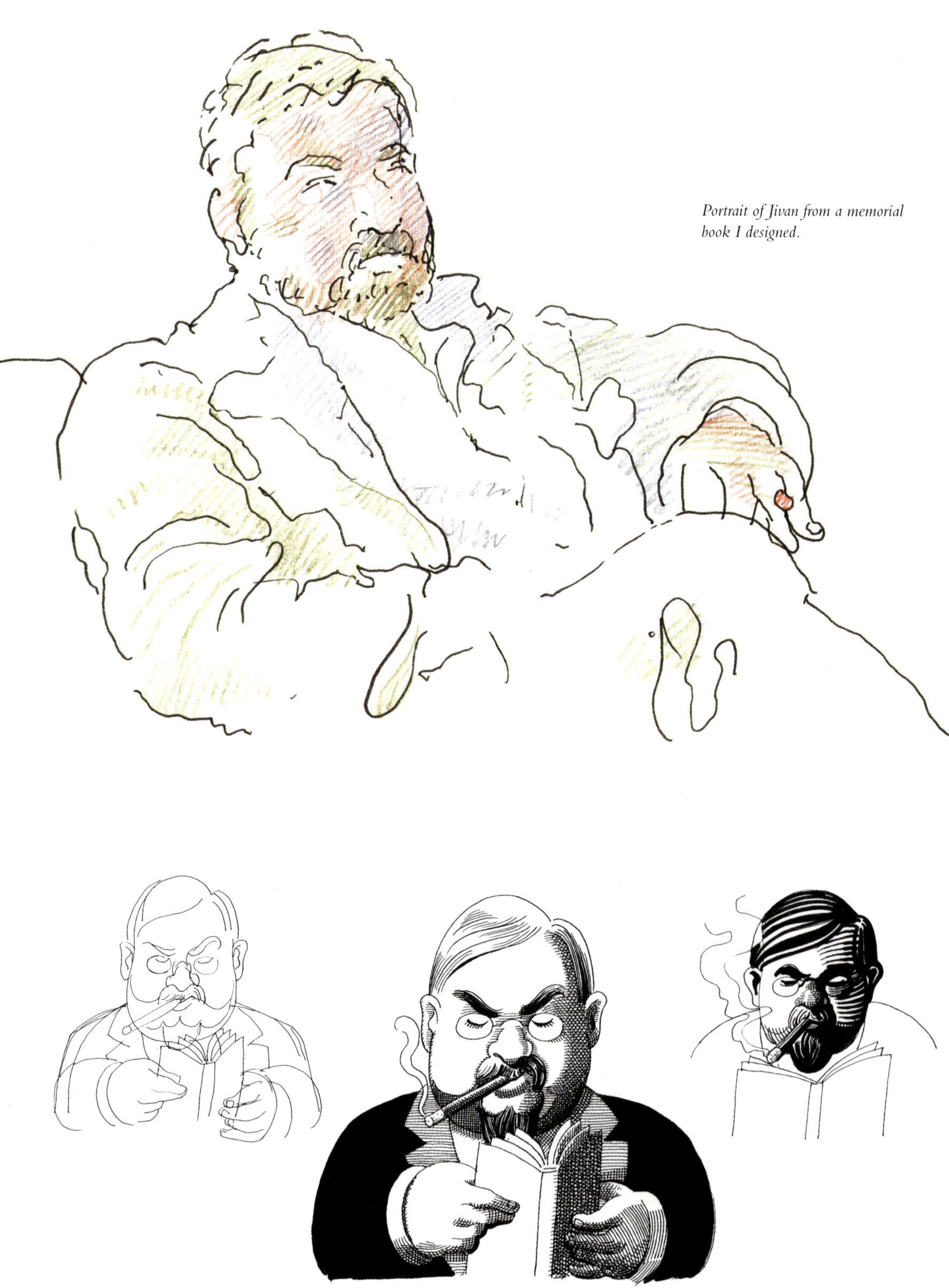

Portrait of Jivan from a memorial book I designed.

Studies for the final portrait.

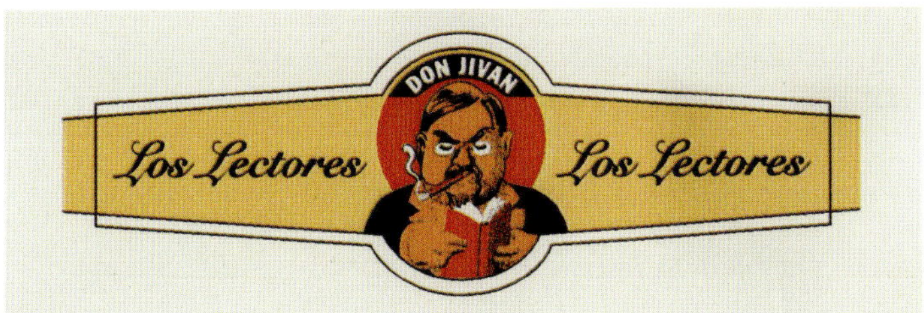

Cigar label.

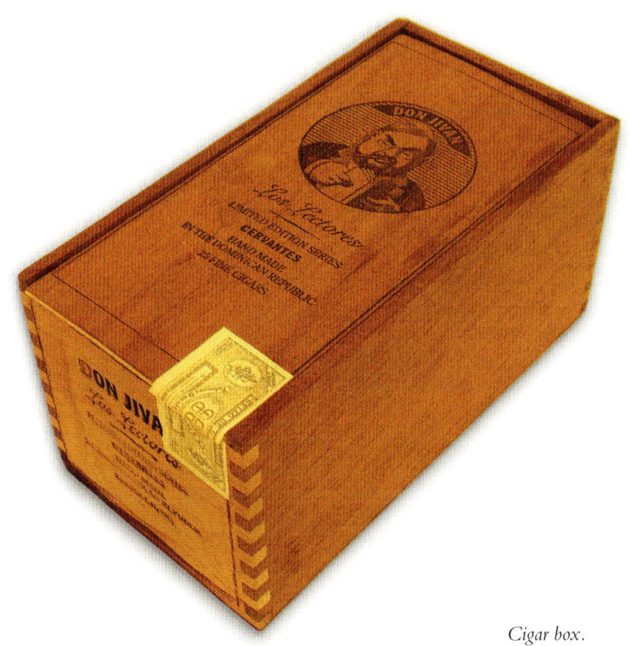

Cigar box.

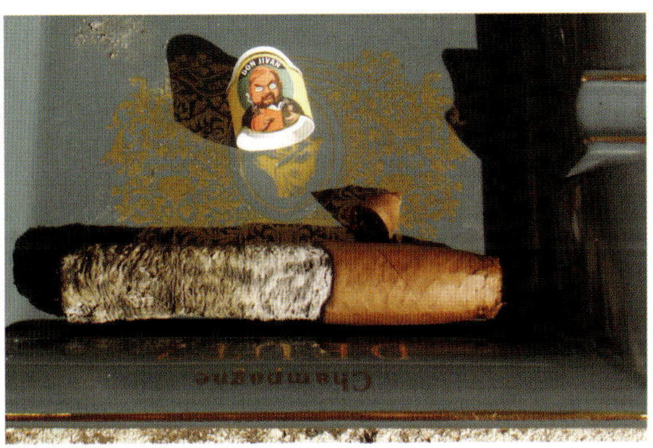

Ashtray.

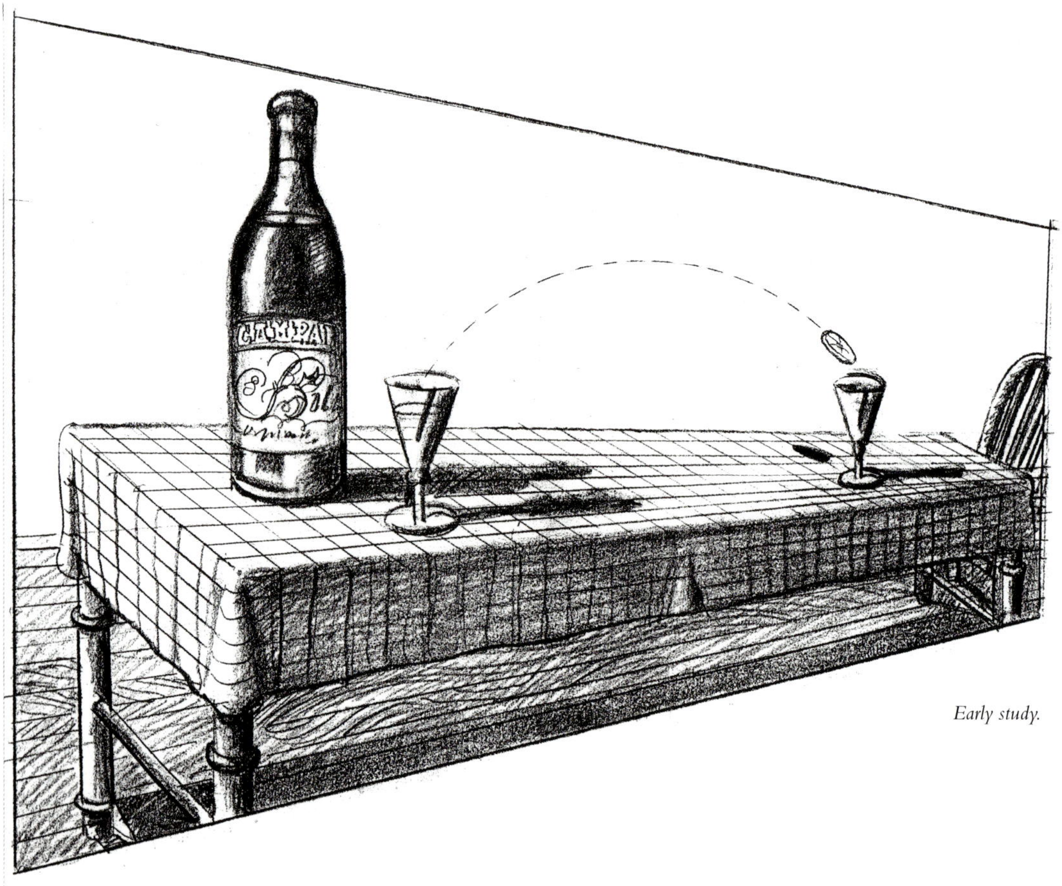

Early study.

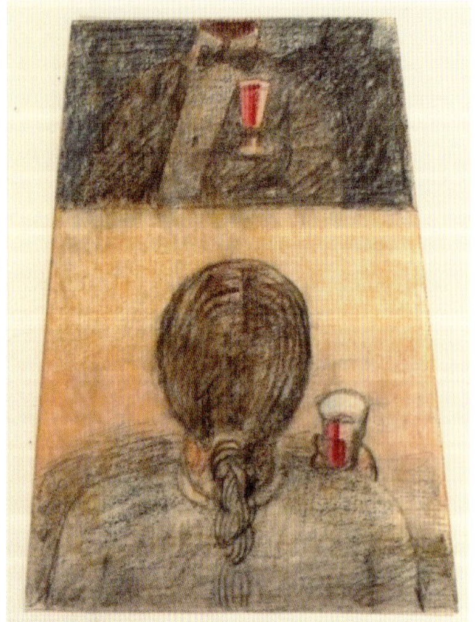

Sketch.

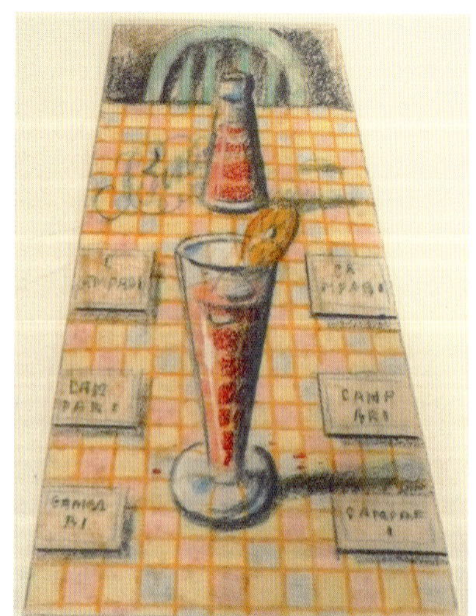

Sketch.

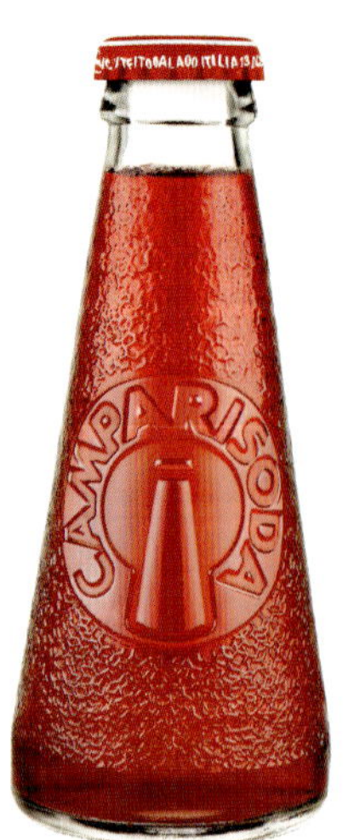

The bottle itself.

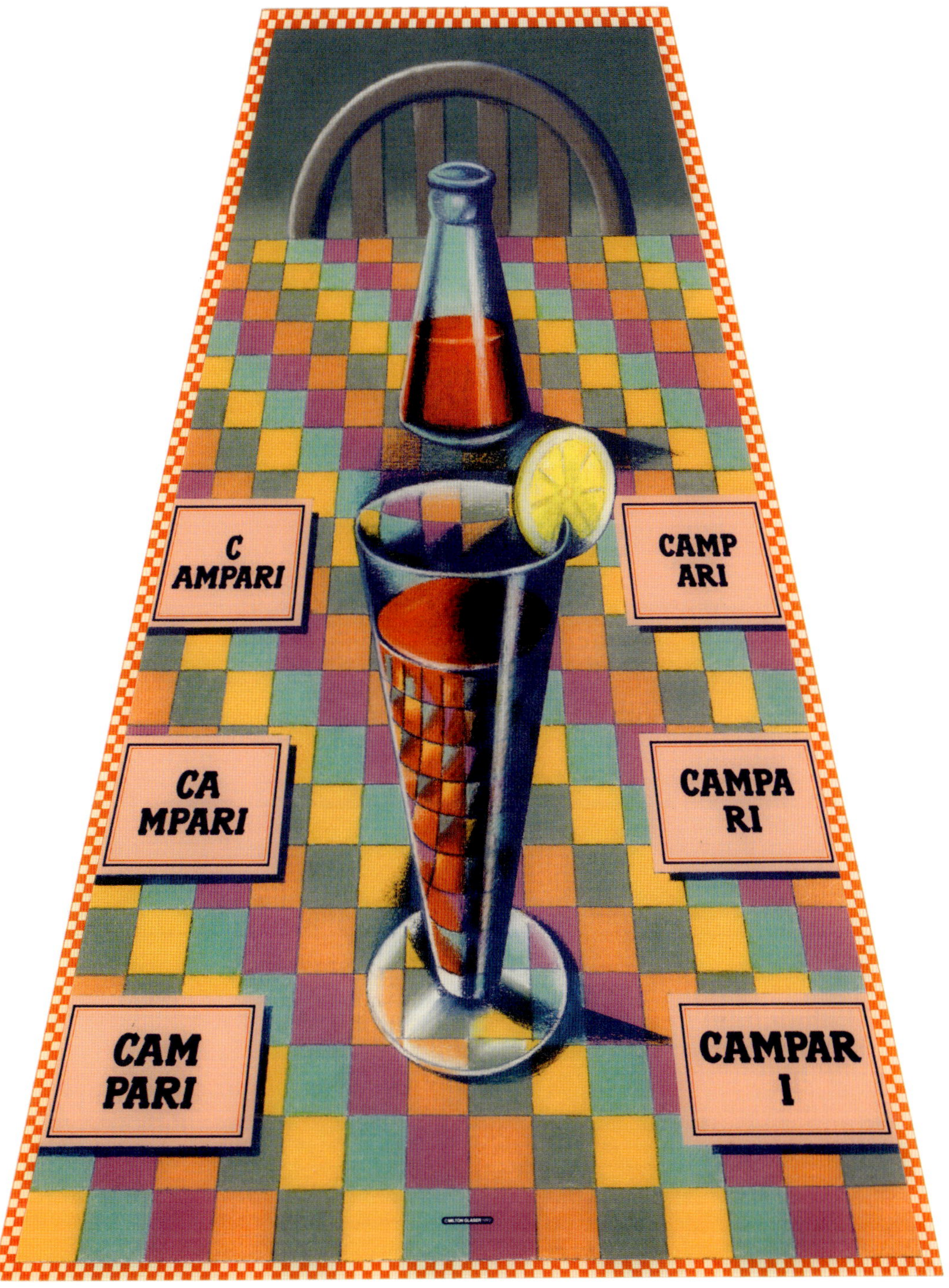

Final poster.

The Vespa poster was first developed using markers to create the image. Adjustments on the computer kept all the elements but changed their relationships to one another.

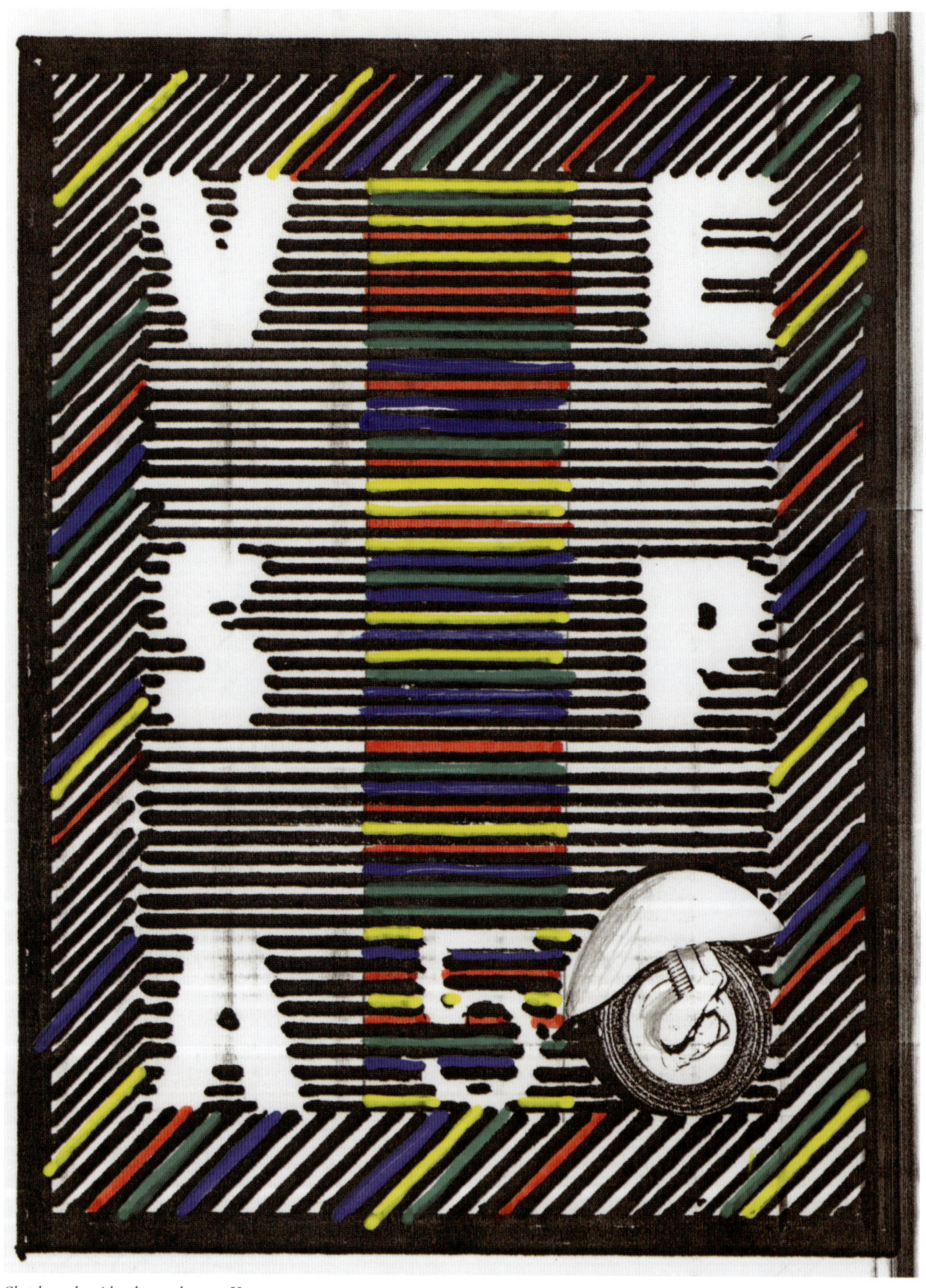

Sketch made with color markers on Xerox copy.

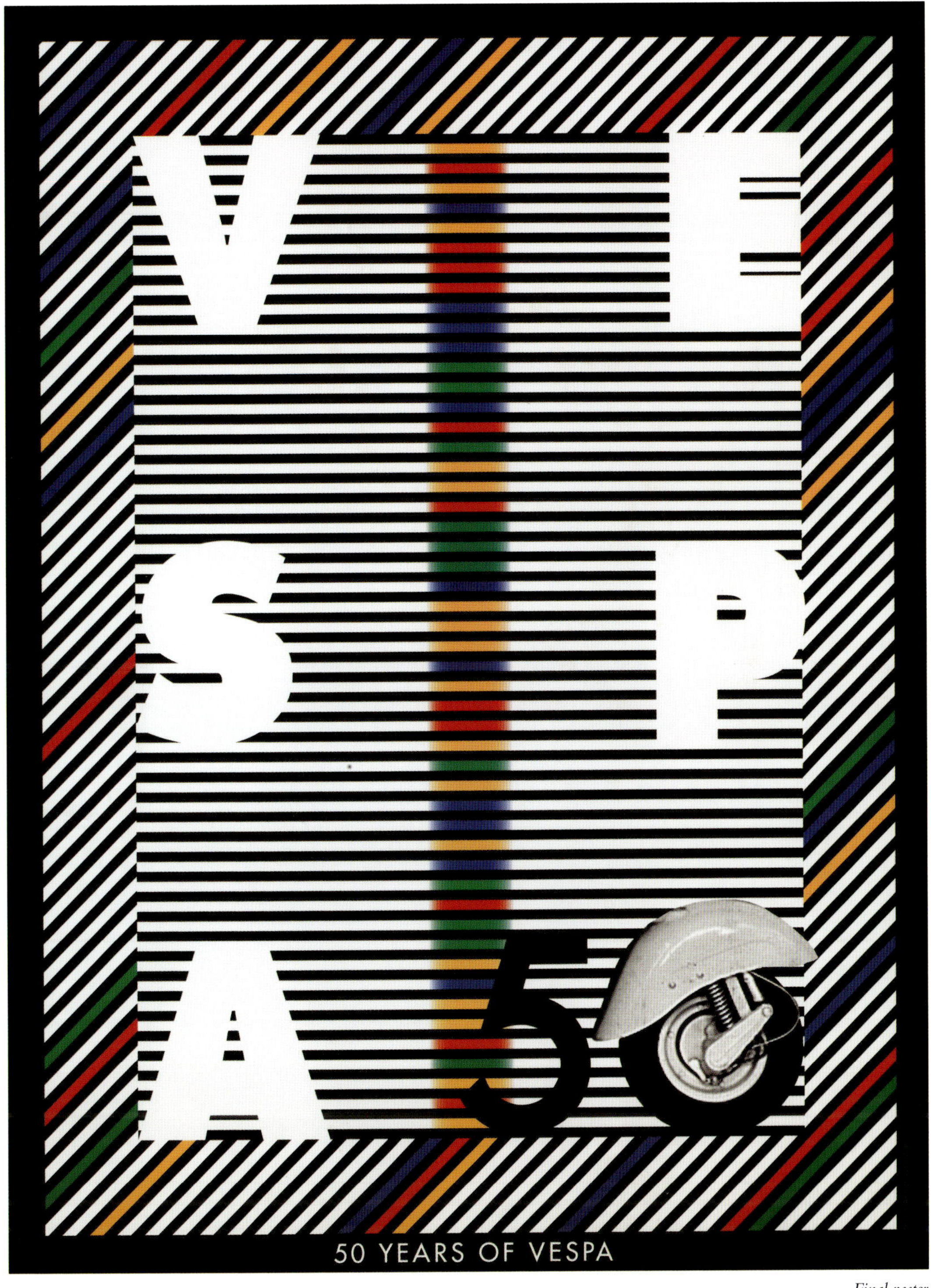

Final poster.

The theater company called Theater for a New Audience (TFANA) uses a series of Shakespeare portraits to represent its identity. Its equivalent of the Oscar is its stylized portrait of Shakespeare in iridescent metal.

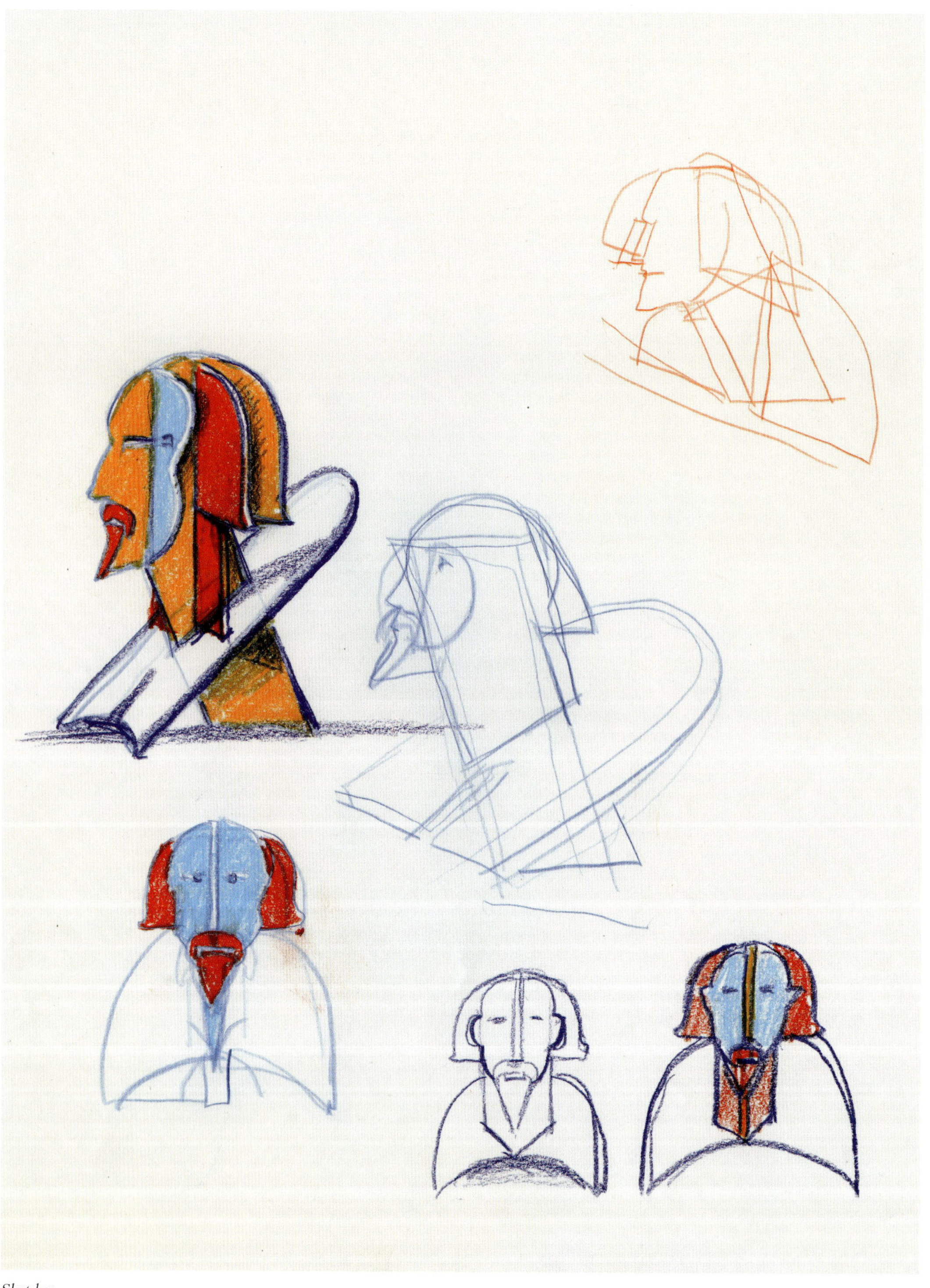

Sketches.

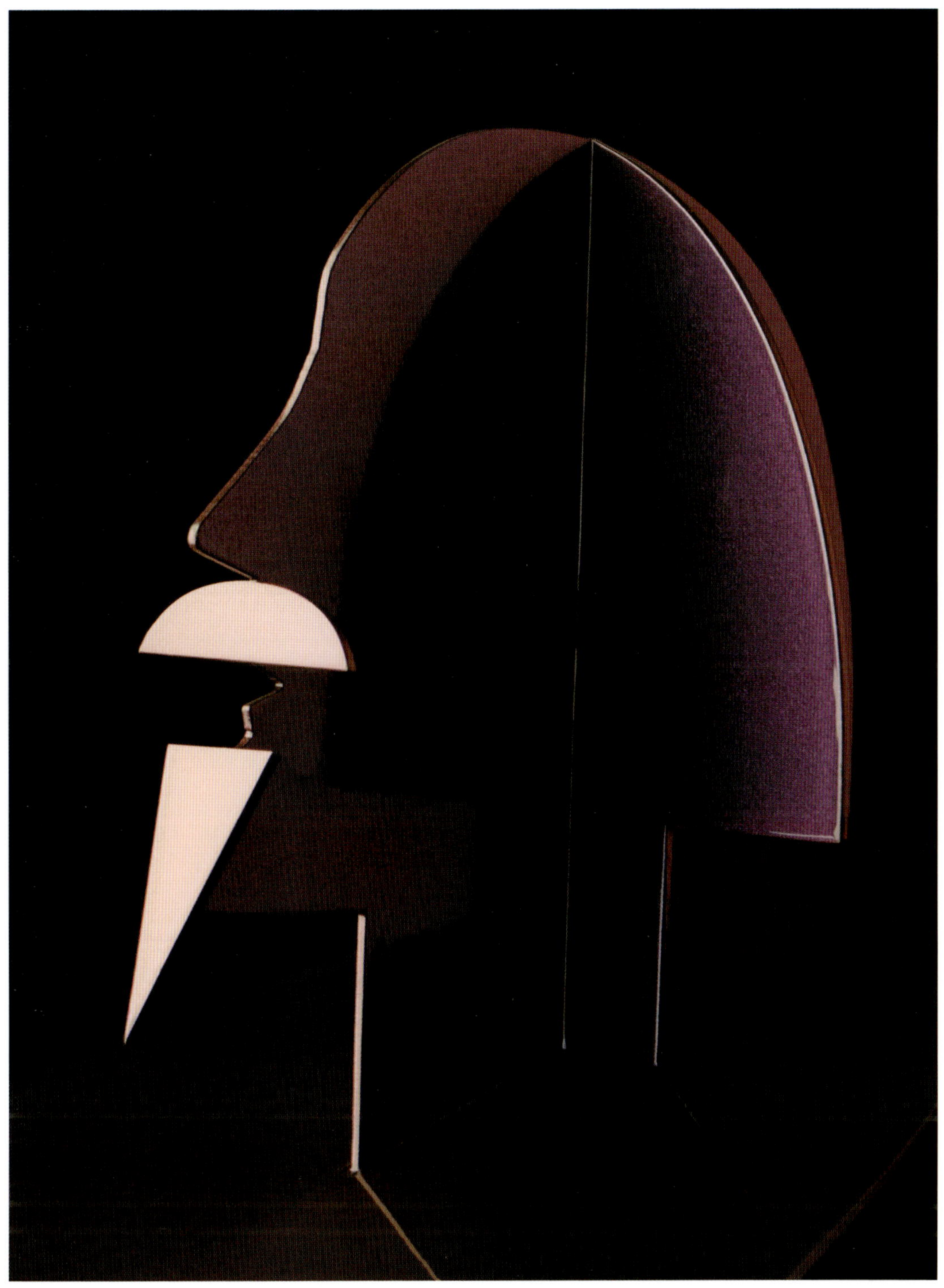

Finished sculpture.

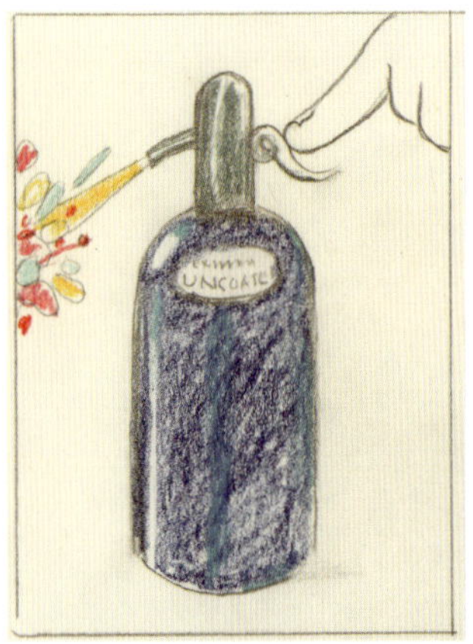

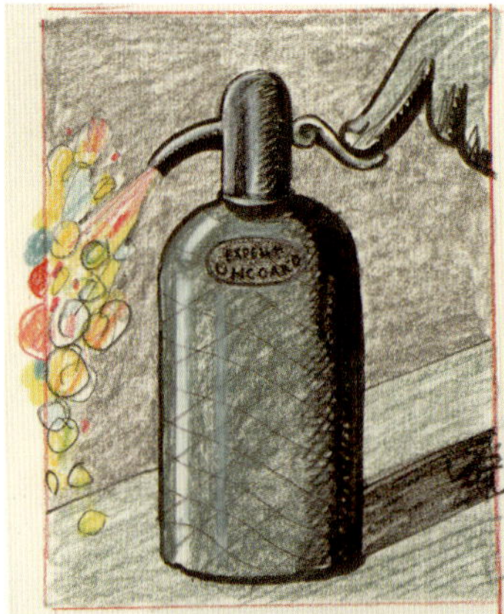

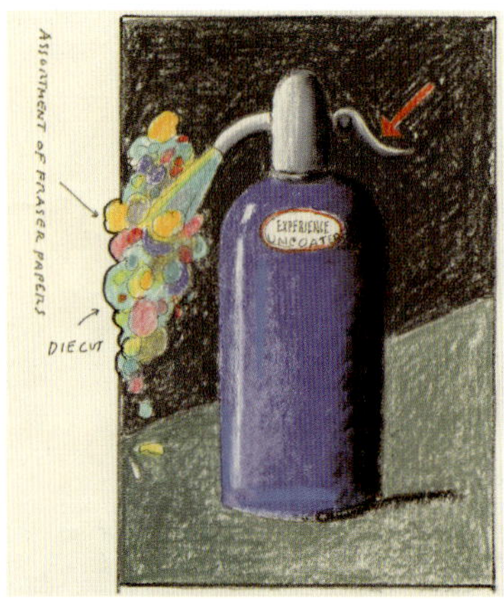

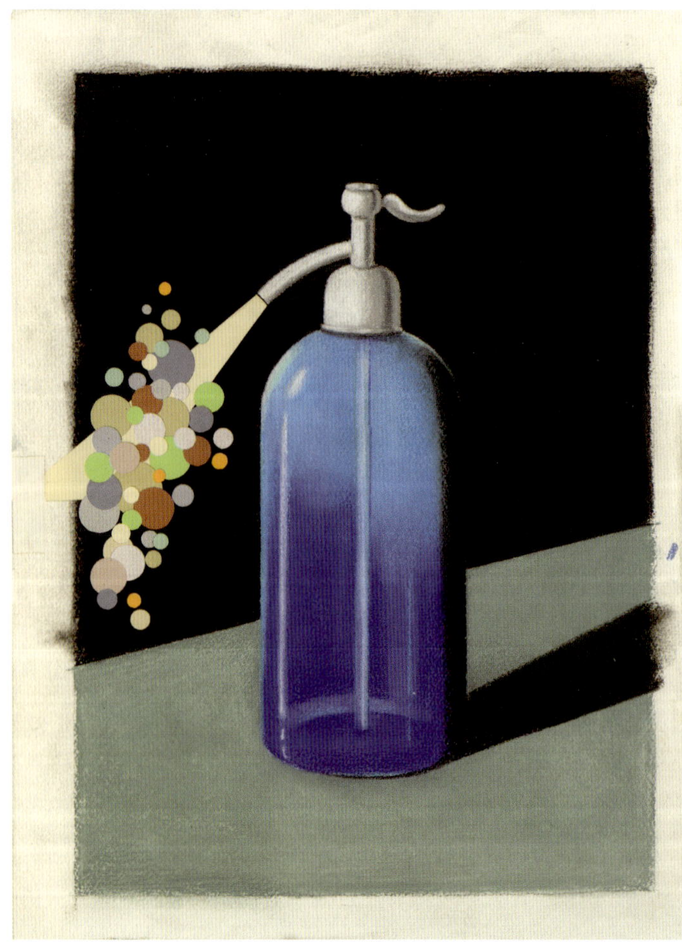

Early sketches.

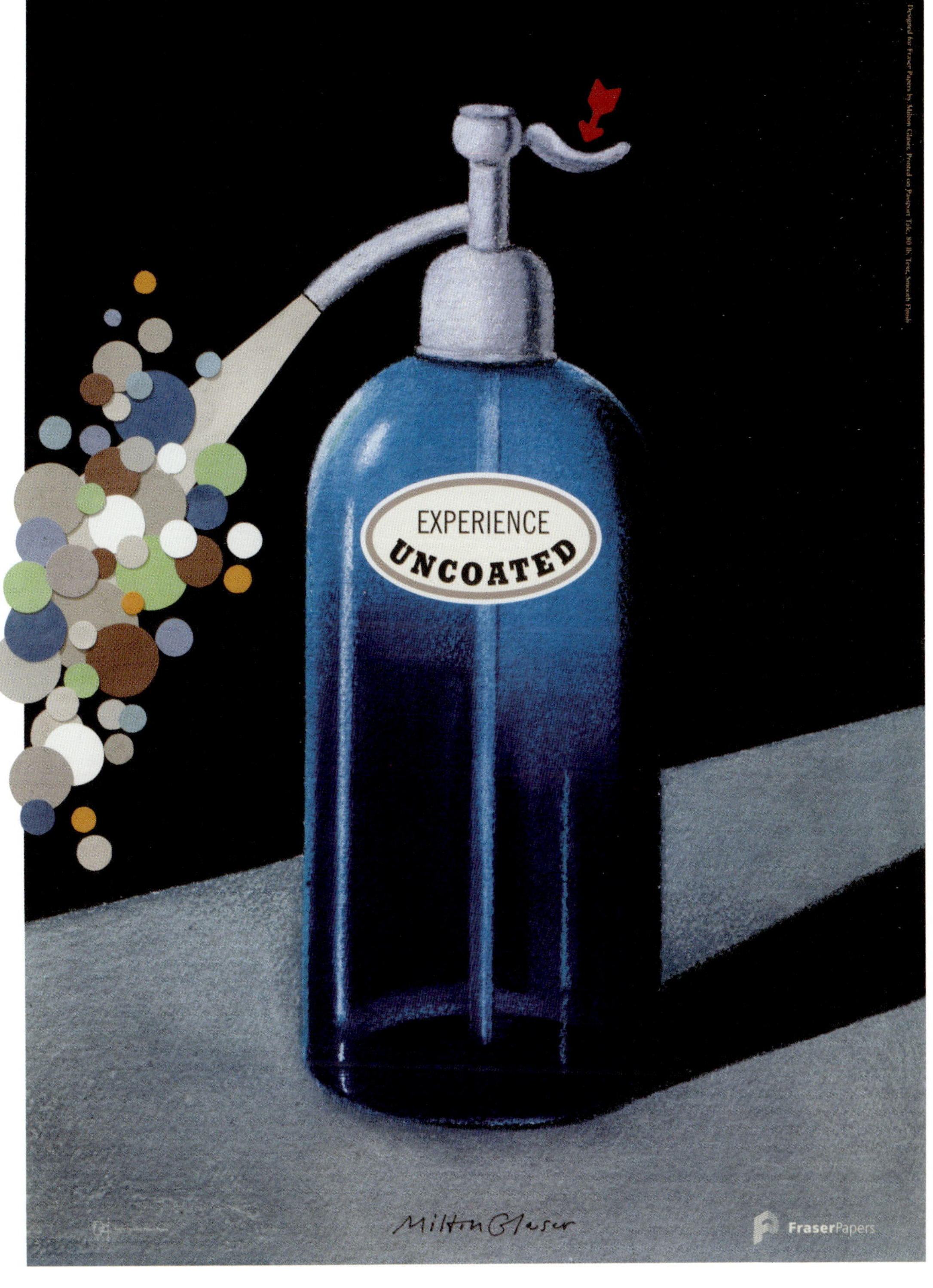
EXPERIENCE
UNCOATED
Milton Glaser
FraserPapers
Designed for Fraser Papers by Milton Glaser. Printed on Passport Talc, 80 lb. Text, Smooth Finish.

These early sketches show how fragments from each drawing found their way into the finished portrait of Aretha Franklin. The final image was installed by the National Portrait Gallery in Washington, DC, in 2018.

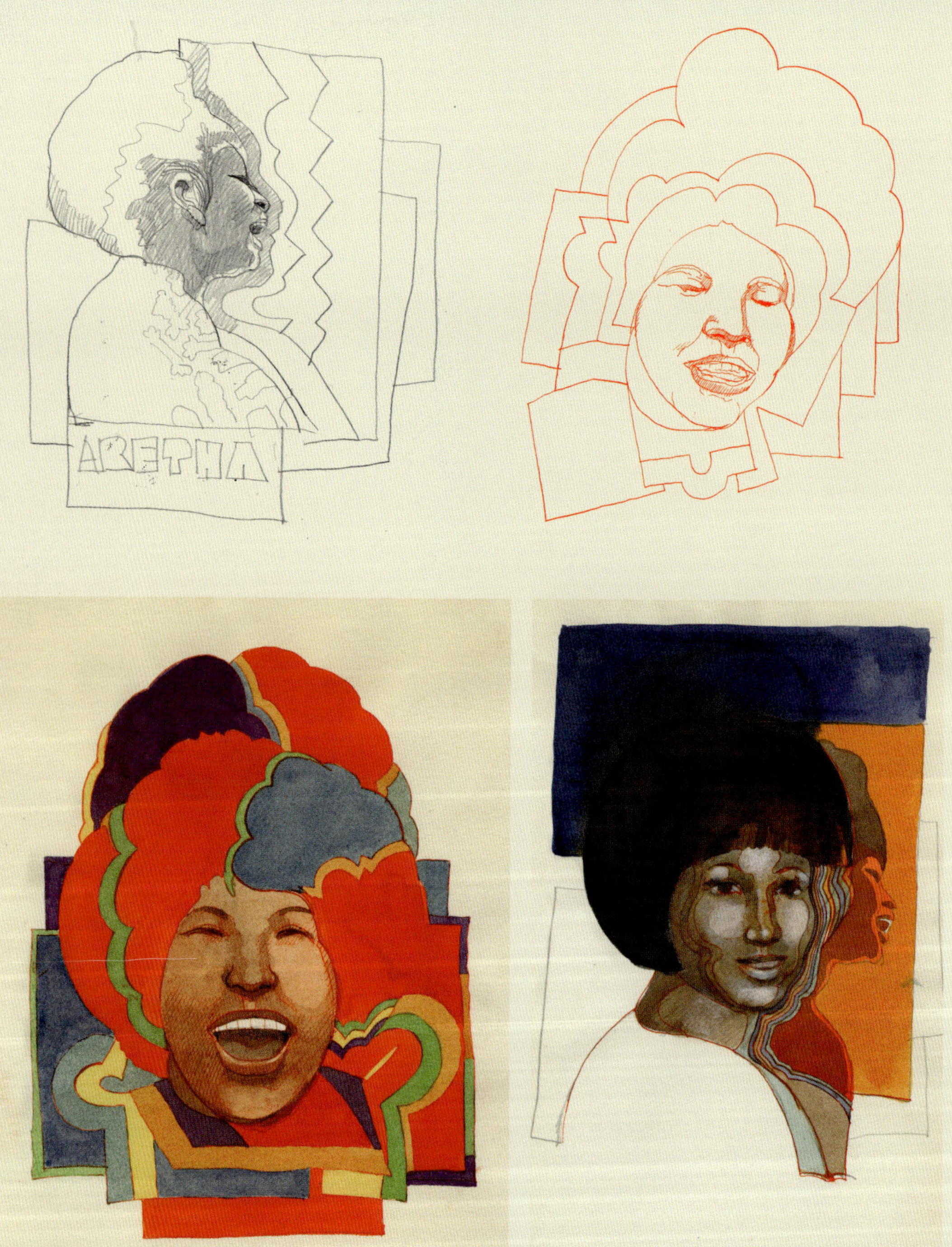

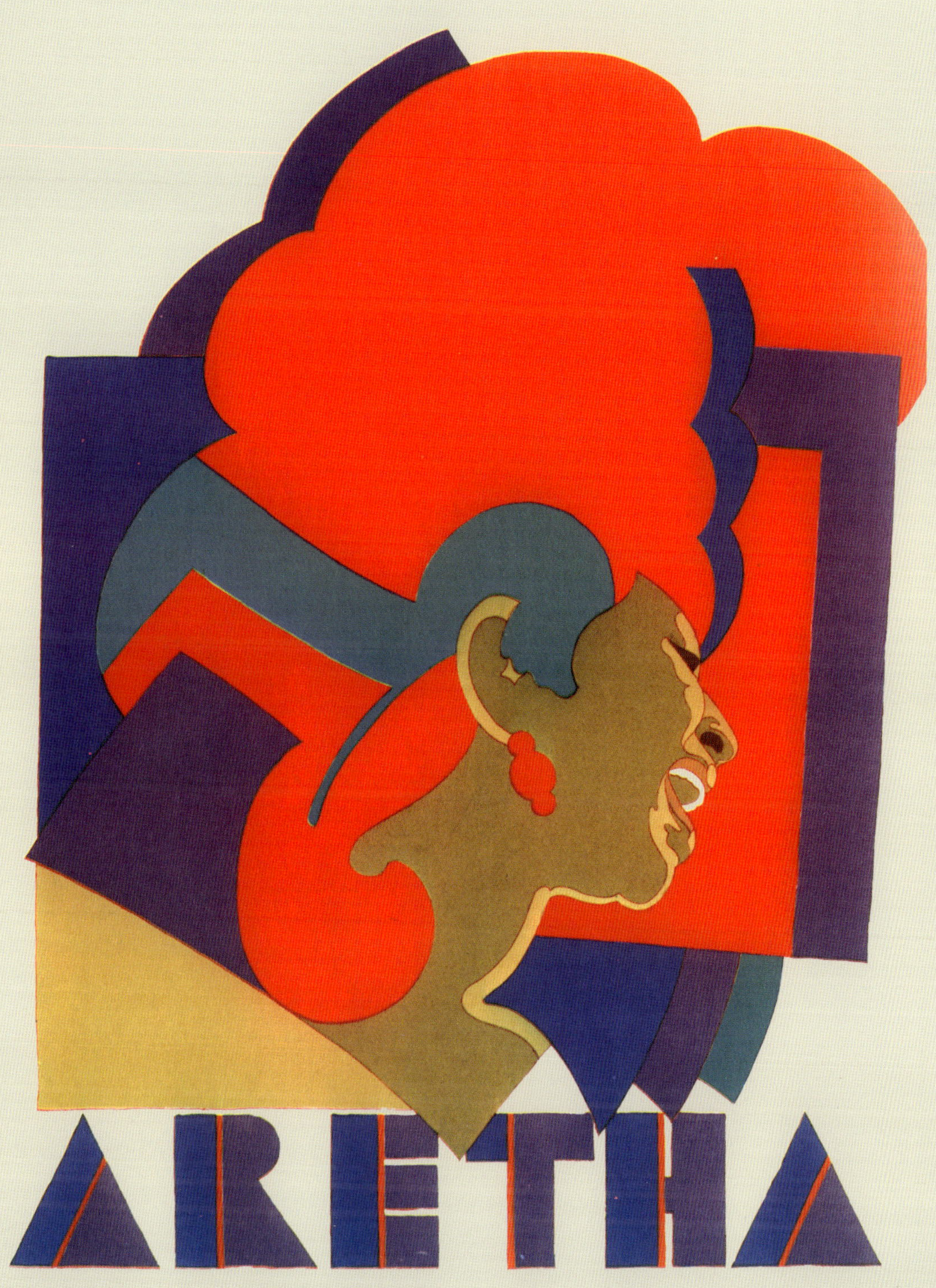
ARETHA

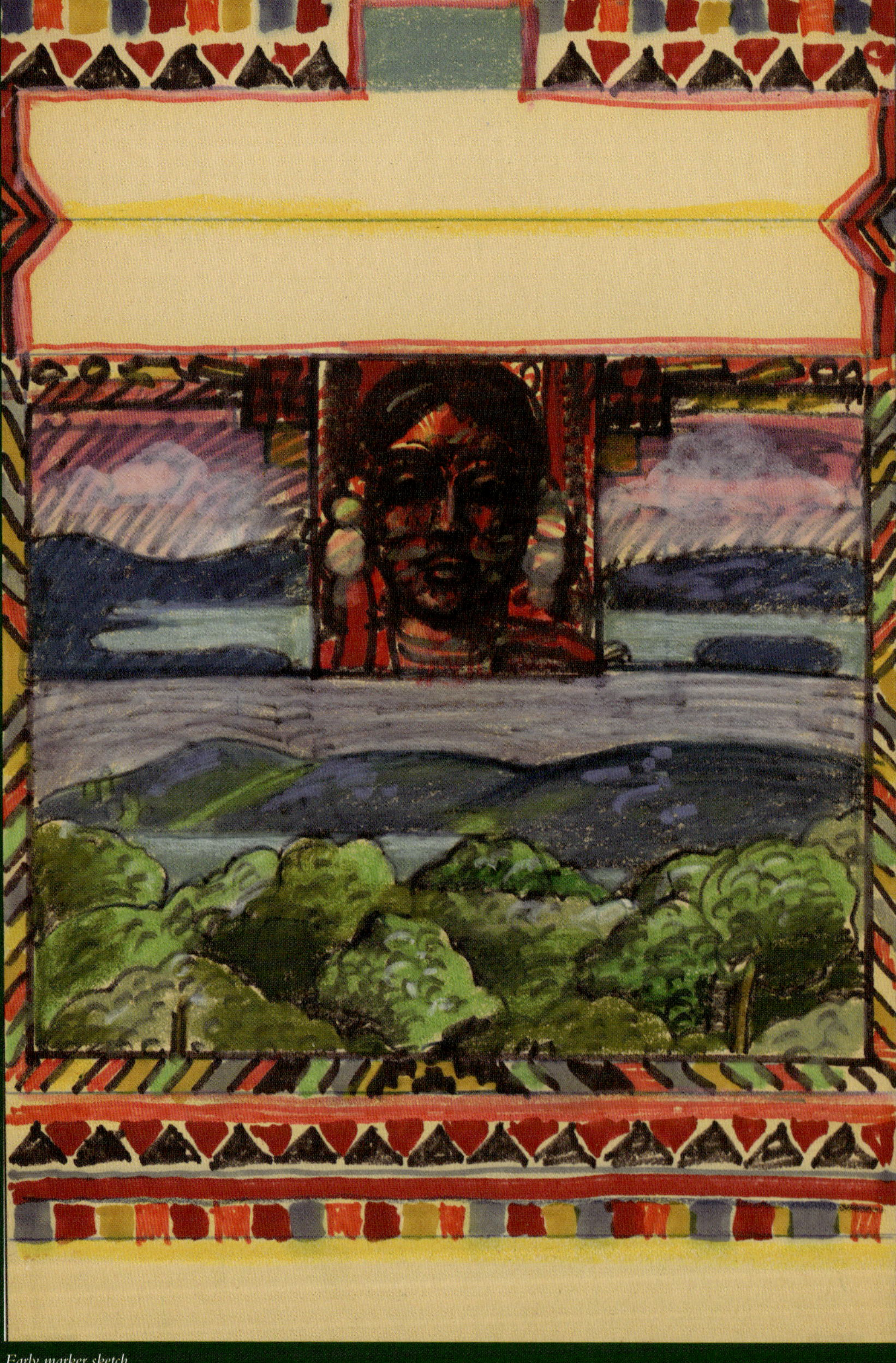

Early marker sketch.

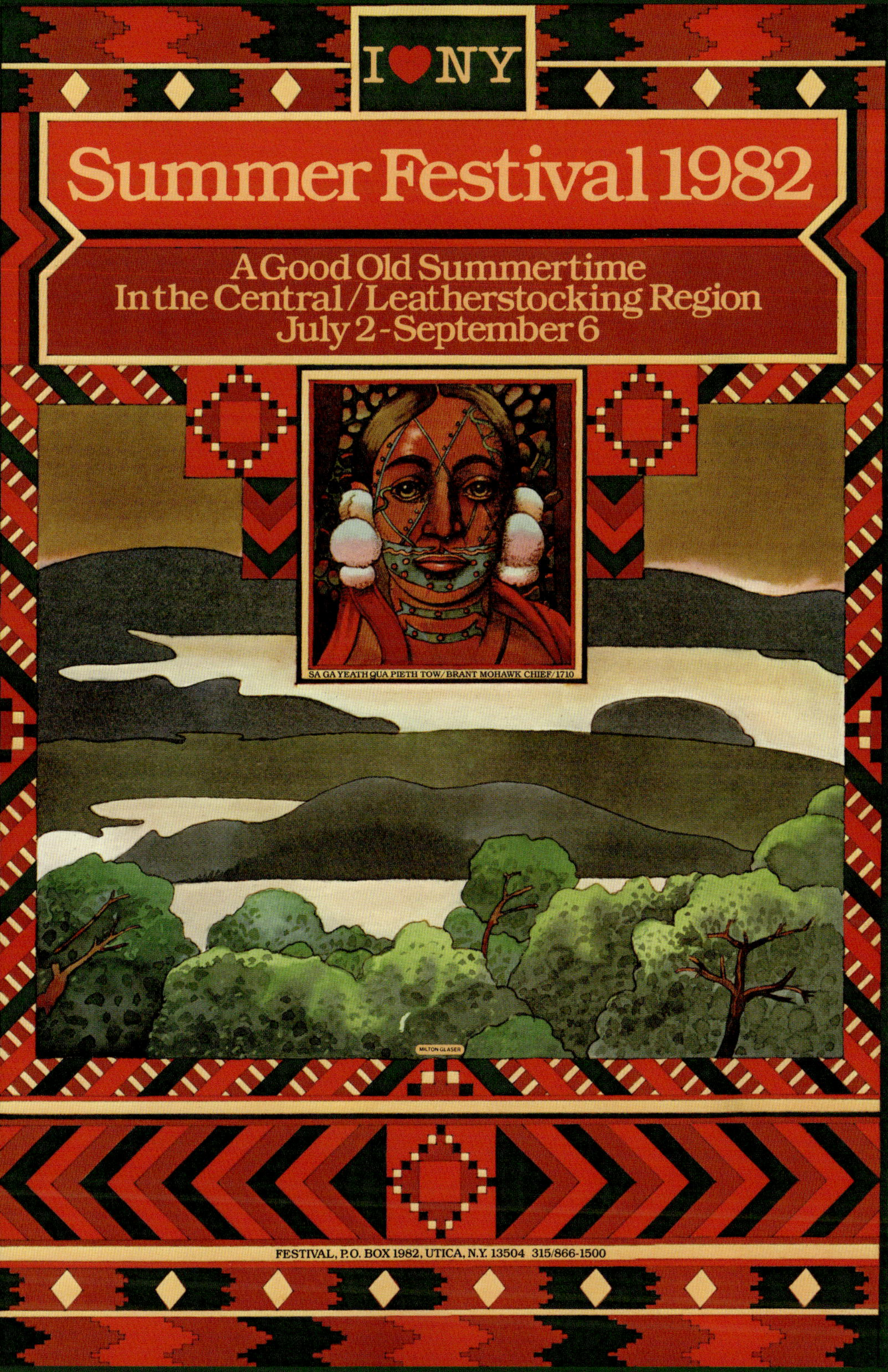

Final poster.

An angel seen from behind was the idea for the cover of the publication of the second part of Tony Kushner's remarkable play *Angels in America*.

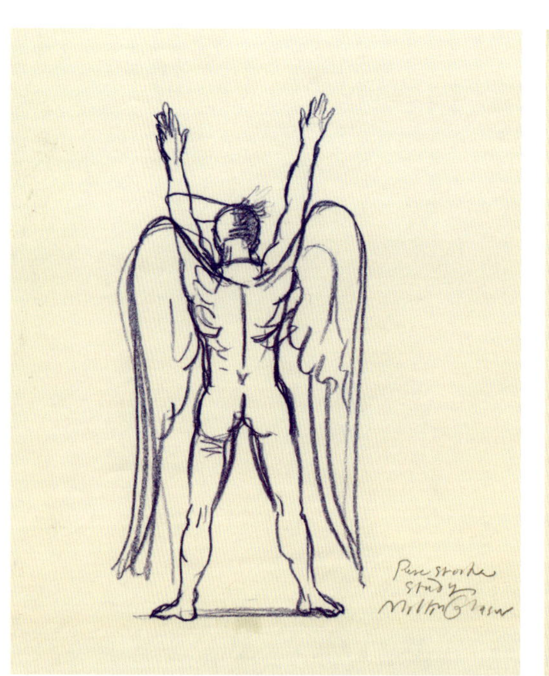

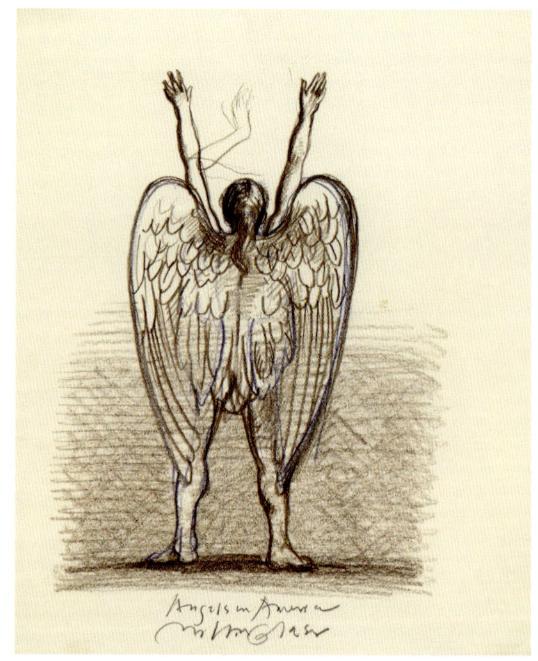

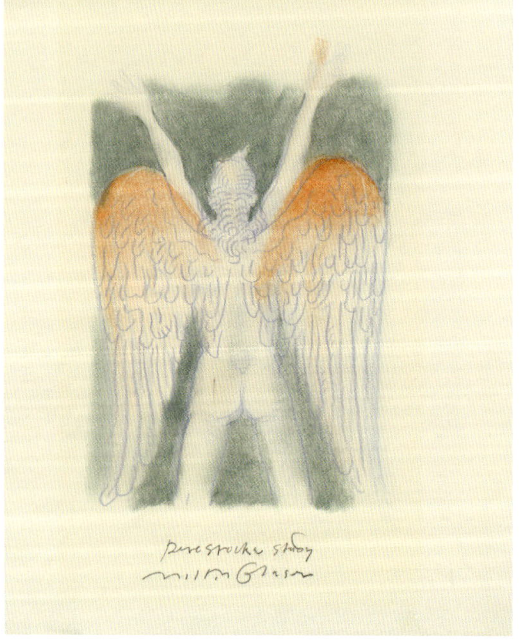

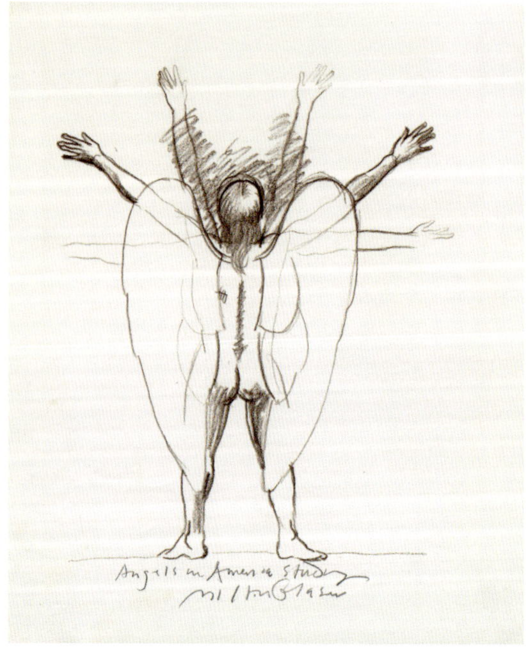

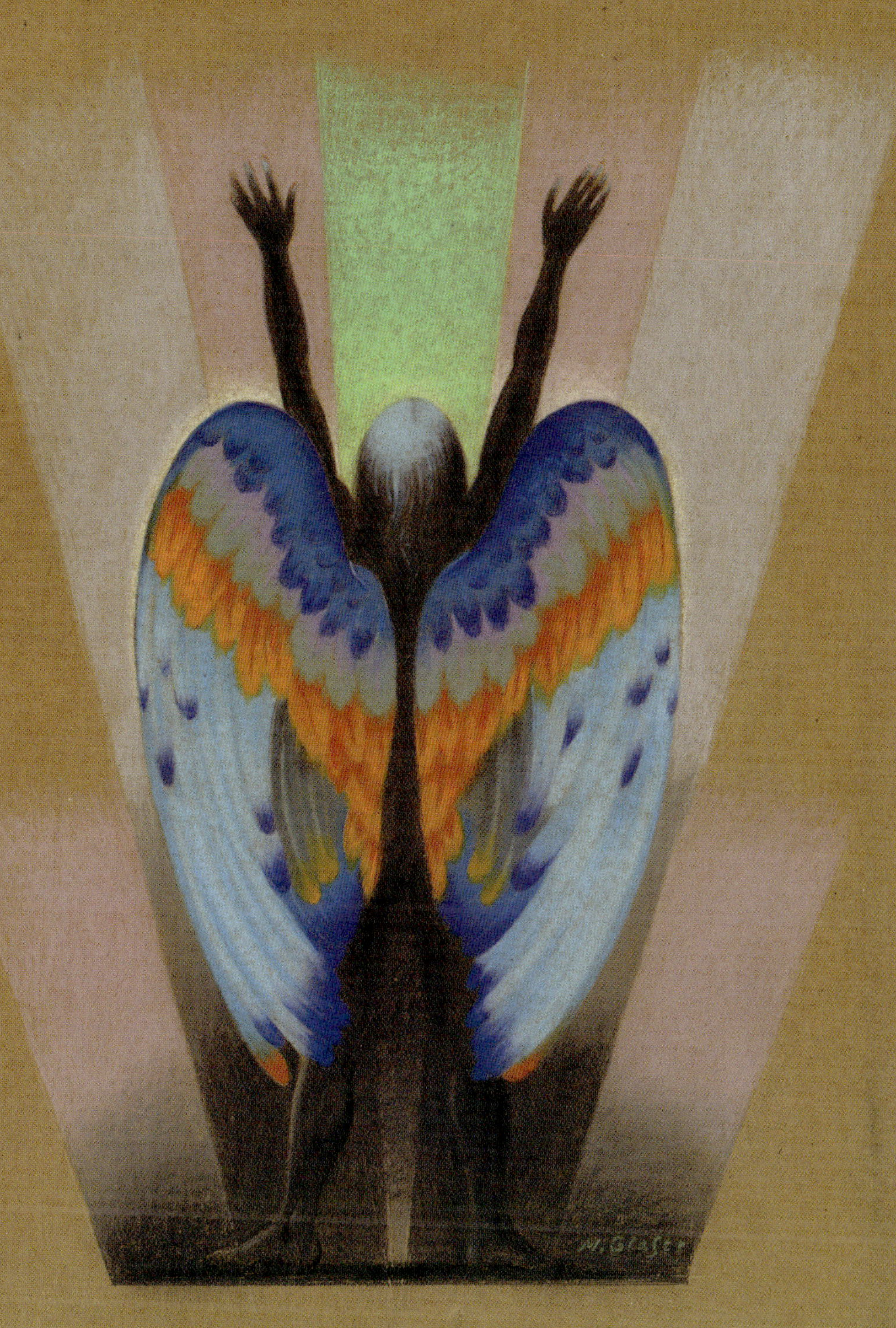

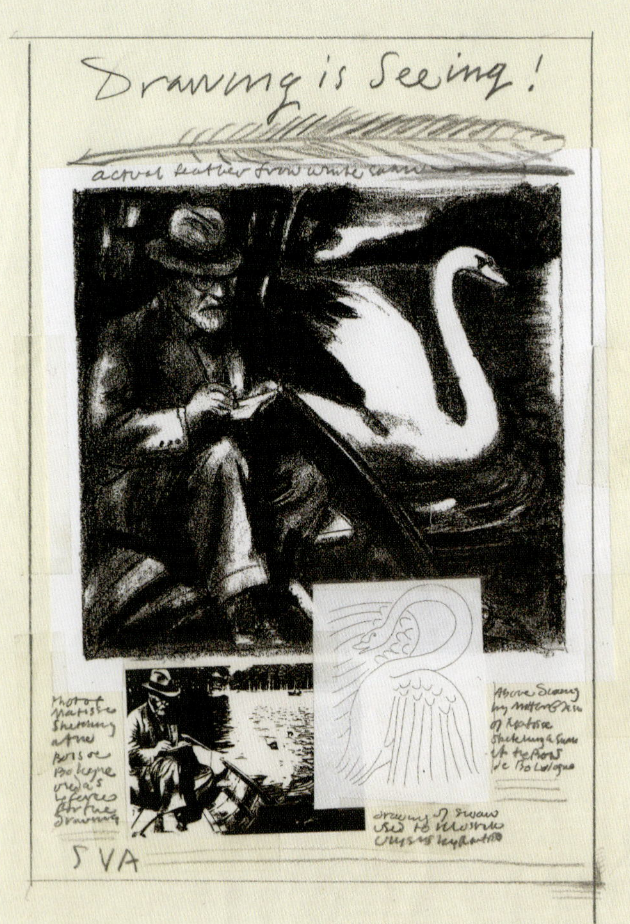

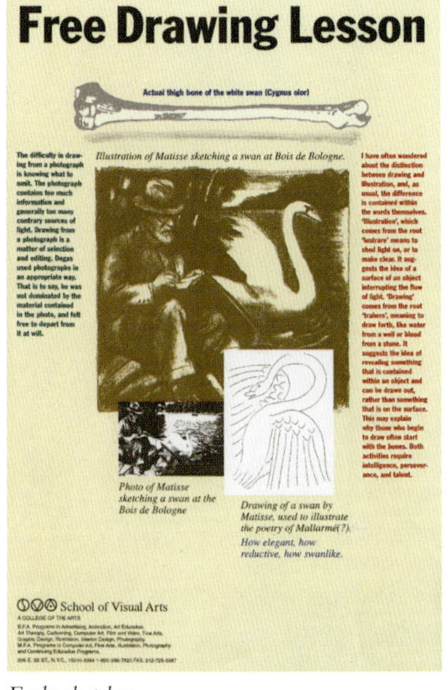

Free Drawing Lesson

Actual thigh bone of the white swan (Cygnus olor)

Illustration of Matisse sketching a swan at Bois de Bologne.

The difficulty in drawing from a photograph is knowing what to omit. The photograph contains too much information and generally too many contrary sources of light. Drawing from a photograph is a matter of selection and editing. Degas used photographs in an appropriate way. That is to say, he was not dominated by the material contained in the photo, and felt free to depart from it at will.

I have often wondered about the distinction between drawing and illustration, and, as usual, the difference is contained within the words themselves. 'Illustration', which comes from the root 'lustrare' means to shed light on, or to make clear. It suggests the idea of a surface of an object interrupting the flow of light. 'Drawing' comes from the root 'trahere', meaning to draw forth, like water from a well or blood from a stone. It suggests the idea of revealing something that is contained within an object and can be drawn out, rather than something that is on the surface. This may explain why those who begin to draw often start with the bones. Both activities require intelligence, perseverance, and talent.

Photo of Matisse sketching a swan at the Bois de Bologne

Drawing of a swan by Matisse, used to illustrate the poetry of Mallarmé(?). How elegant, how reductive, how swanlike.

School of Visual Arts

A COLLEGE OF THE ARTS

B.F.A. Programs in Advertising, Animation, Art Education, Art Therapy, Cartooning, Computer Art, Film and Video, Fine Arts, Graphic Design, Illustration, Interior Design, Photography. M.F.A. Programs in Computer Art, Fine Arts, Illustration, Photography and Continuing Education Programs.
209 E. 23 ST., N.Y.C., 10010-3994 1-800-366-7820 FAX: 212-725-3587

Early sketches

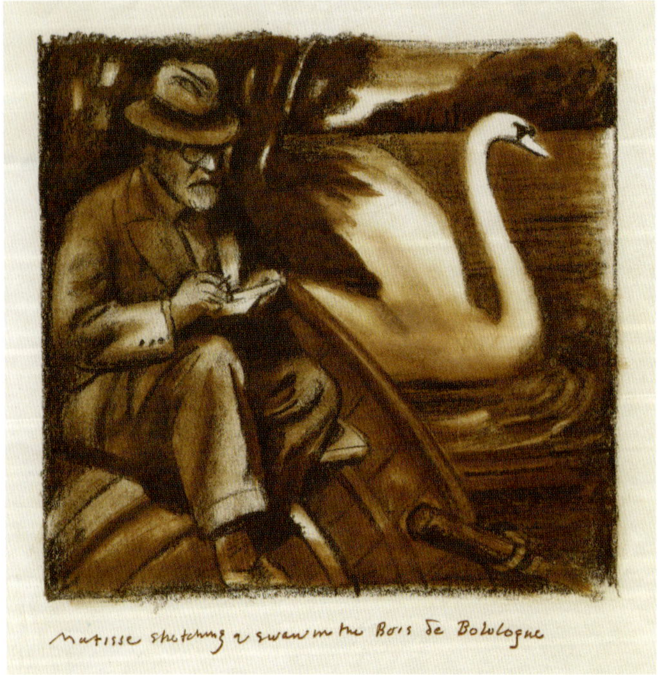

Original drawing.

A Drawing Lesson

The difficulty in drawing from a photograph is knowing what to omit. The photograph contains too much information and generally too many contrary sources of light. Drawing from a photograph is a matter of selection and editing. Degas used photographs in an appropriate way. That is to say, he was not dominated by the material contained in the photo, and felt free to depart from it at will.

Illustration of Matisse sketching a swan at Bois de Bologne

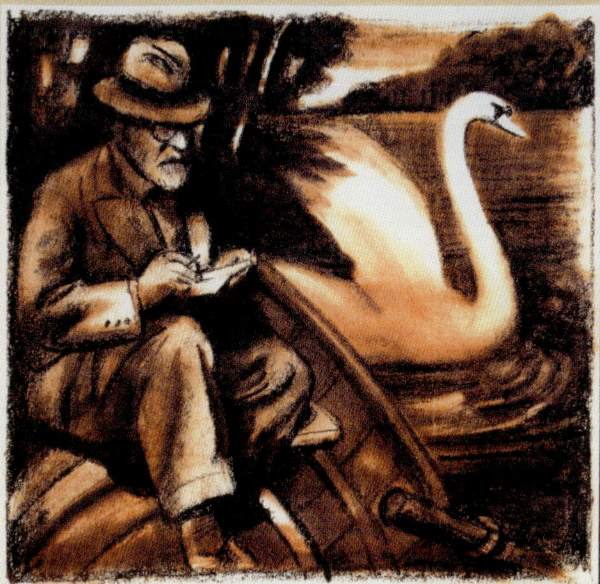

Photo of Matisse sketching a swan at the Bois de Bologne

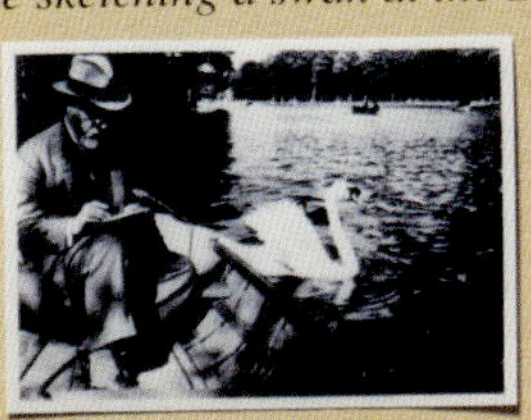

I have often wondered about the distinction between drawing and illustration, and, as usual, the difference is contained within the words themselves. 'Illustration', which comes from the root 'lustrare' means to shed light on, or to make clear. It suggests the idea of a surface of an object interrupting the flow of light. 'Drawing' comes from the root 'trahere', meaning to draw forth, like water from a well or blood from a stone. It suggests the idea of revealing something that is contained within an object and can be drawn out, rather than something that is on the surface. This may explain why those who begin to draw often start with the bones. Both activities require intelligence, perseverance, and talent.

Milton Glaser

Characteristic bones of the white swan (Cygnus olor)

School of Visual Arts
A COLLEGE OF THE ARTS

B.F.A. Programs in Advertising, Animation, Art Education,
Art Therapy, Cartooning, Computer Art, Film and Video, Fine Arts,
Graphic Design, Illustration, Interior Design, Photography.
M.F.A. Programs in Computer Art, Fine Arts, Illustration, Photography,
and Continuing Education Programs.

209 E. 23 ST., N.Y.C., 10010-3994 1-800-366-7820 FAX: 212-725-3587

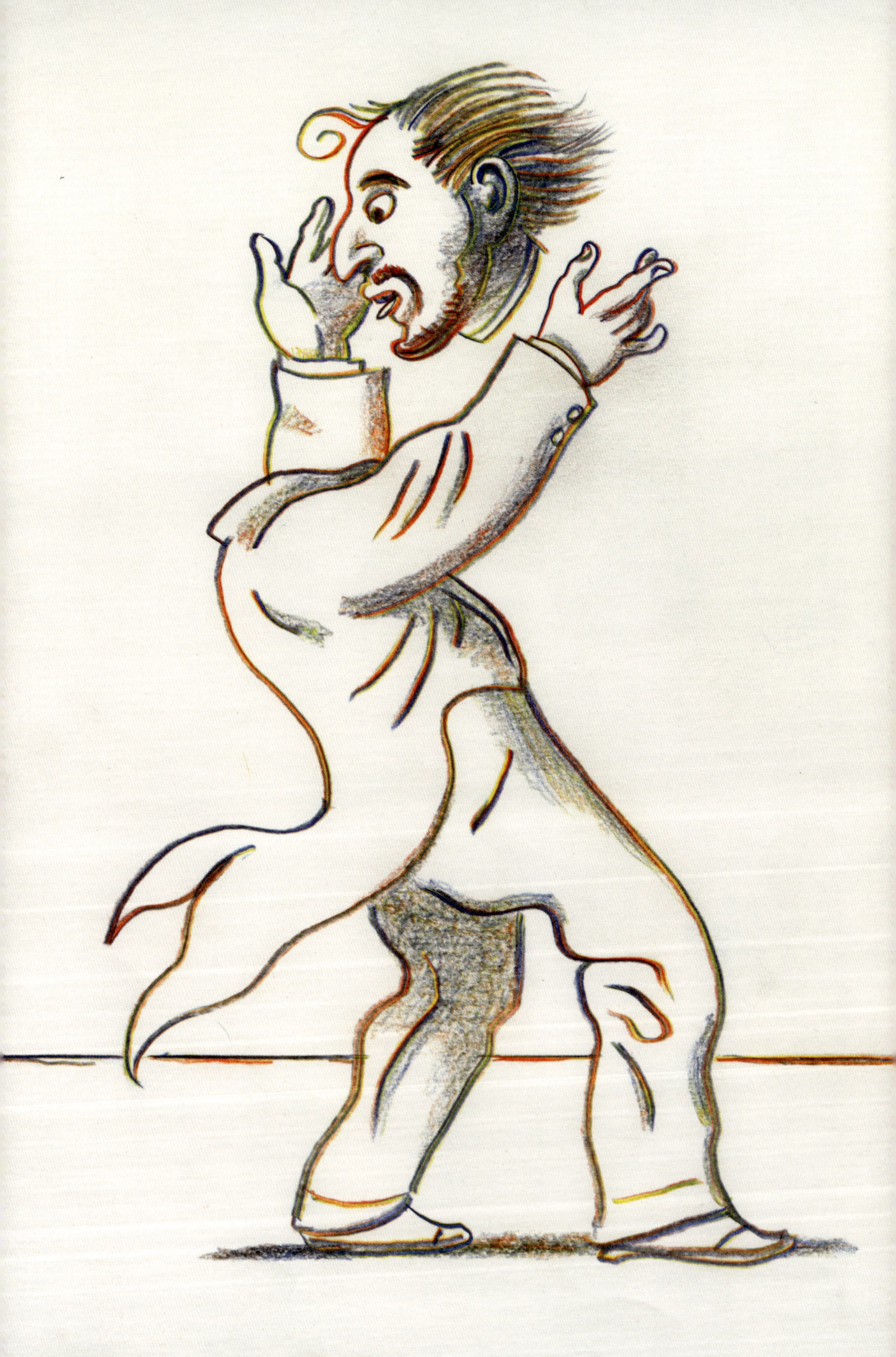

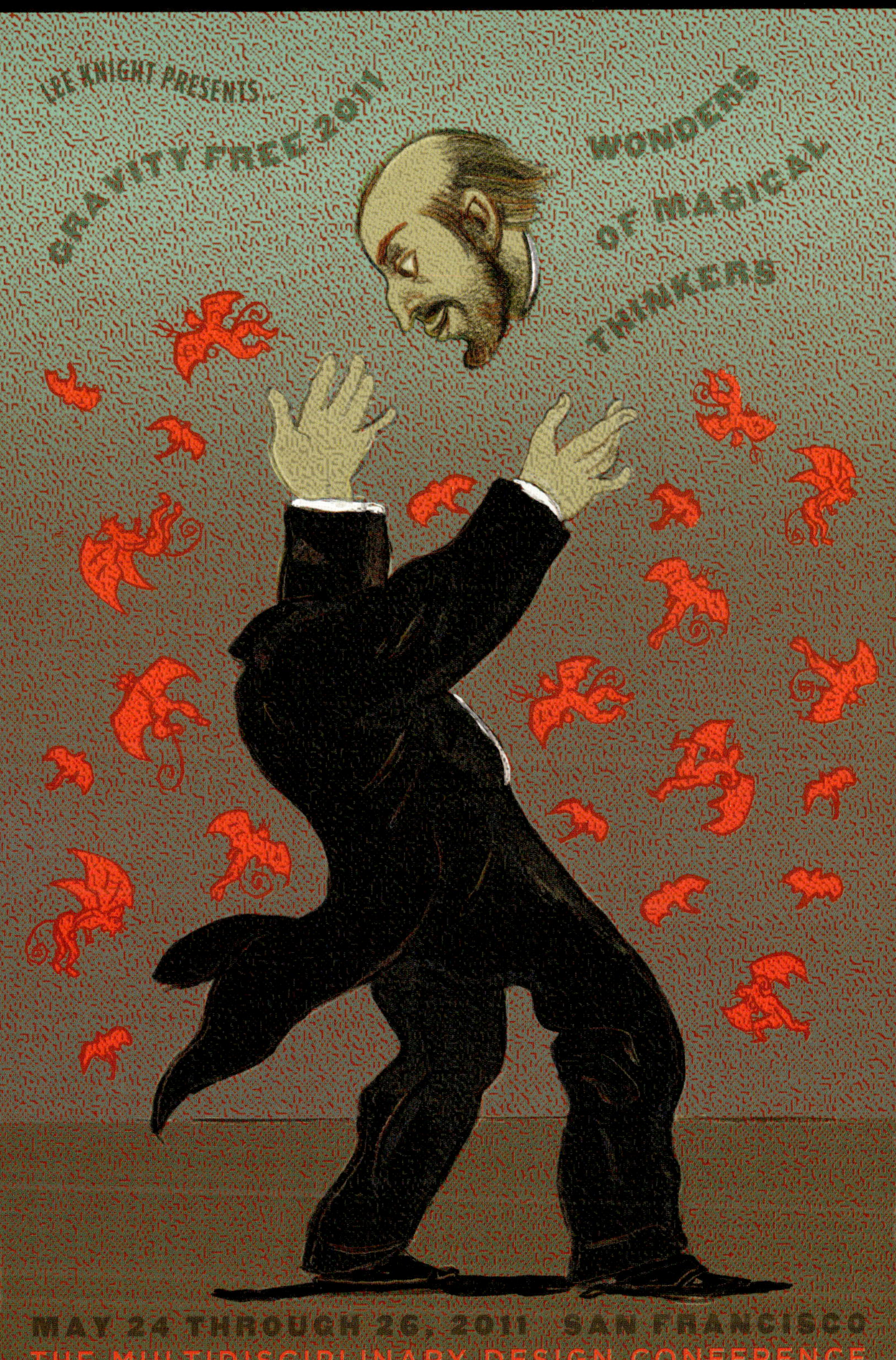
LEE KNIGHT PRESENTS
GRAVITY FREE 2011
WONDERS OF MAGICAL THINKERS
MAY 24 THROUGH 26, 2011 SAN FRANCISCO
THE MULTIDISCIPLINARY DESIGN CONFERENCE

I developed a group of alternative images to depict the corruption of the Catholic Church. The one finally chosen is less outrageous than the others.

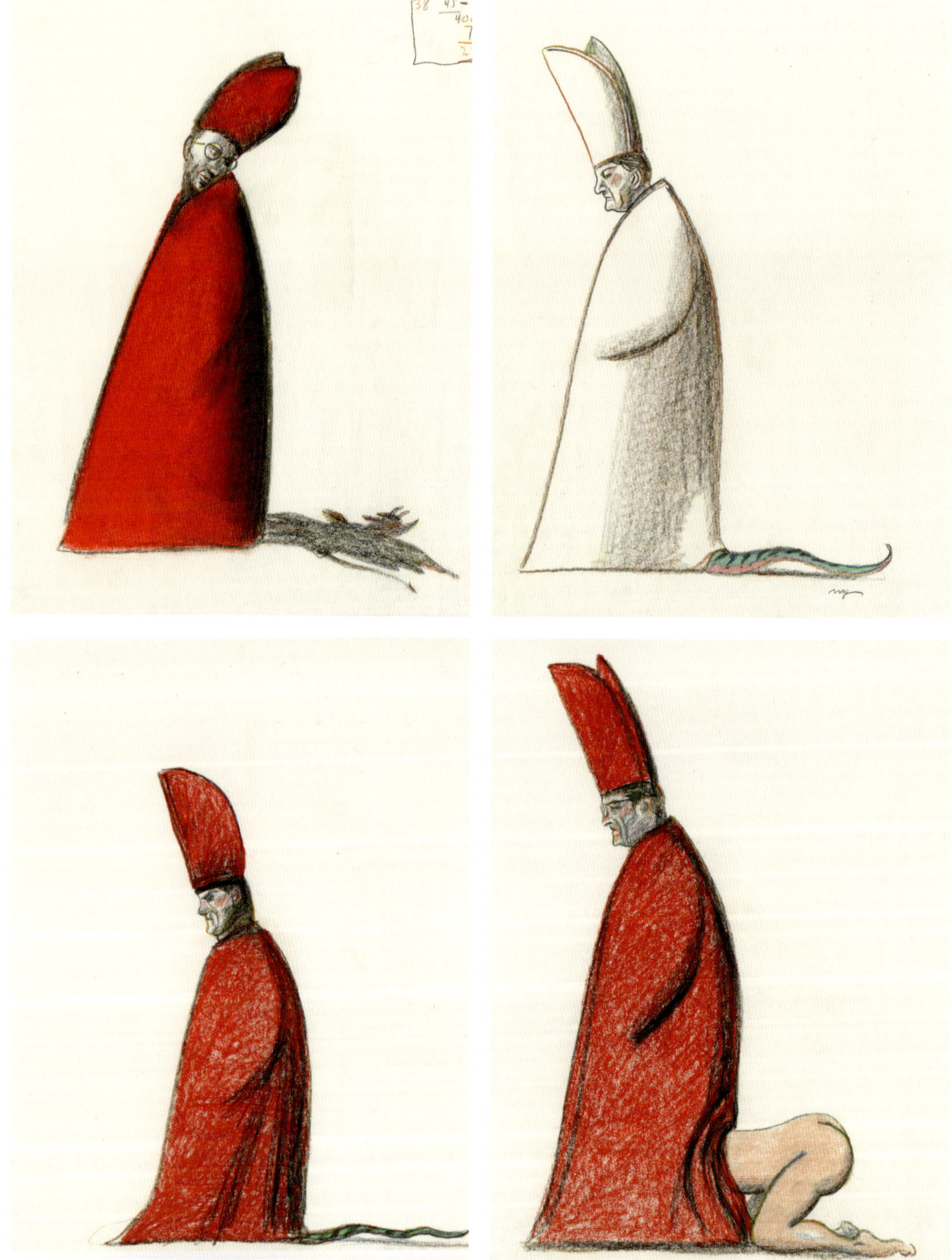

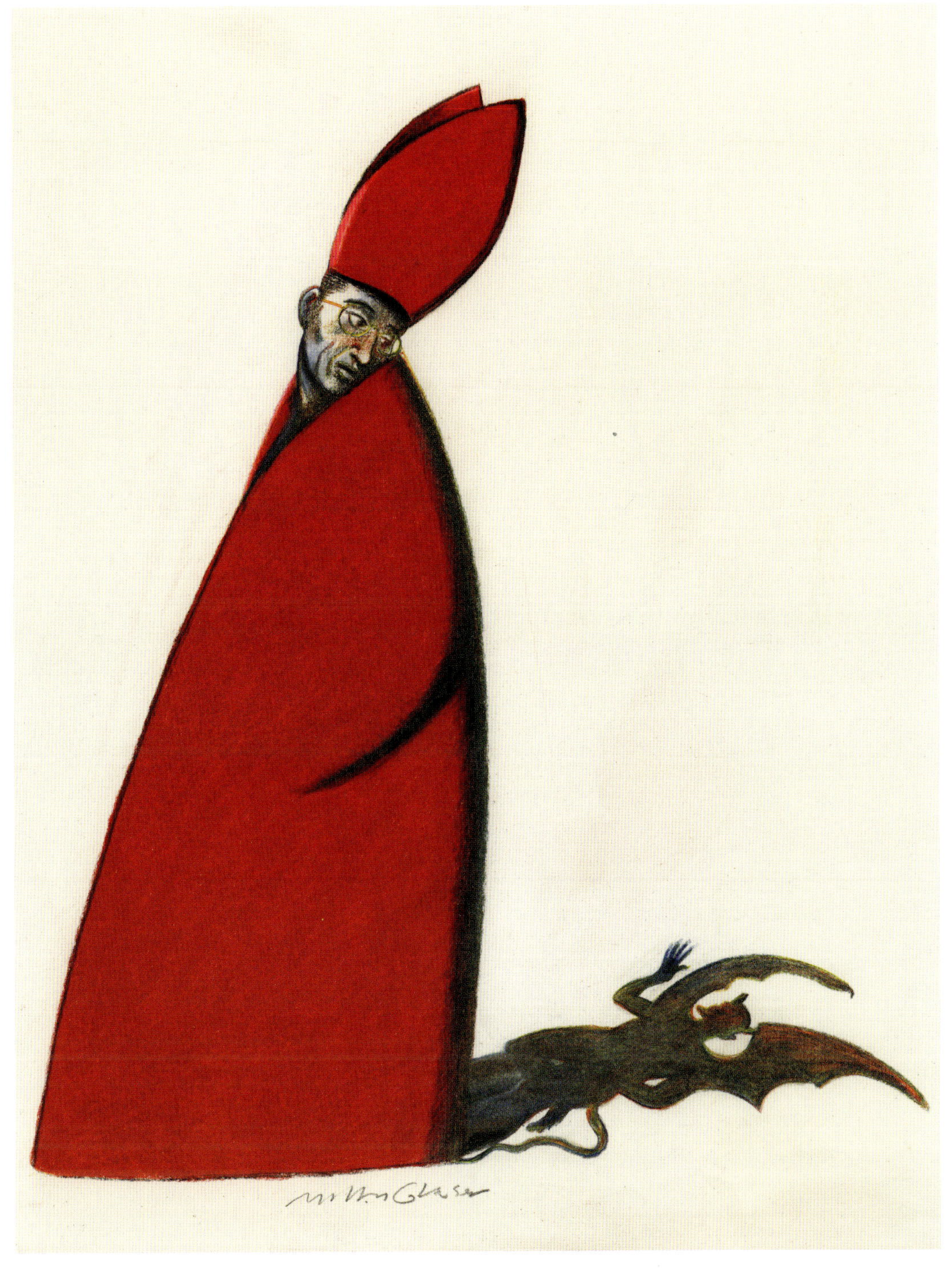

I've never seen a photograph of Albert Camus without a cigarette, so I decided to make this the central motif of this poster.

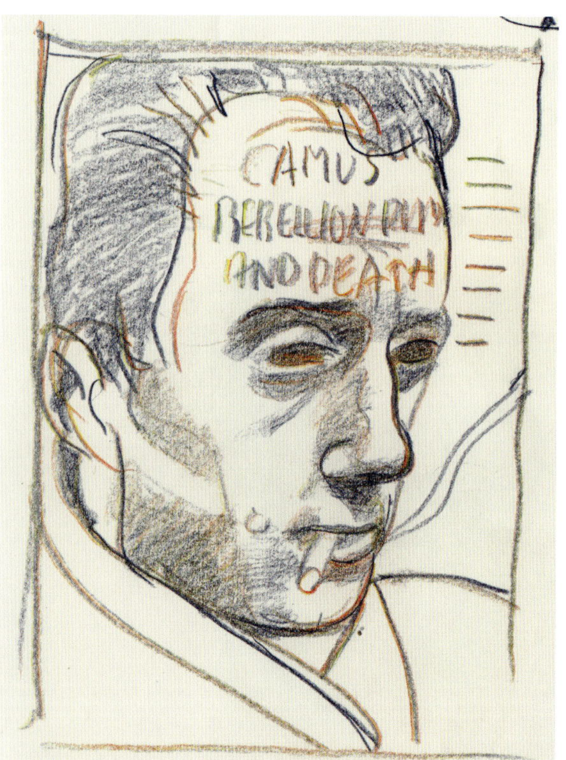
CAMUS
REBELLION AND
AND DEATH

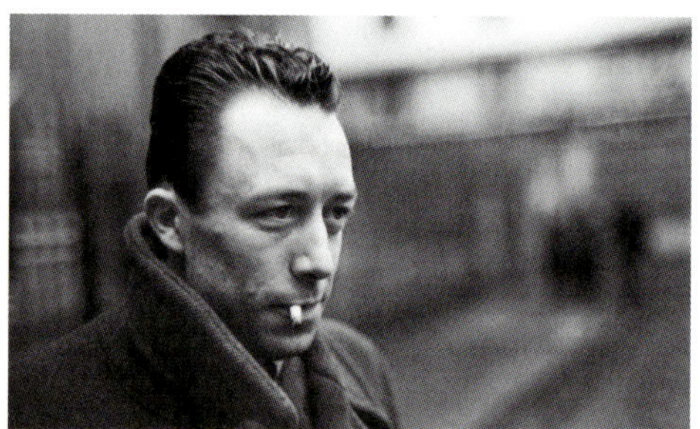

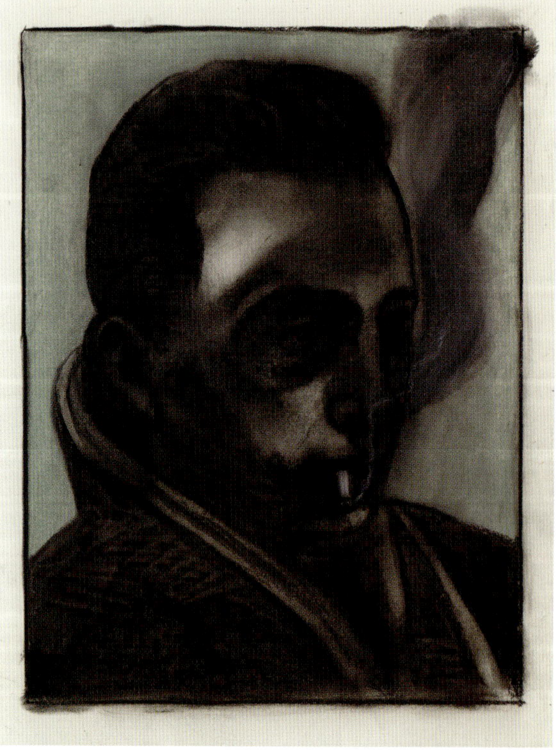

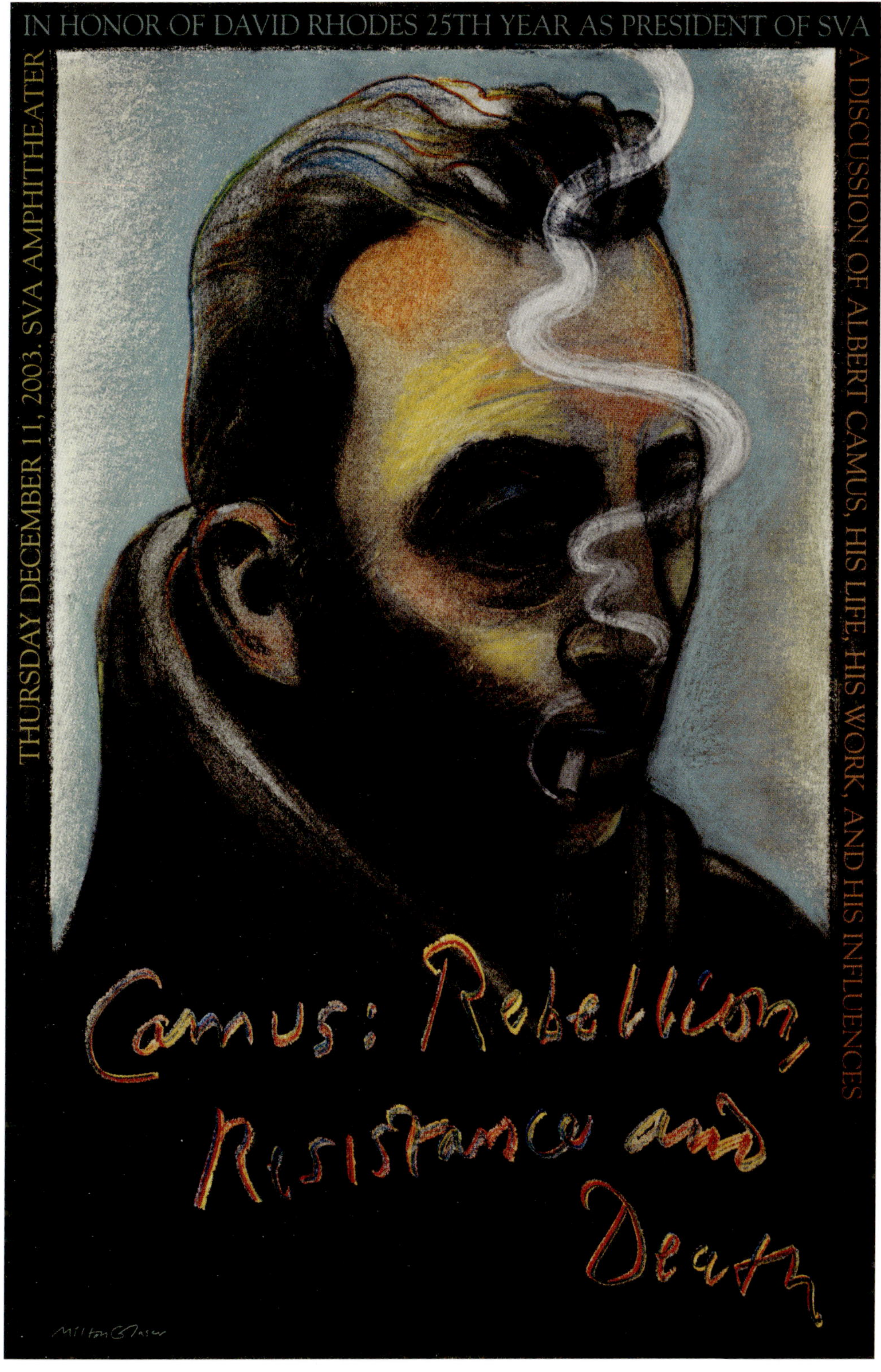
IN HONOR OF DAVID RHODES 25TH YEAR AS PRESIDENT OF SVA
THURSDAY DECEMBER 11, 2003. SVA AMPHITHEATER
A DISCUSSION OF ALBERT CAMUS, HIS LIFE, HIS WORK, AND HIS INFLUENCES
Camus: Rebellion, Resistance and Death
Milton Glaser

The finished art of *Monet Reaching for His Brush* started with a photograph of the event informed by my memory of a beautiful painting by Matisse. The abstract nature of the painting's red field influenced my decision to transform the line drawing into a colored print. The synthesis of actual reference and memory creates a powerful combination.

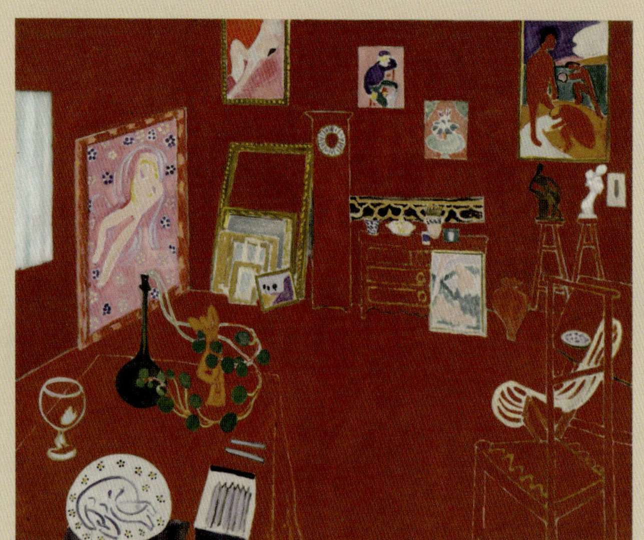

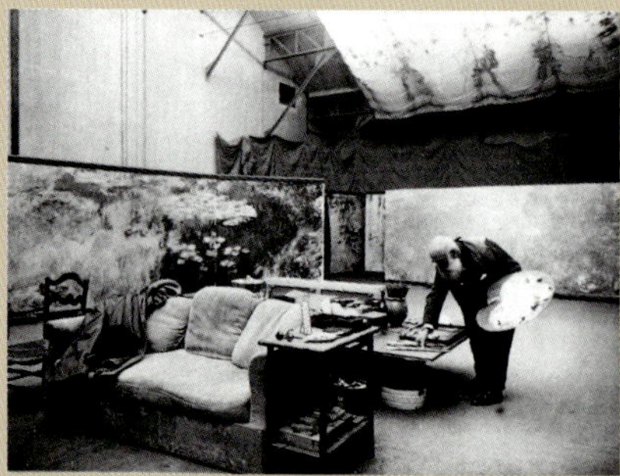

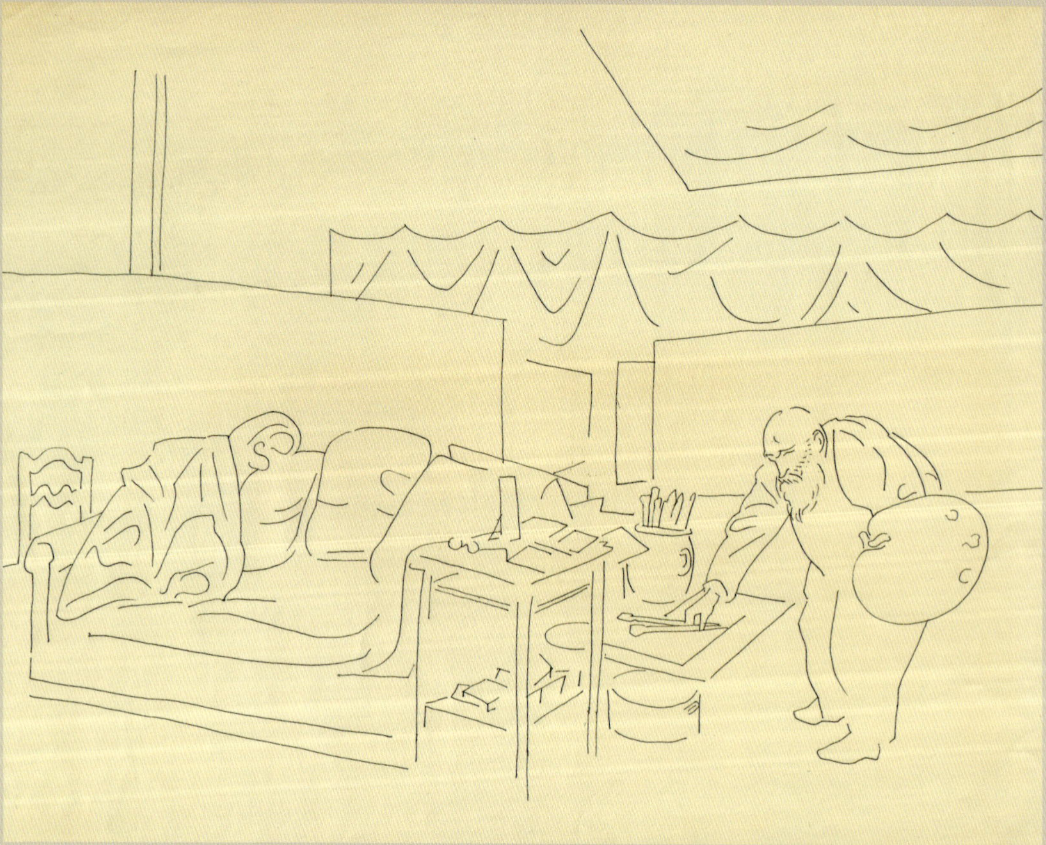

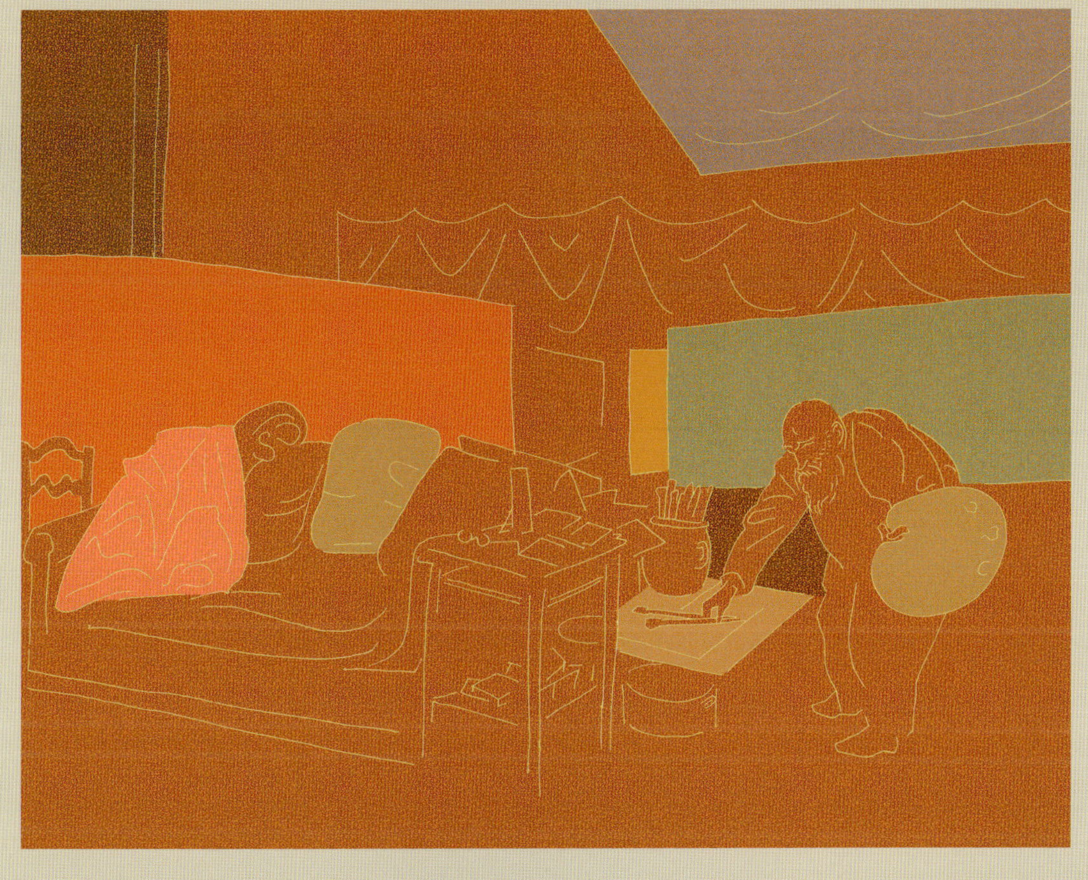

A line drawing can establish the entire structure of an illustration, while the use of tonality and color can create the opportunity for changing the meaning. The most significant element of the work to me is the red light that illuminates Othello's face, an idea that occurred to me on the path to executing the finish.

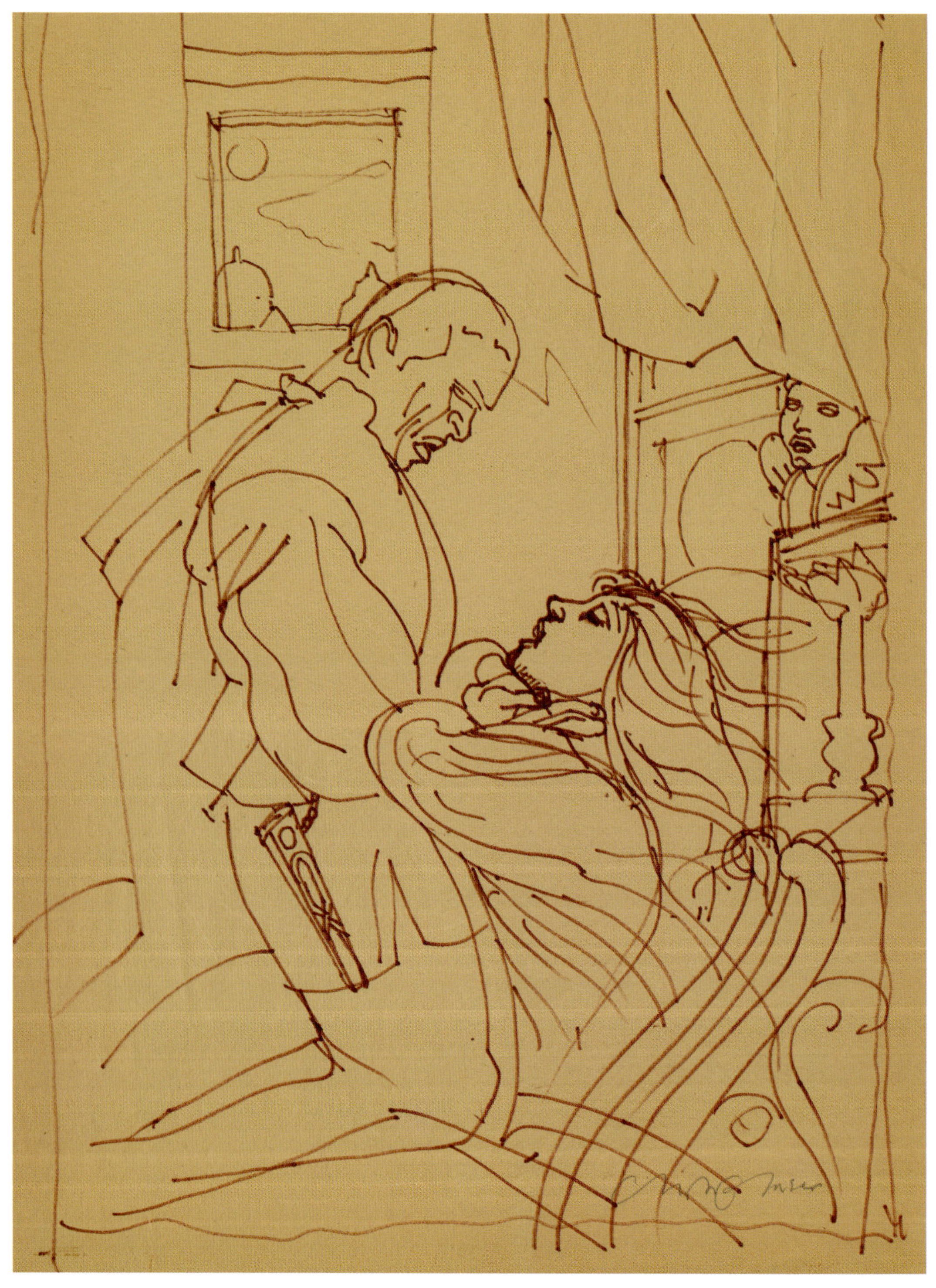

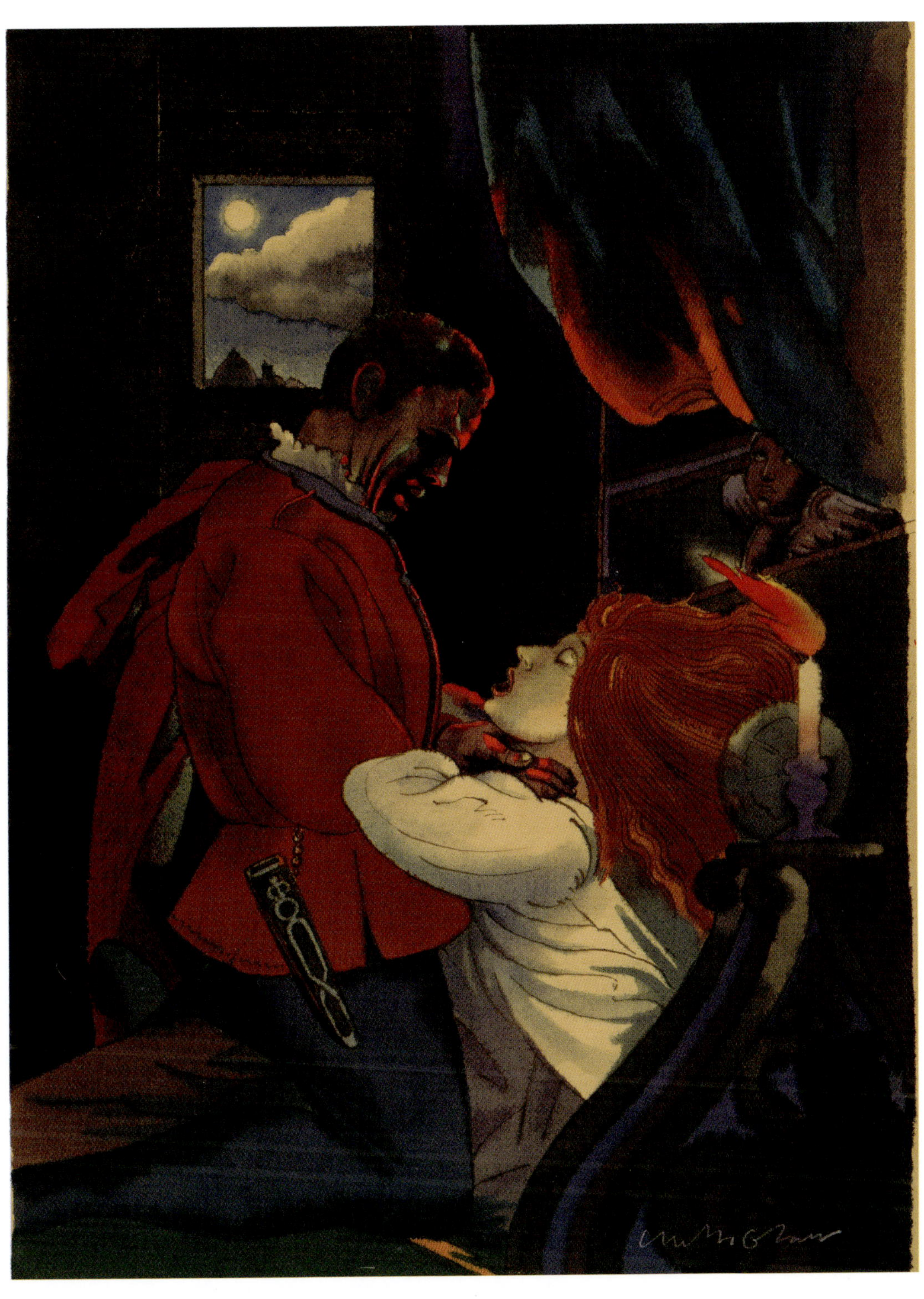

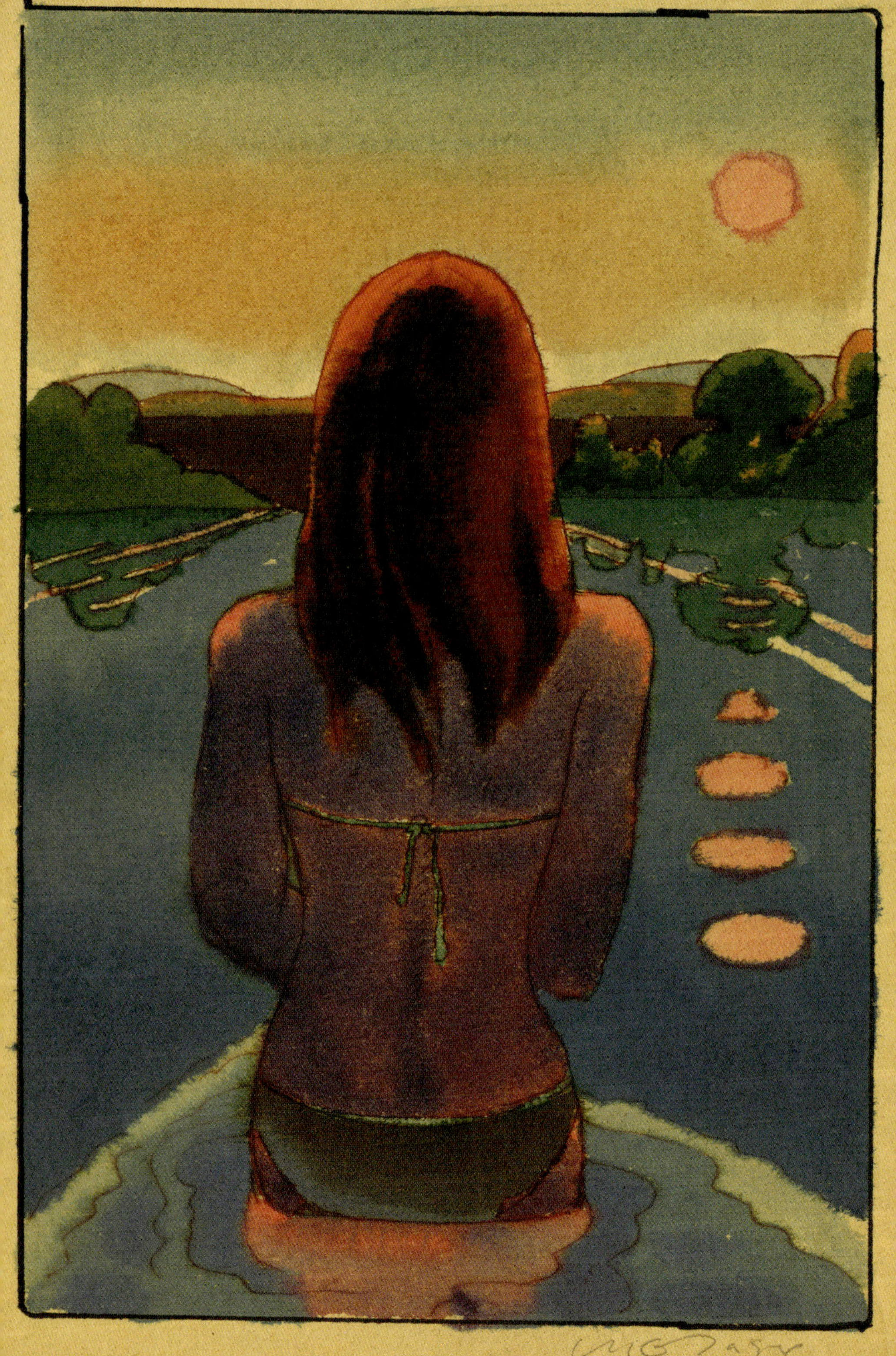

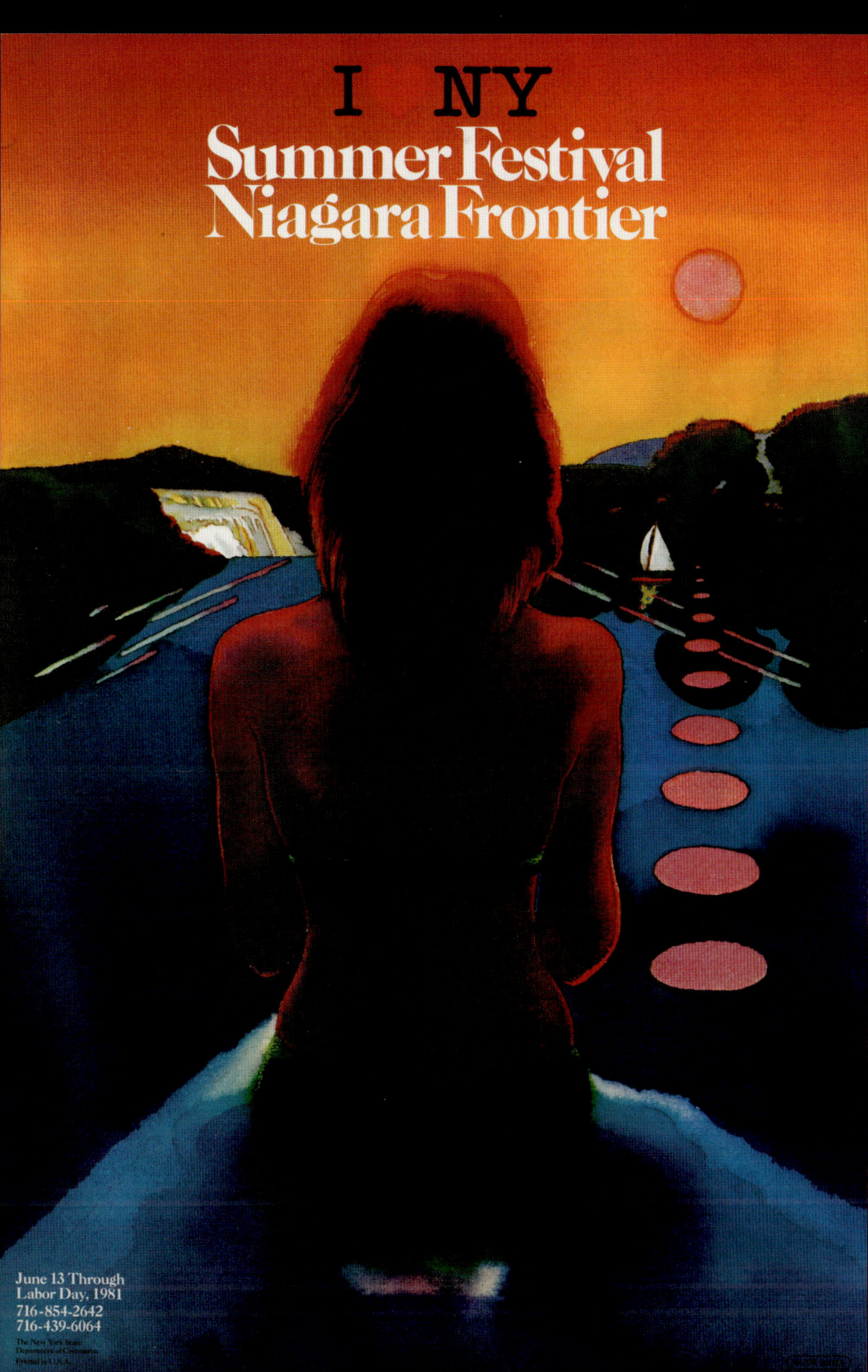
I ♥ NY
Summer Festival
Niagara Frontier
June 13 Through
Labor Day, 1981
716-854-2642
716-439-6064
The New York State
Department of Commerce
Printed in U.S.A.

The first insight that the word "luck" could become the eyes of a cat shows more expressive content than the more refined and studied version that became the finish.

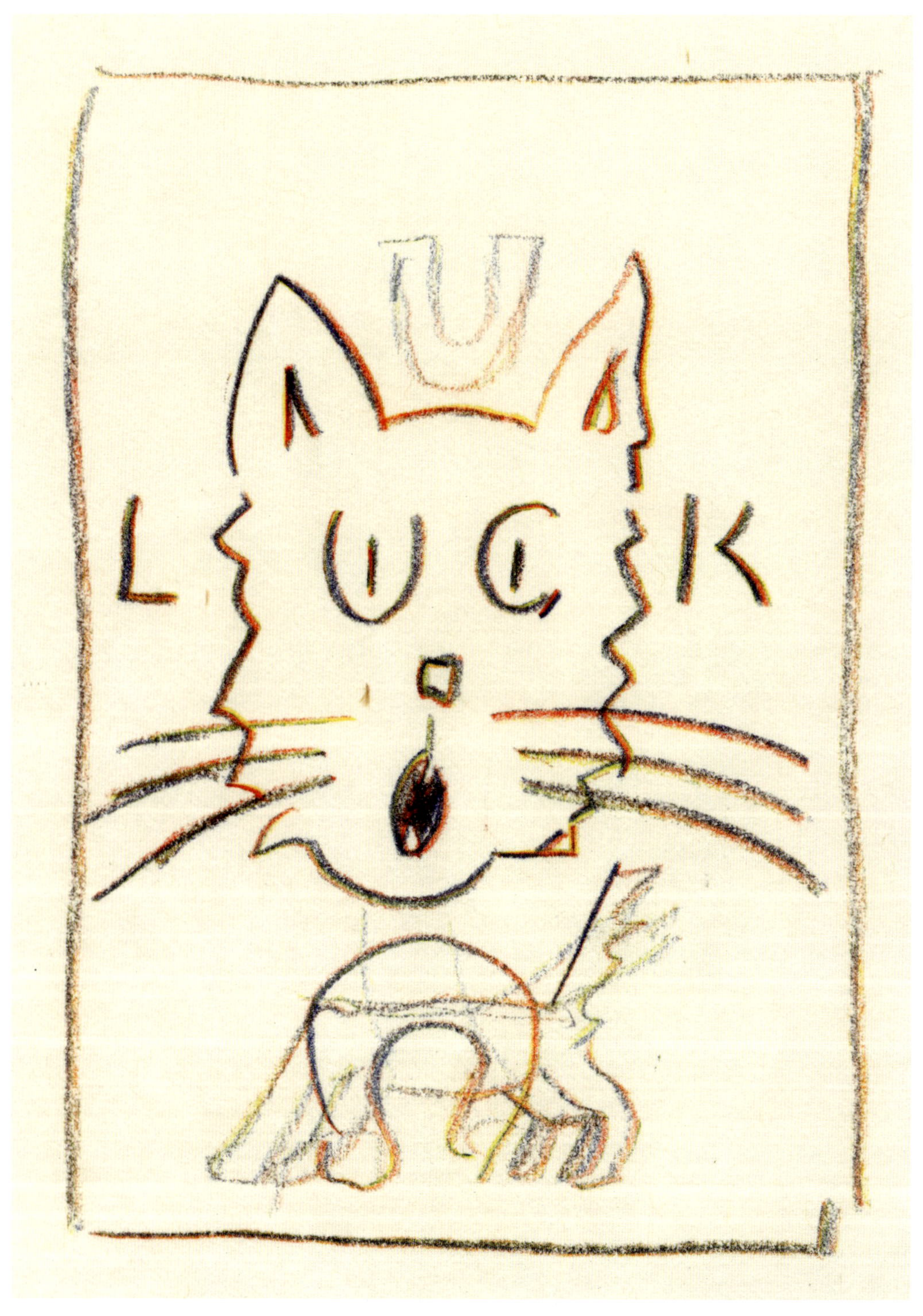

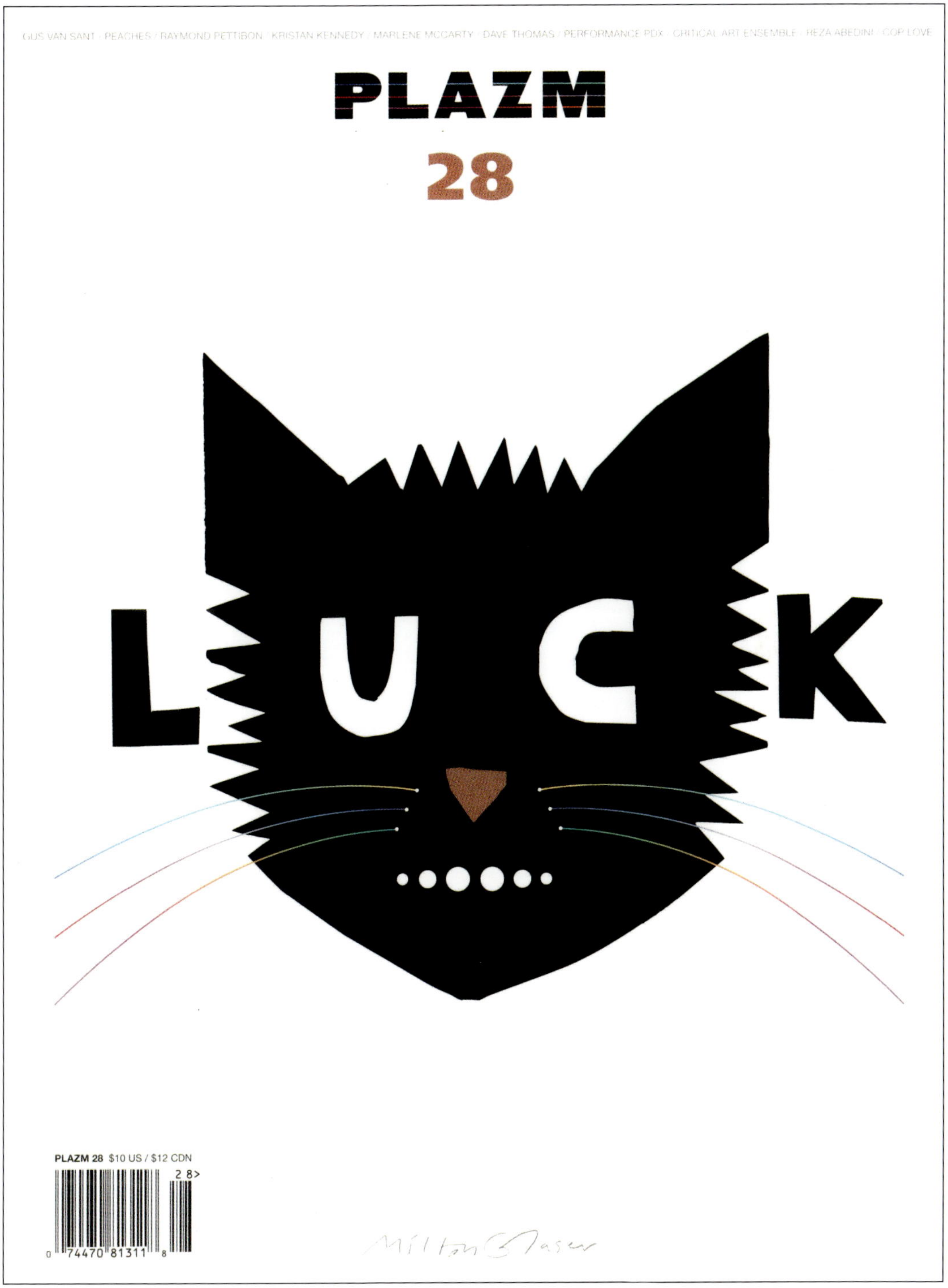

GUS VAN SANT · PEACHES / RAYMOND PETTIBON · KRISTAN KENNEDY / MARLENE MCCARTY · DAVE THOMAS · PERFORMANCE PDX · CRITICAL ART ENSEMBLE · REZA ABEDINI / COP LOVE

PLAZM
28

LUCK

PLAZM 28 $10 US / $12 CDN
2 8>

0 74470 81311 8

The original drawing didn't seem to have enough interest, so I added a purely decorative element in the final.

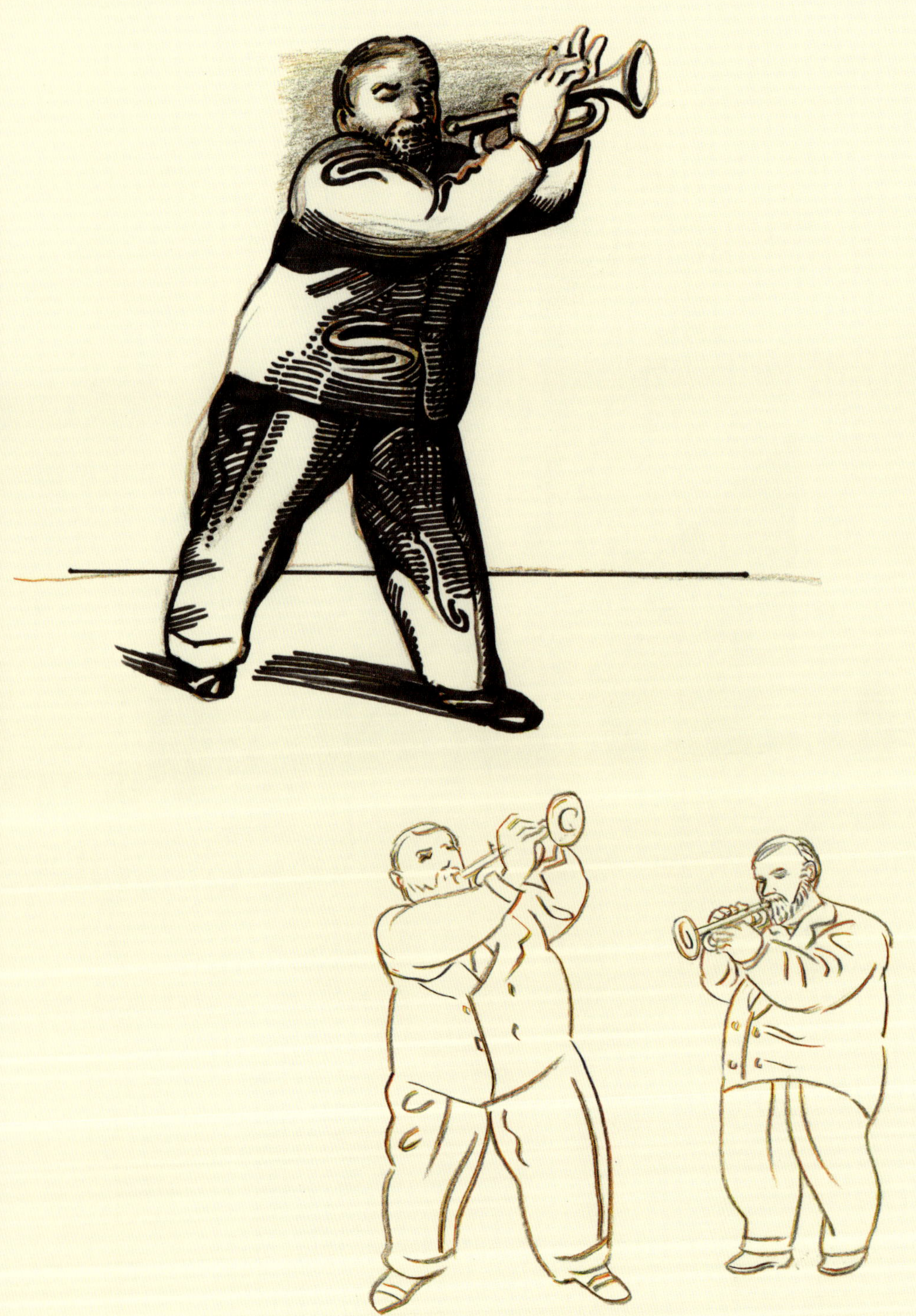

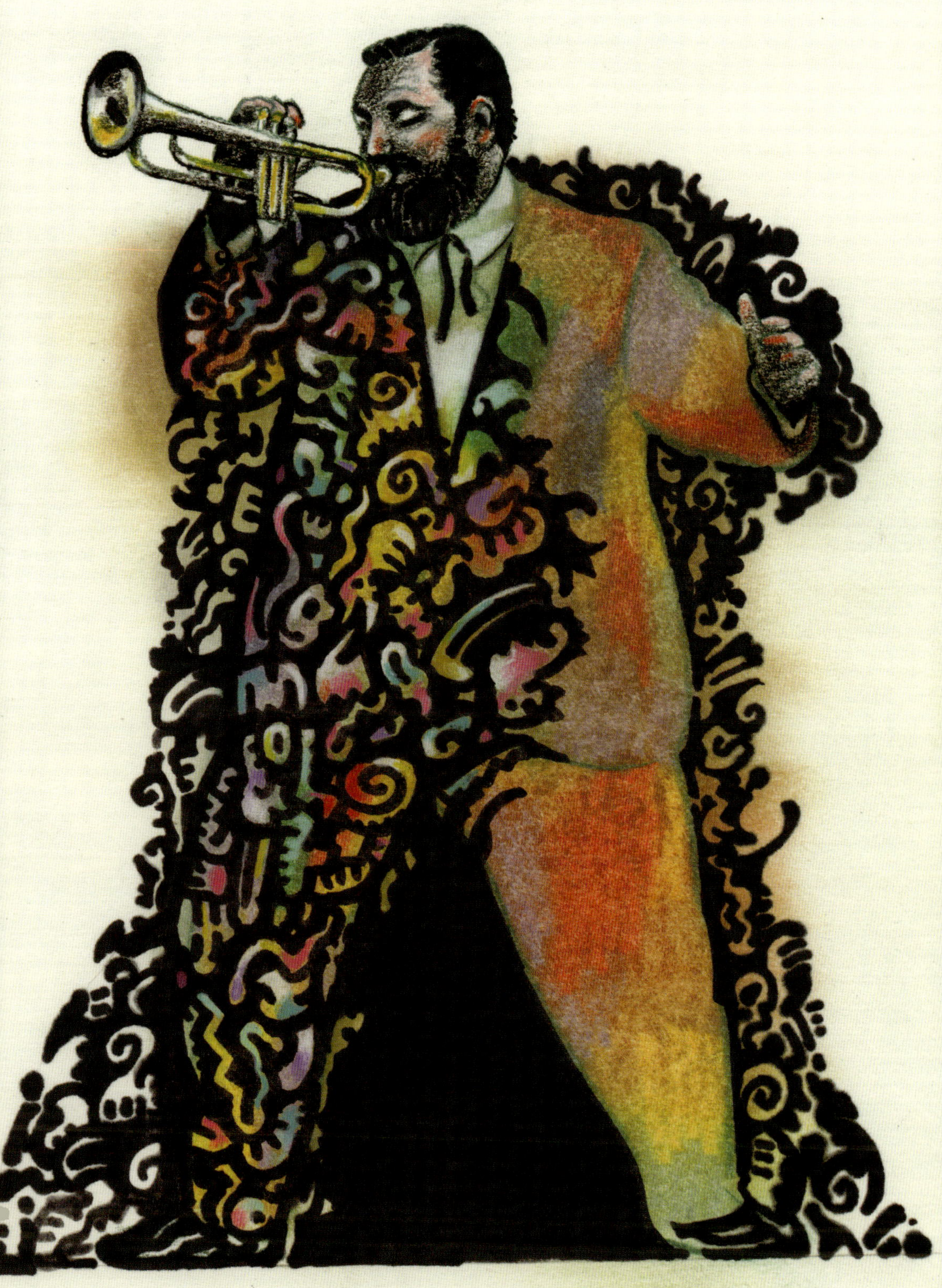

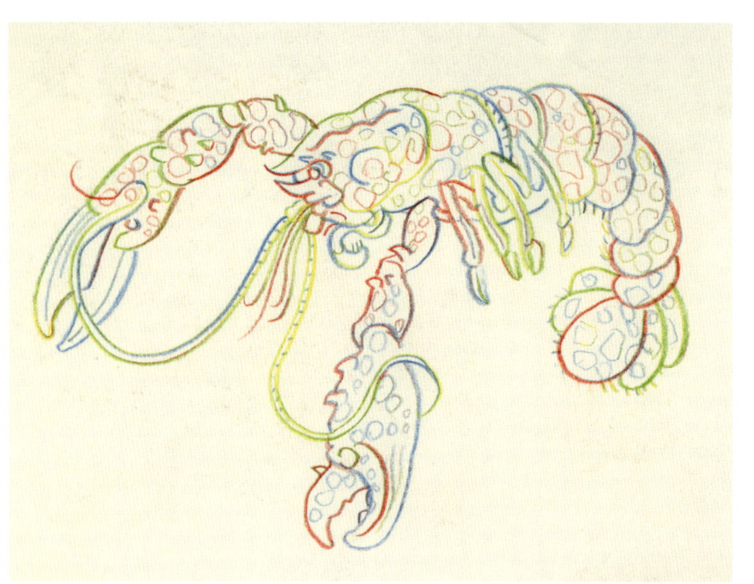

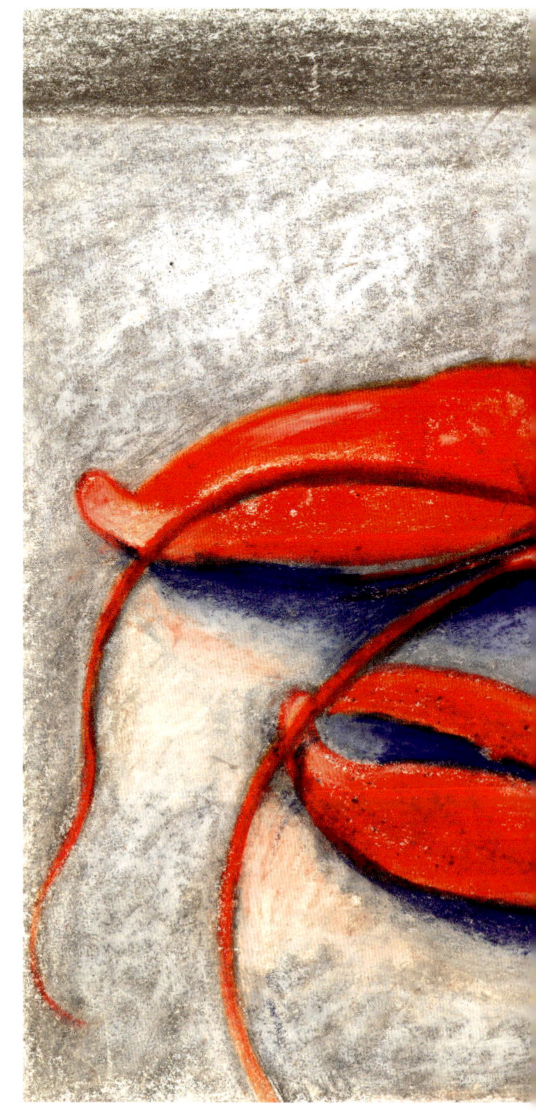

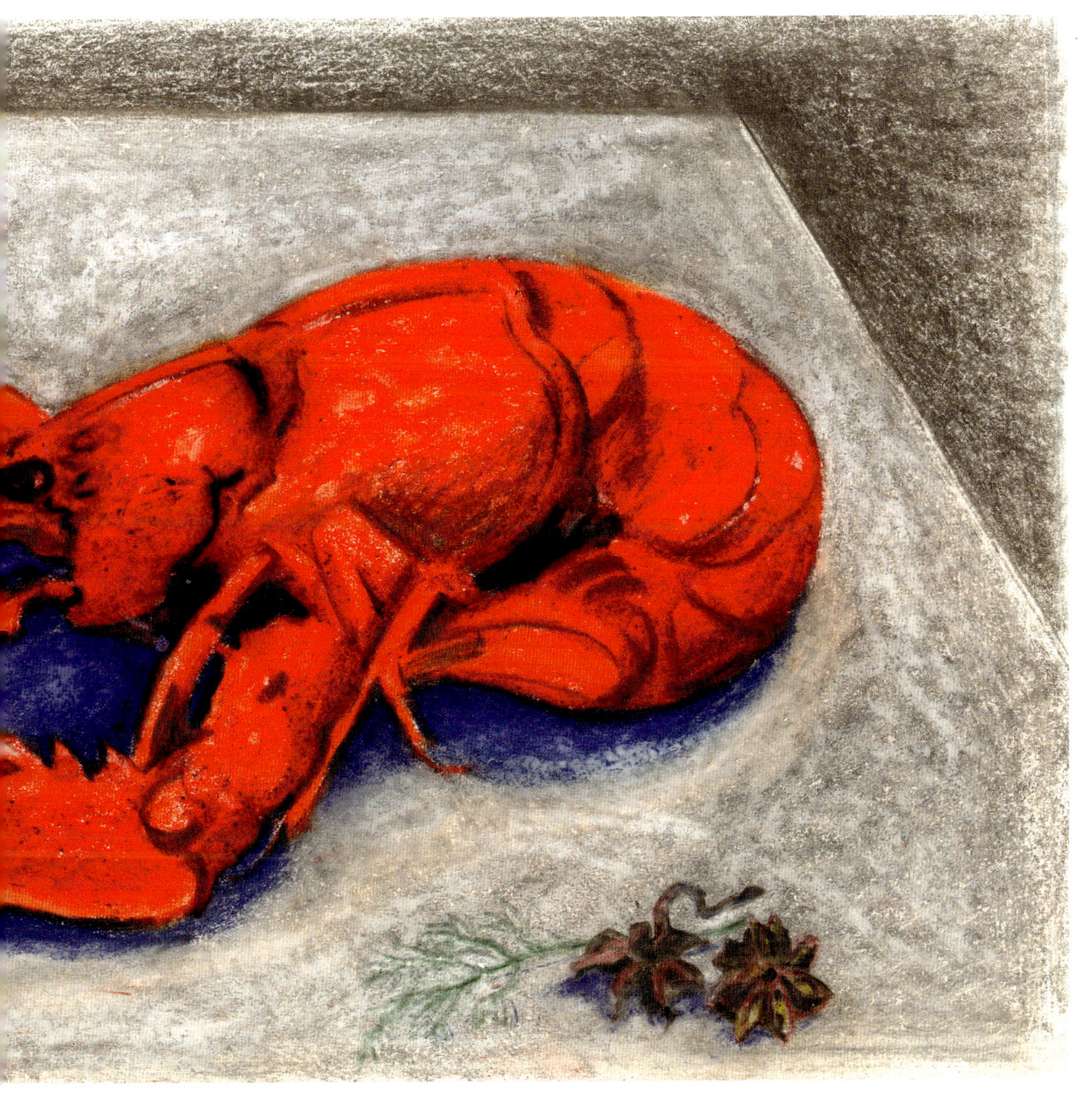

Some preliminary studies for the menu of Cellar in the Sky—a restaurant within the Windows on the World restaurant. The basic drawing remains the same, but there is a change in texture and surface.

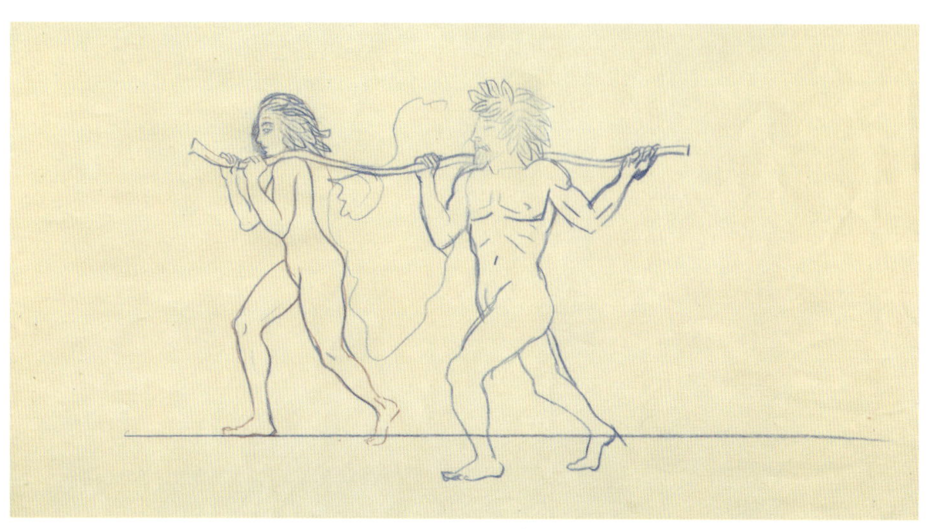

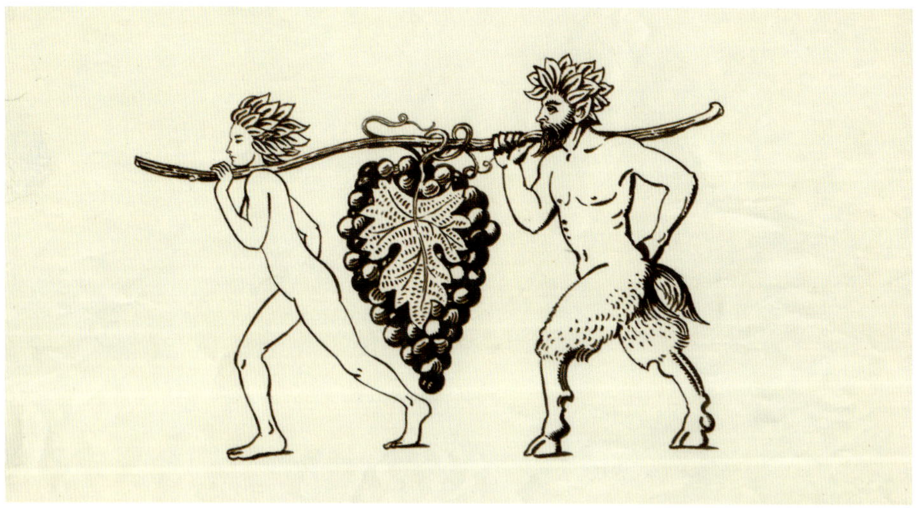

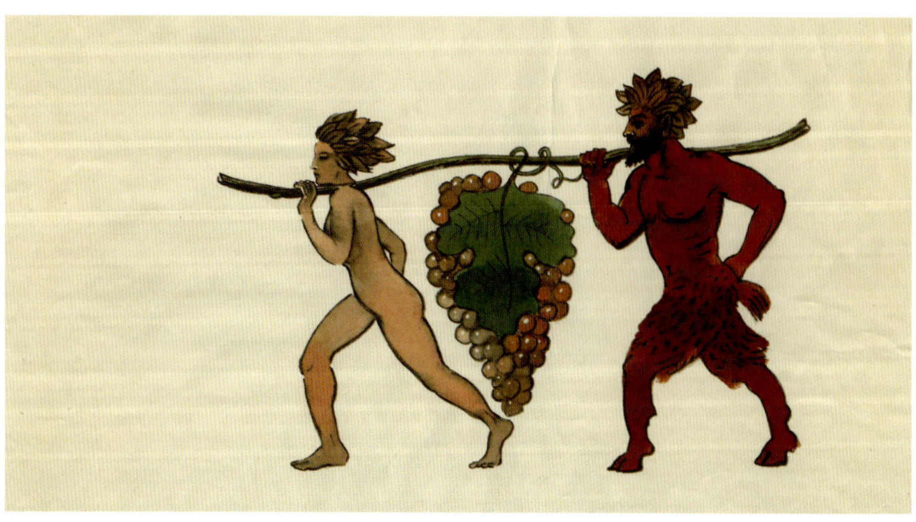

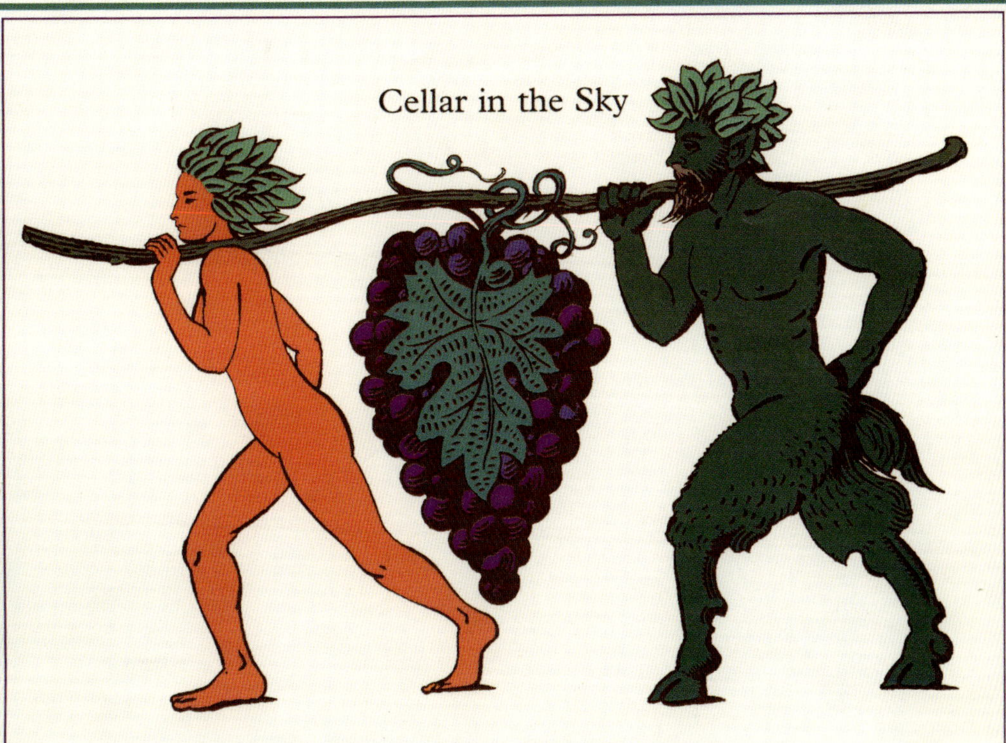

Tribute to Burgundy and the Rhone Valley

Champagne Veuve Clicquot Brut NV

Scallops w/truffle
Meursault 1st Cru les Bouches Cheres, Rene Manuel 1994

Game bird
Chambolle Musigny, Domaine Cottin 1993

Cheese course
Chateauneuf du Pape, Chateau de la Nerthe 1990

Apricot Fruit tart
Muscat de Beaumes de Venise, Domaine de Coyeaux 1993

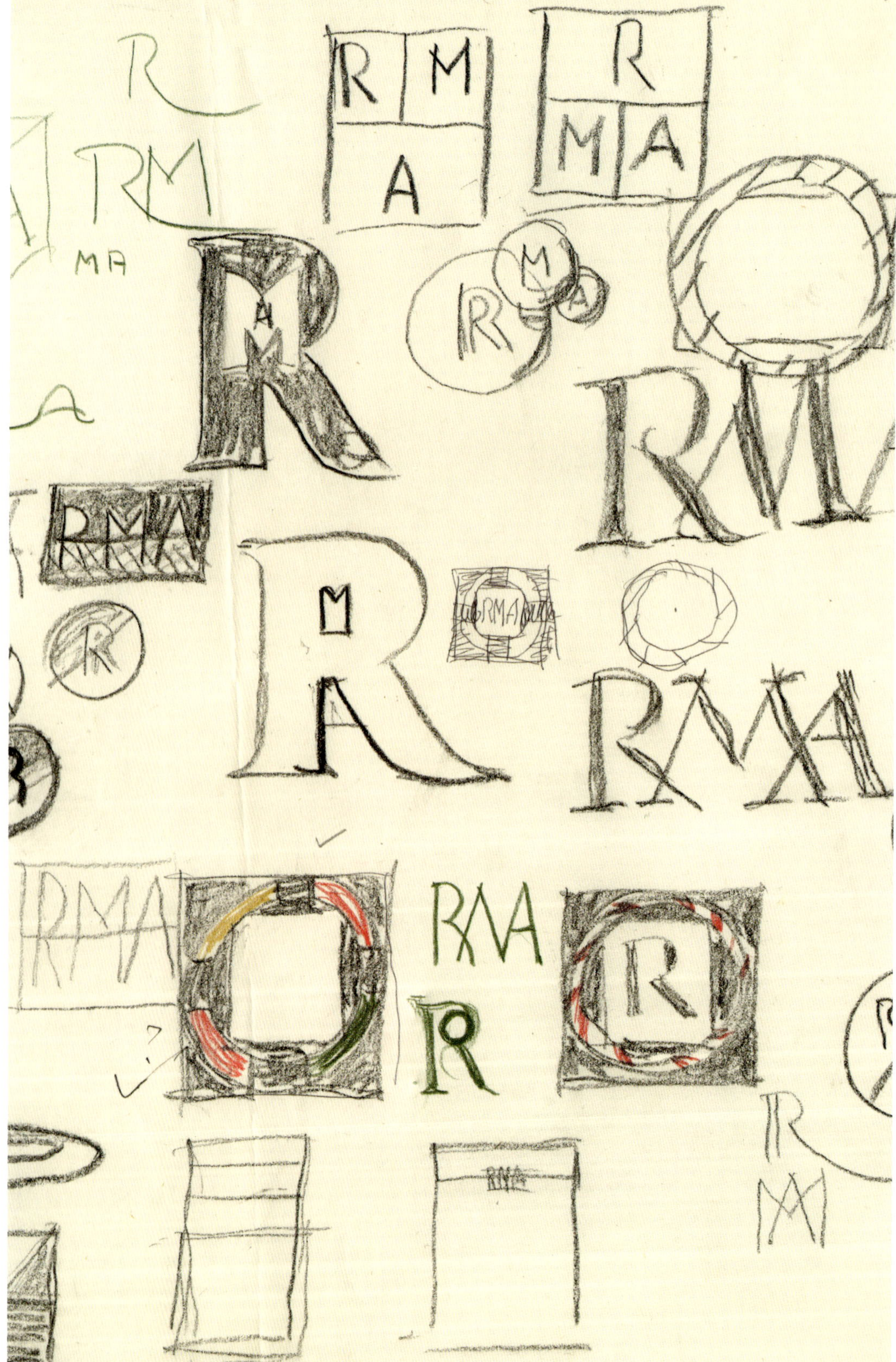

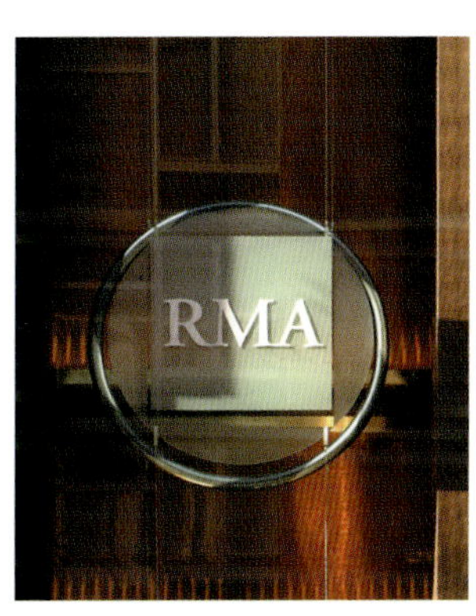

I dragged my wife, cat, and Persian rug out in front of our house in Woodstock as the basis for this drawing, which I later developed in full color.

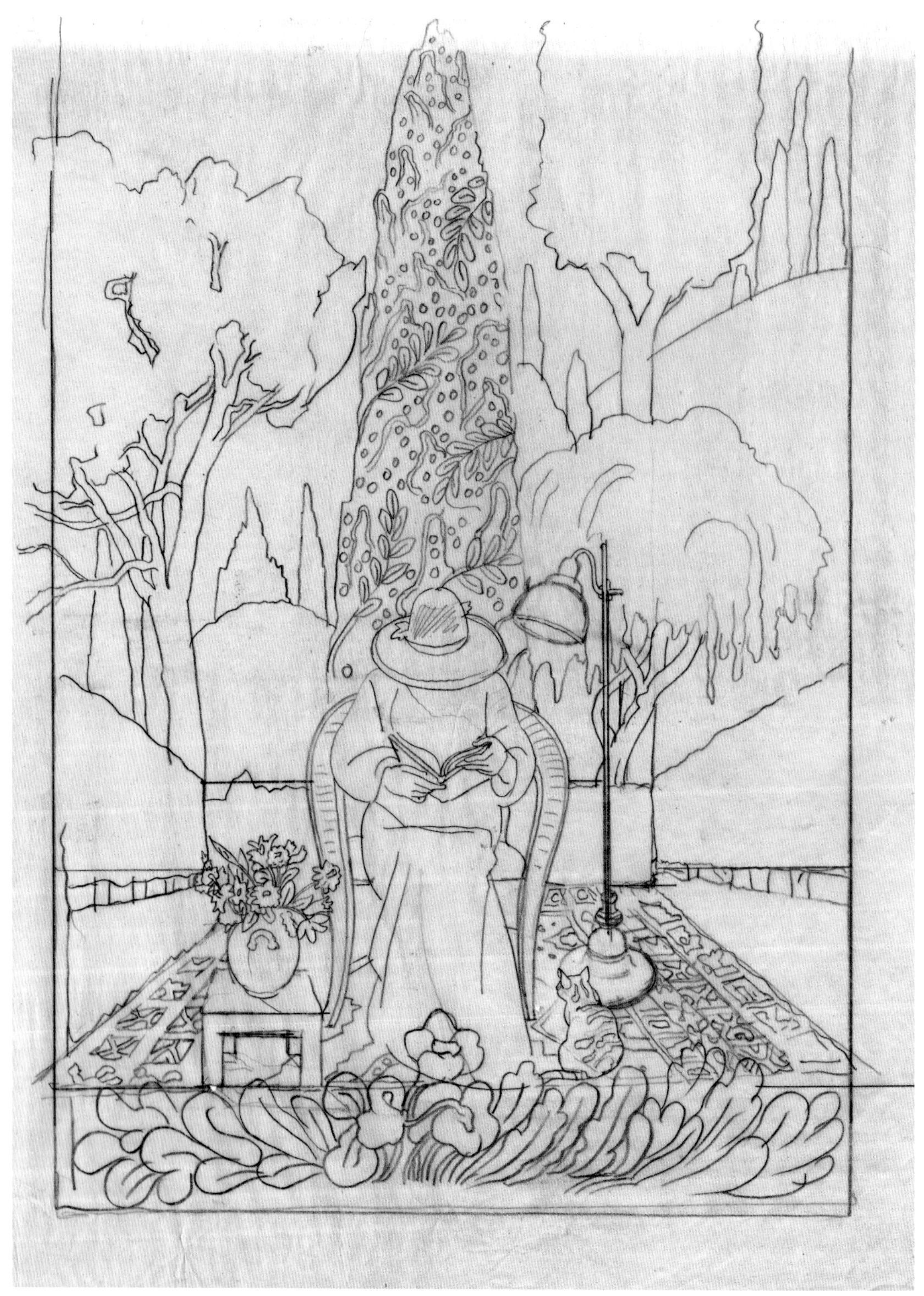

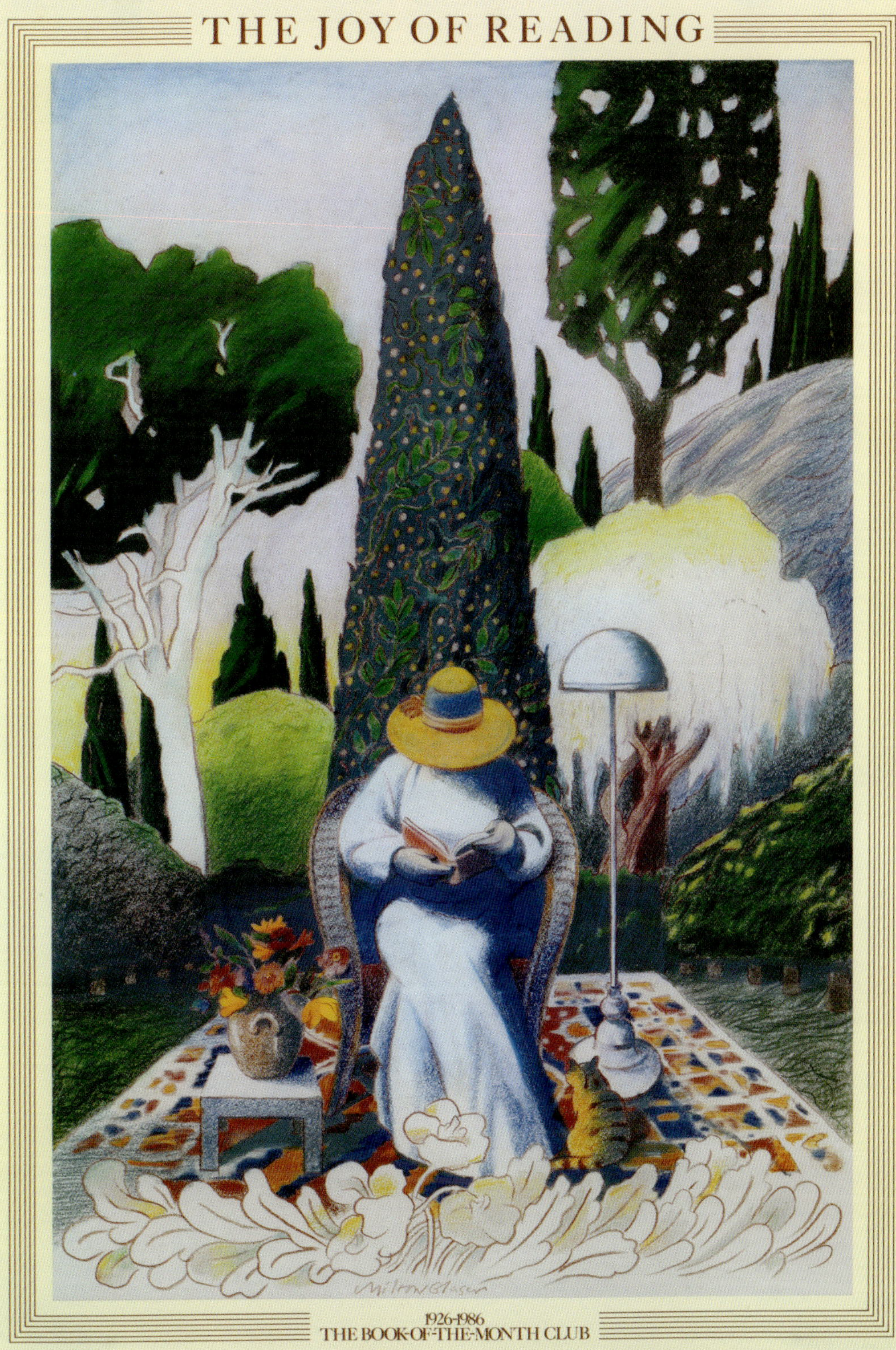

THE JOY OF READING
Milton Glaser
1926-1986
THE BOOK-OF-THE-MONTH CLUB

A poster for a chair manufacturer led to the series of proto-Cubist explorations to let the audience know that we were talking about contemporary furniture.

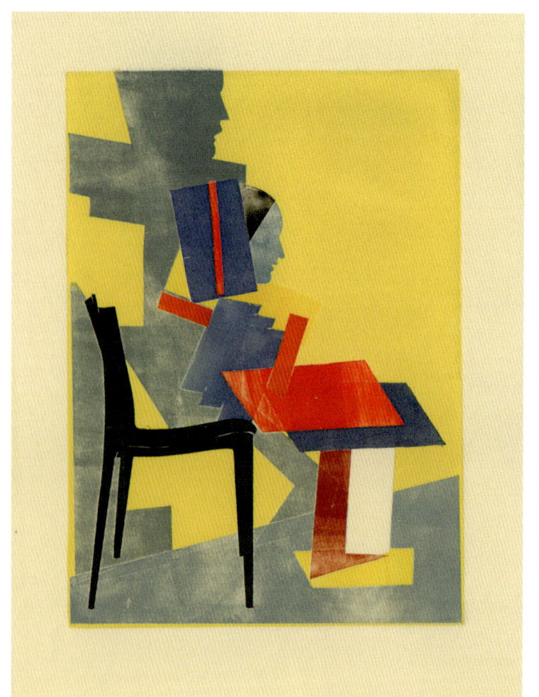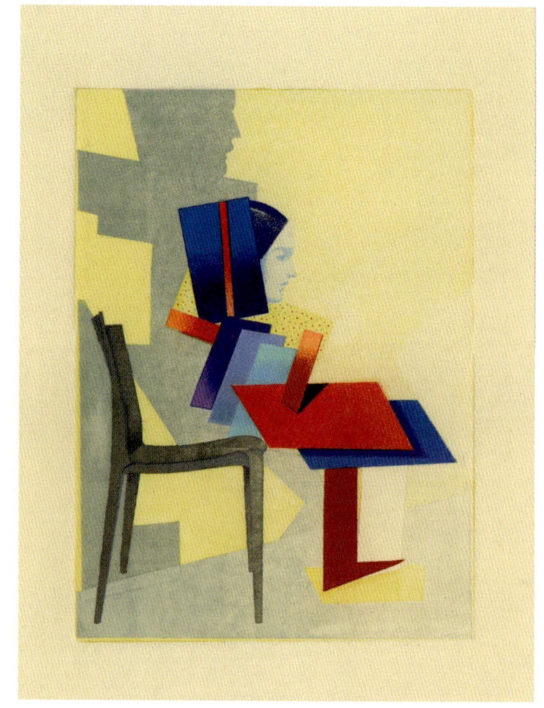

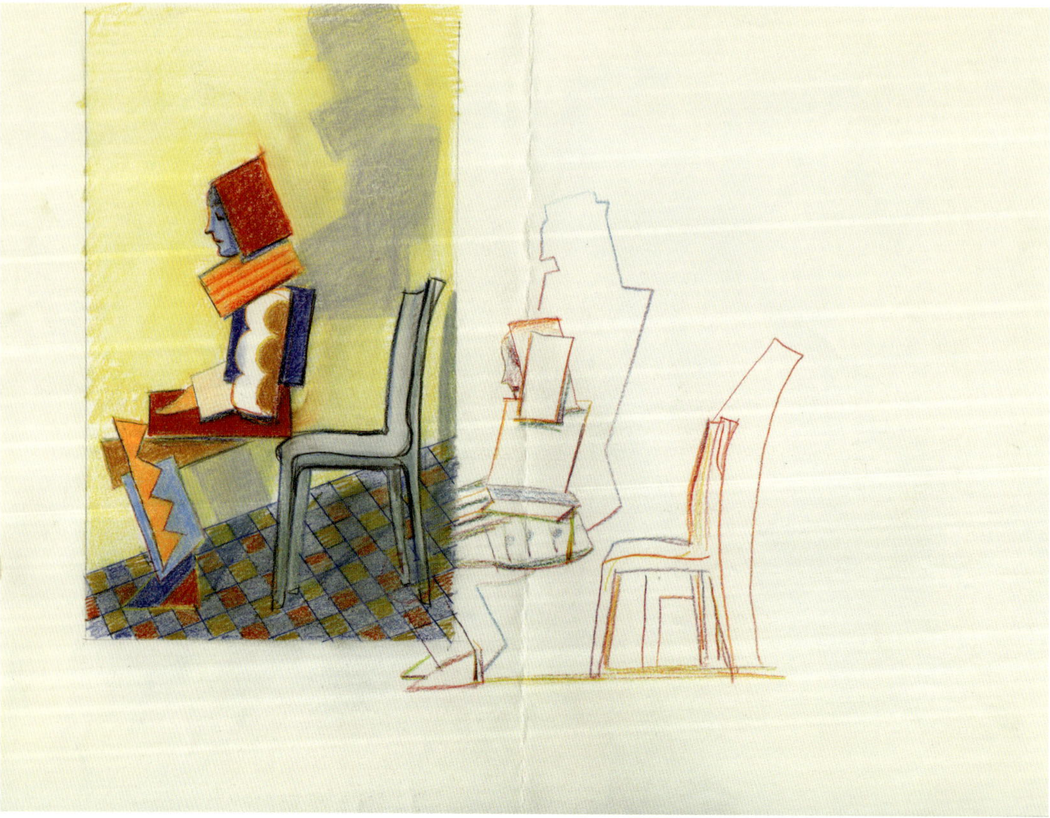

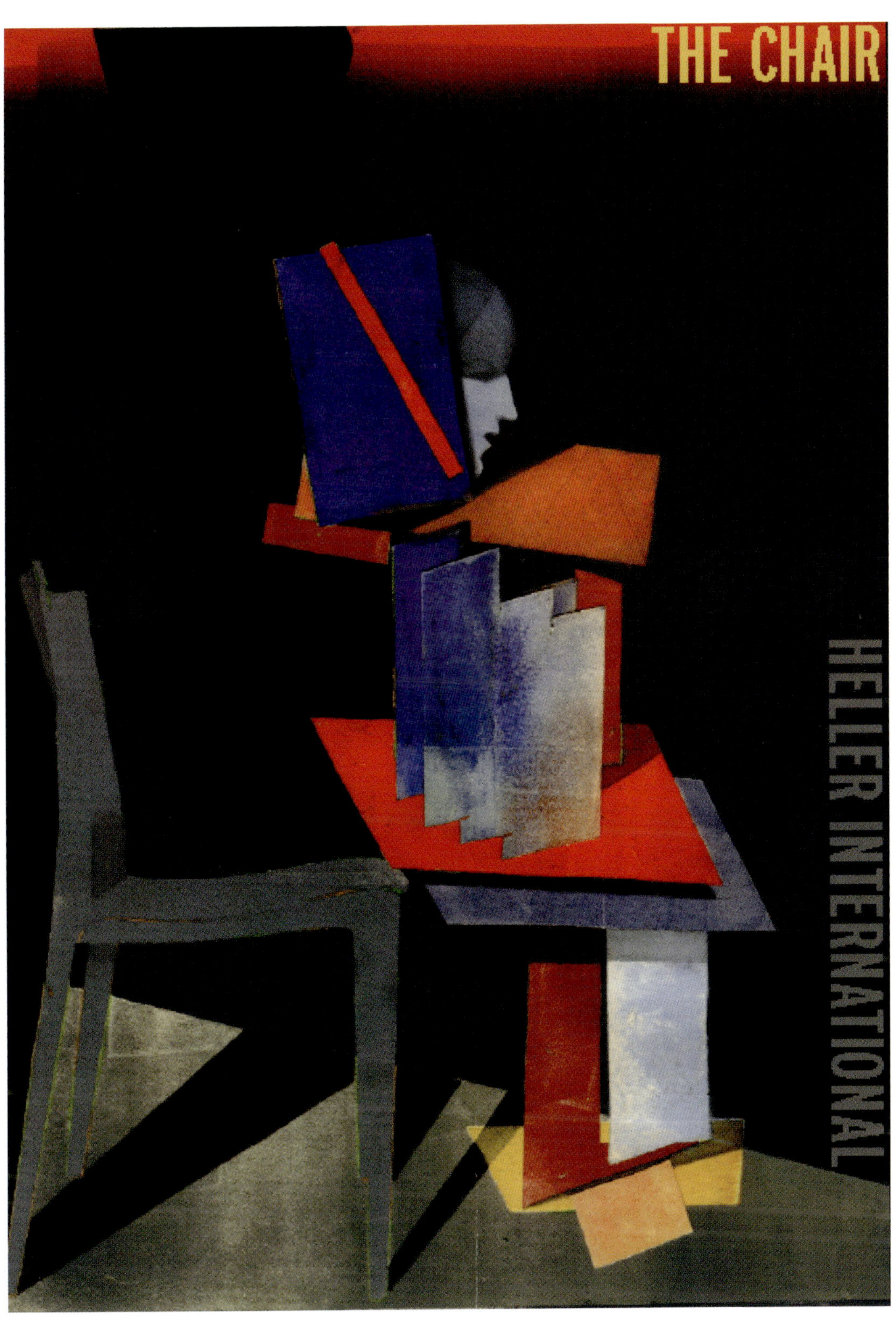
THE CHAIR
HELLER INTERNATIONAL

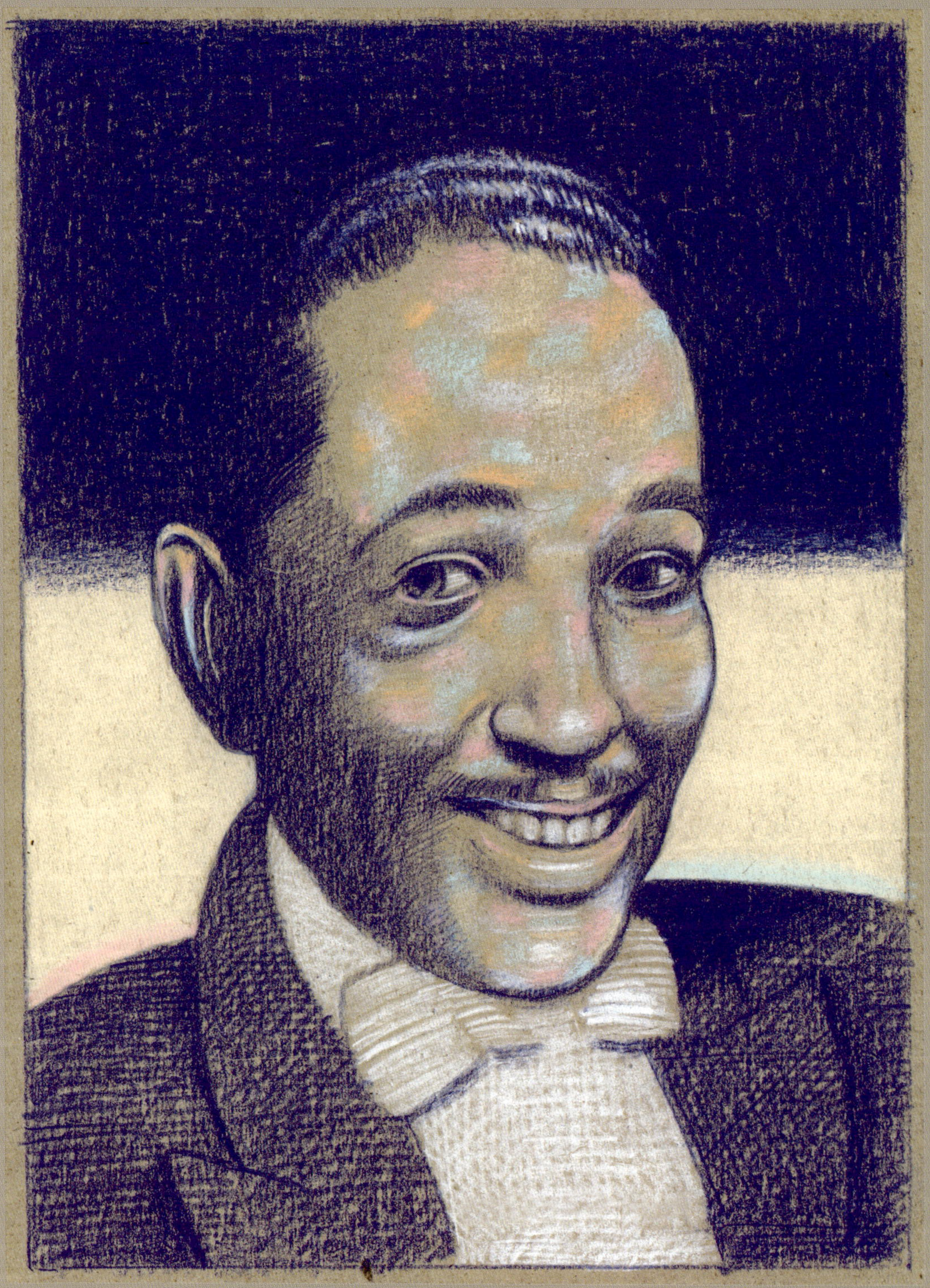

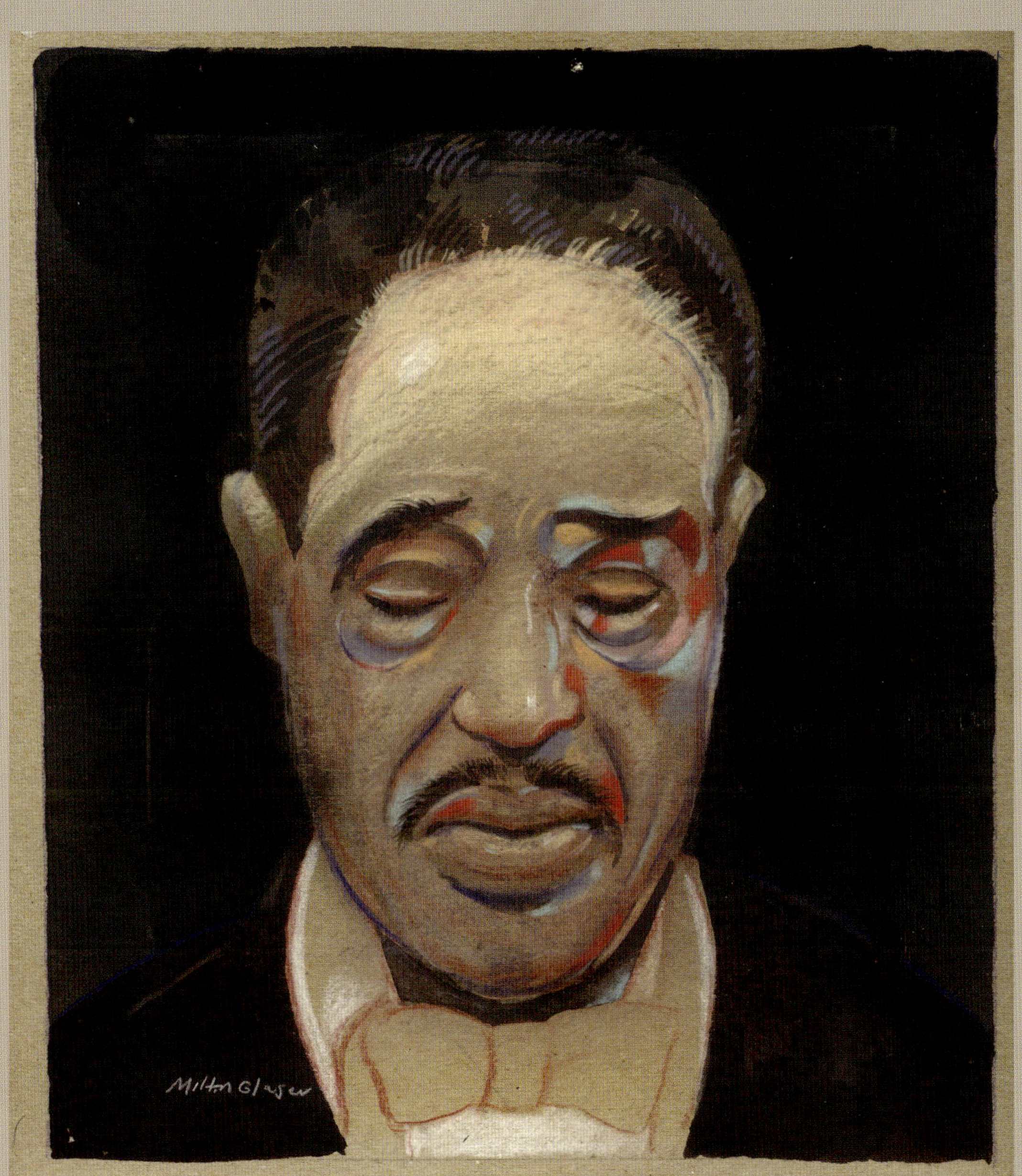
Milton Glaser

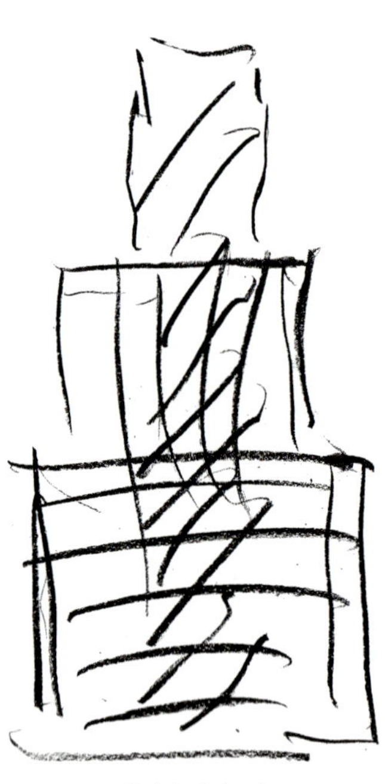

Original sketch.

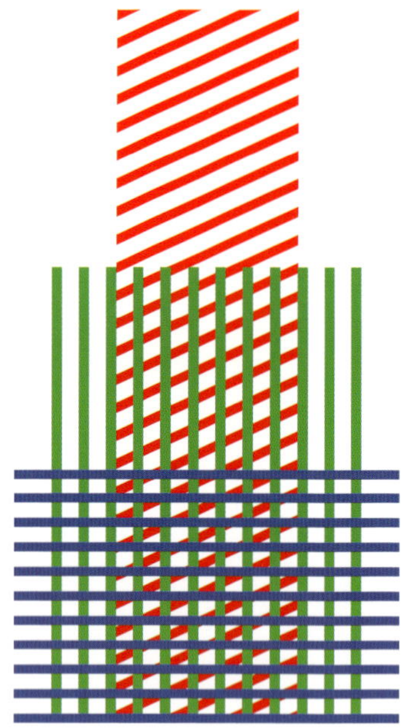

Finished logo.

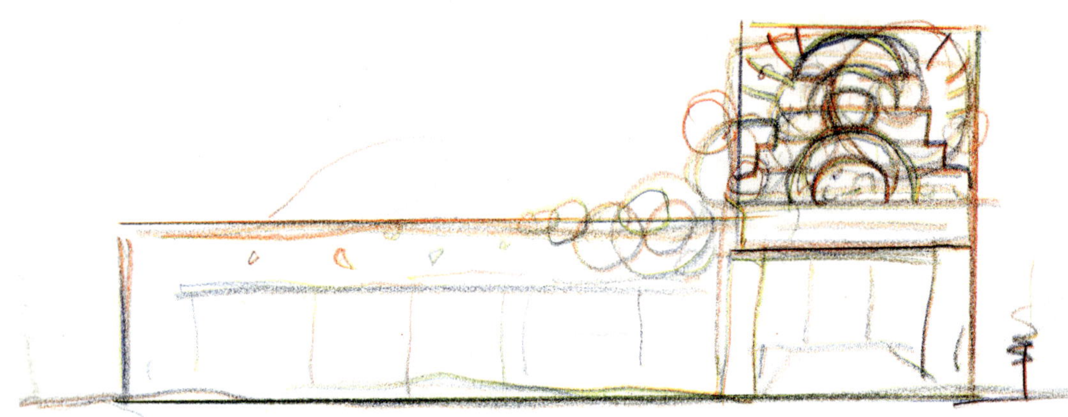

Early sketch for facade of the theatre.

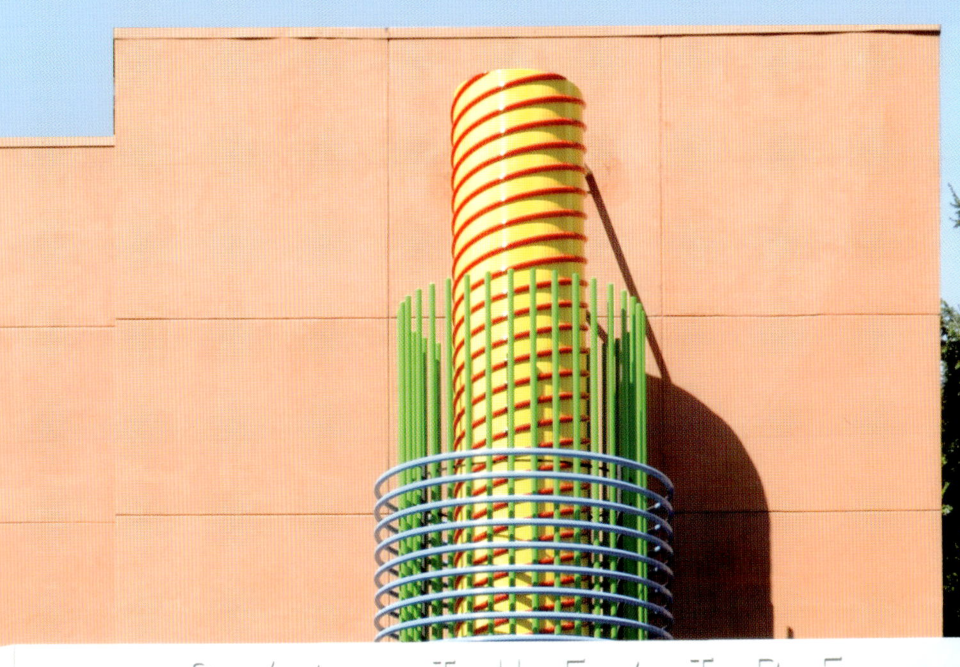

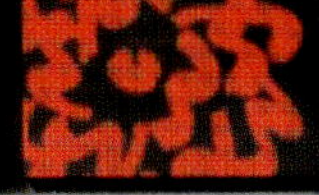

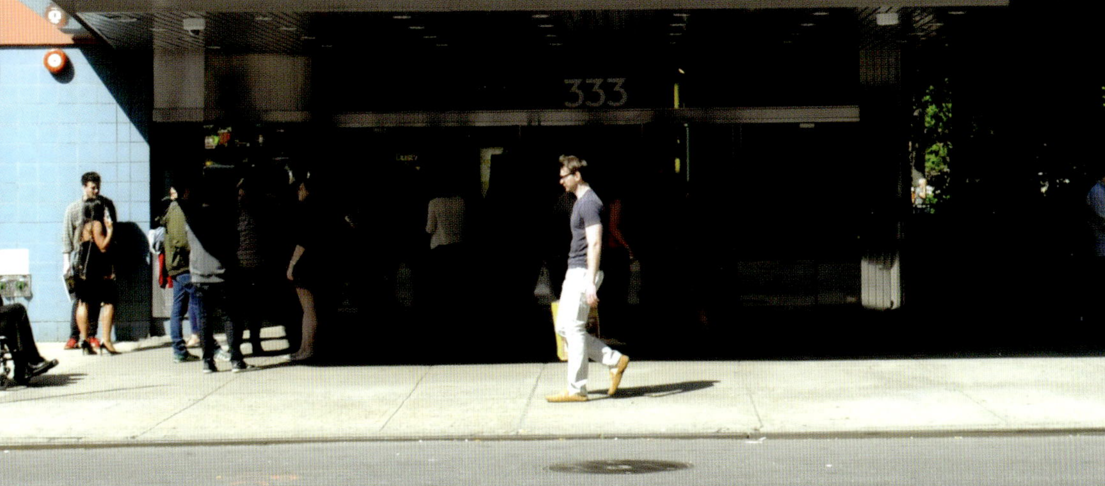

Existing facade.

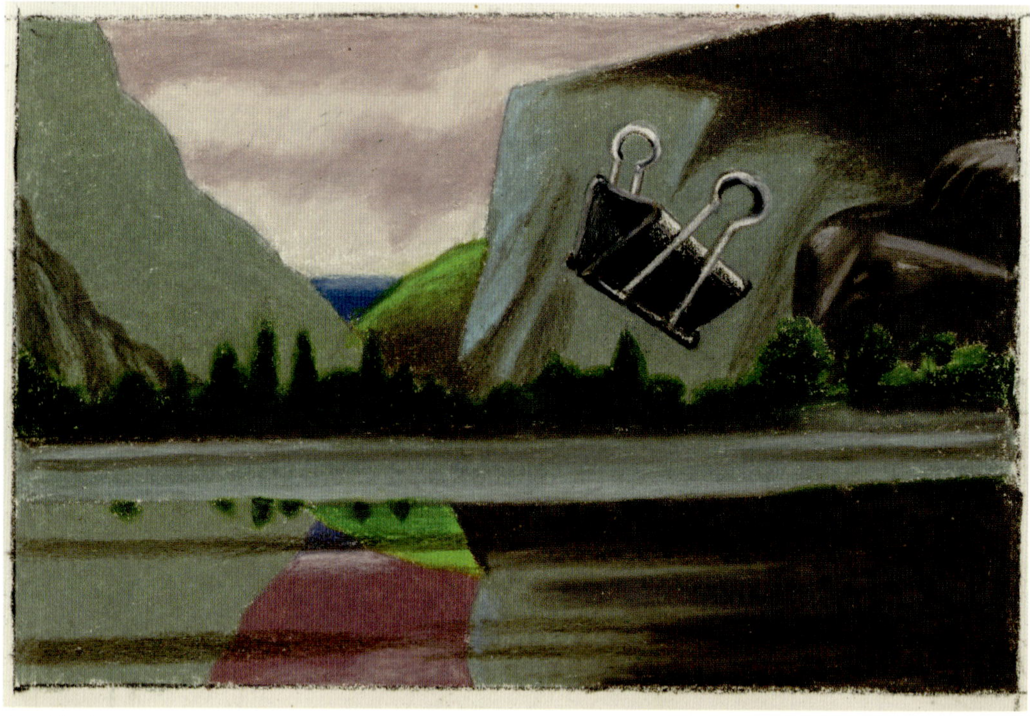

Initial sketch.

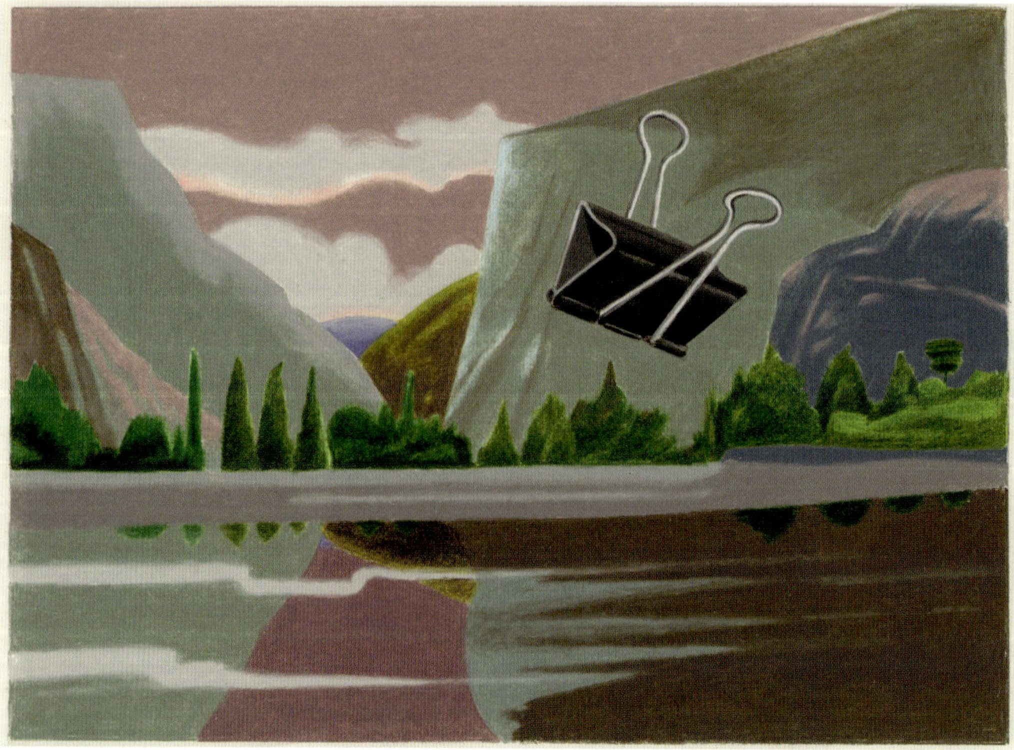

Finished illustration.

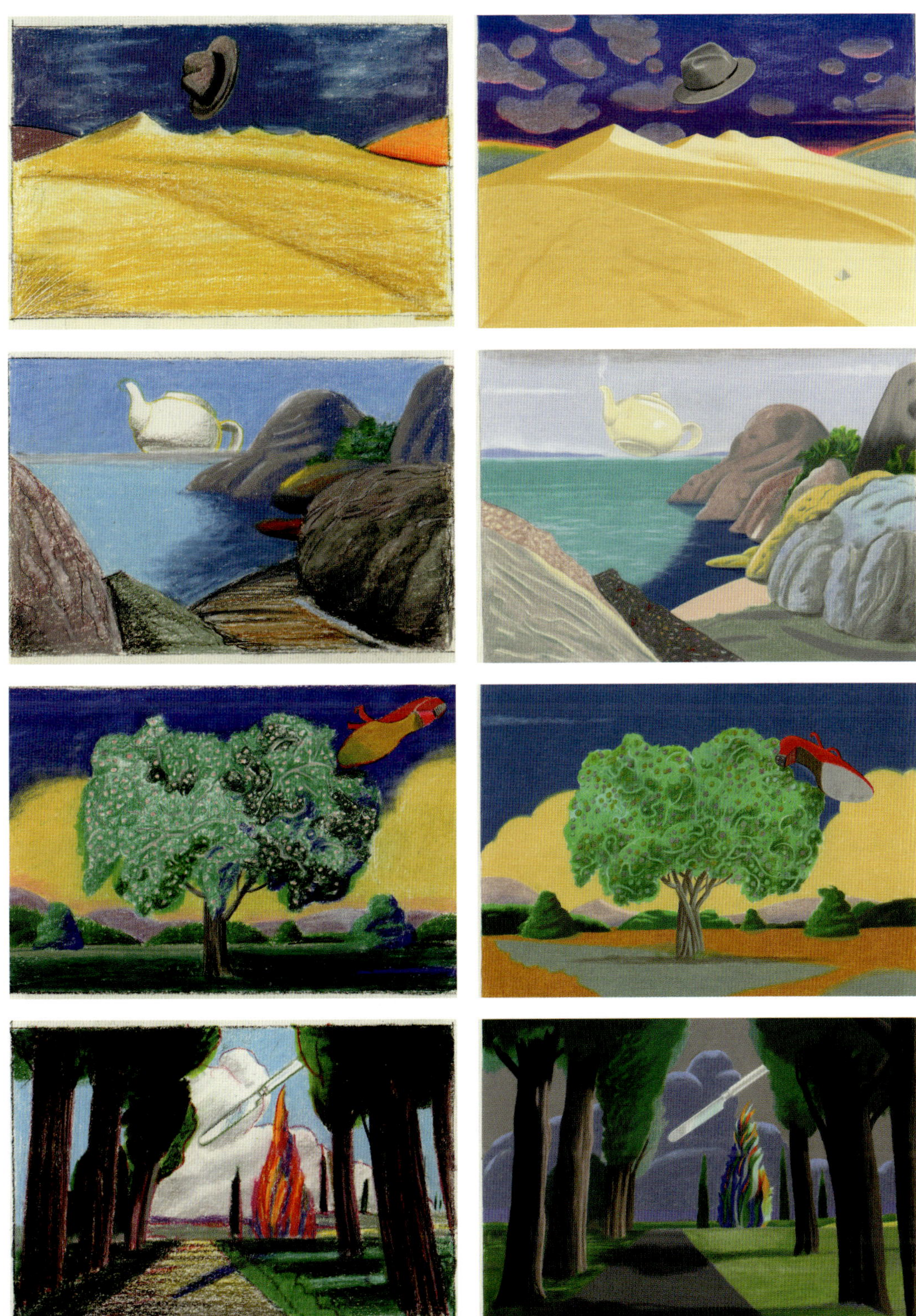

Initial sketches.

Final illustrations.

A pencil portrait of George Gershwin started with many elements that were not included in the final product. The figure on the left in the background, the cigar, and the pose of writing, all disappeared on the final. The finish also changed by turning the figure to a frontal pose, adding musical notes to his suit, and enlarging the scale of the piano.

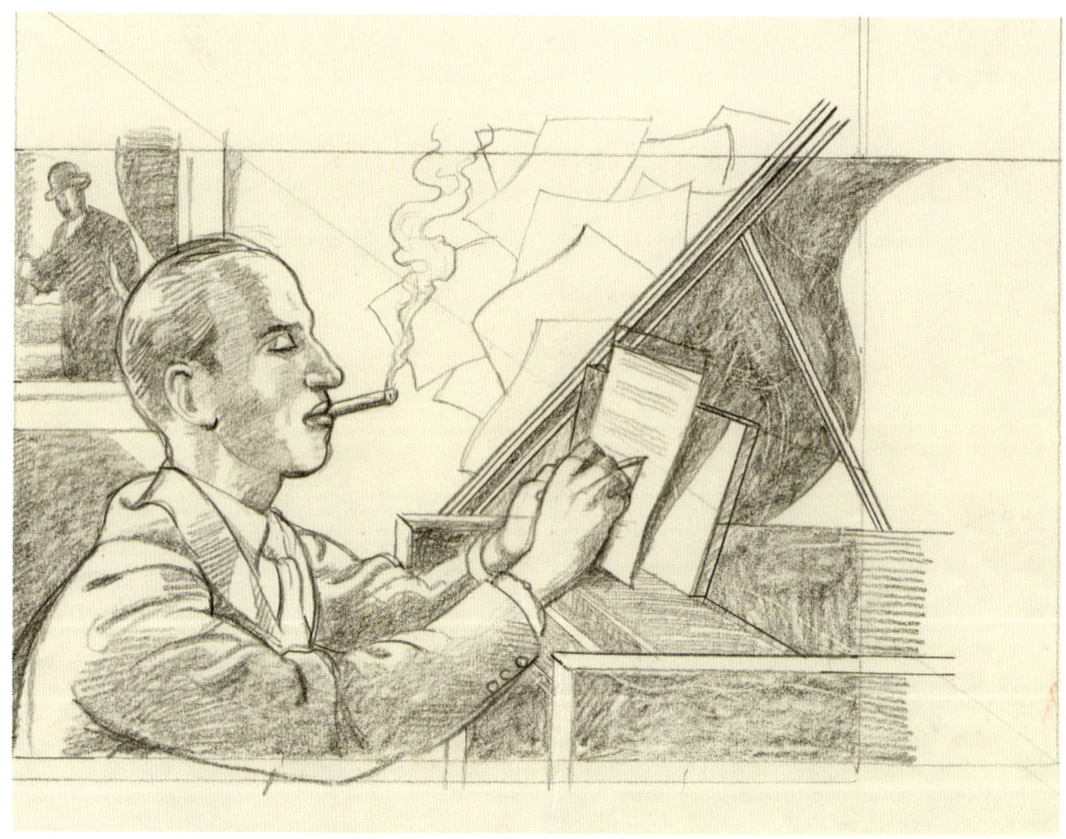

Pencil sketch.

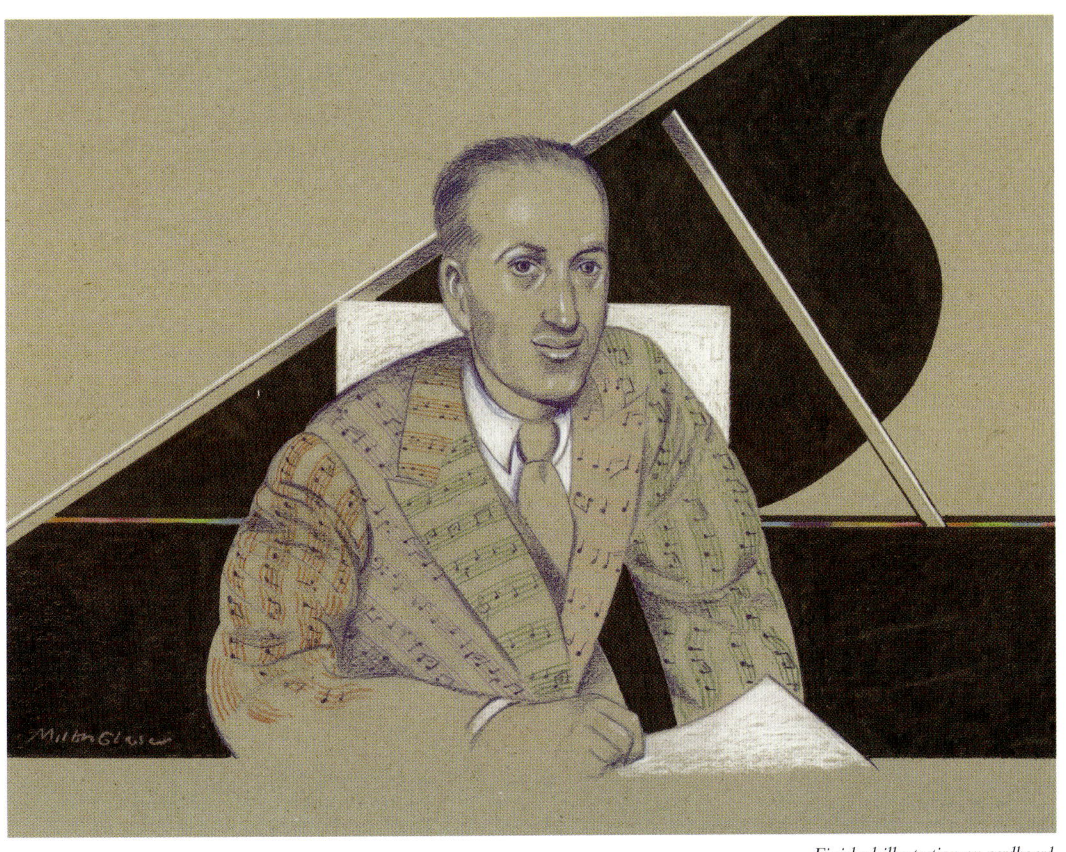

Finished illustration on cardboard.

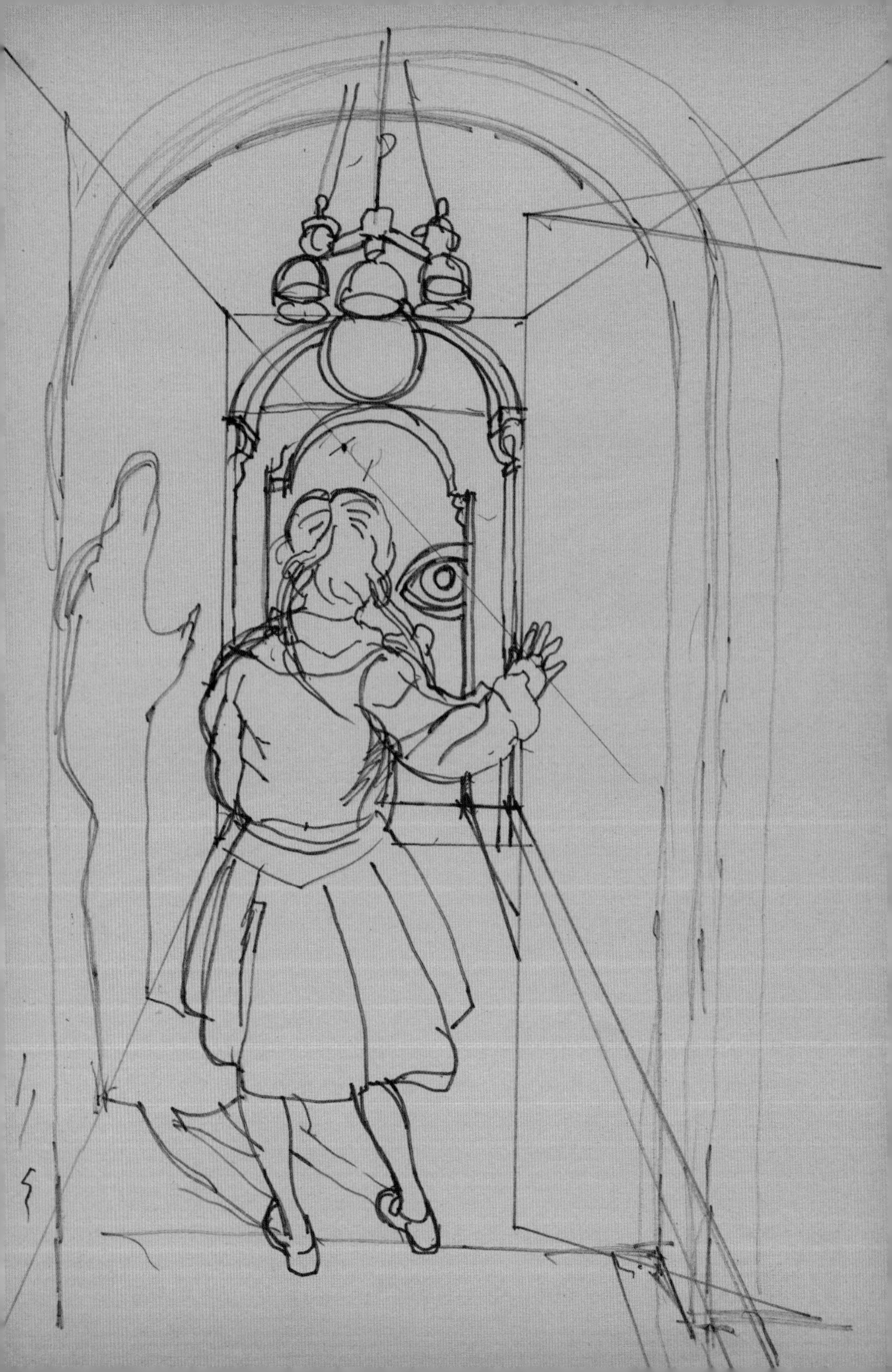

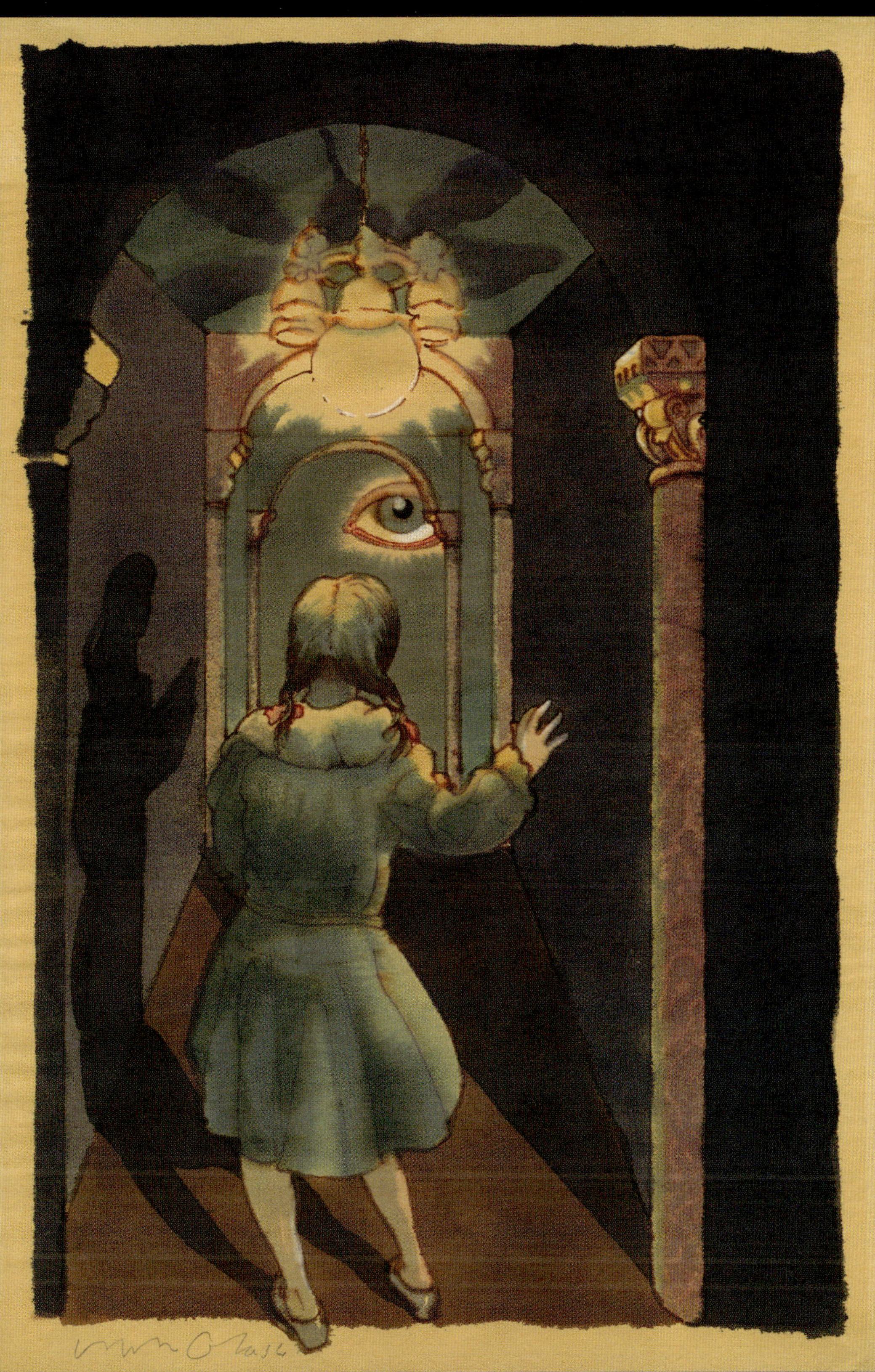

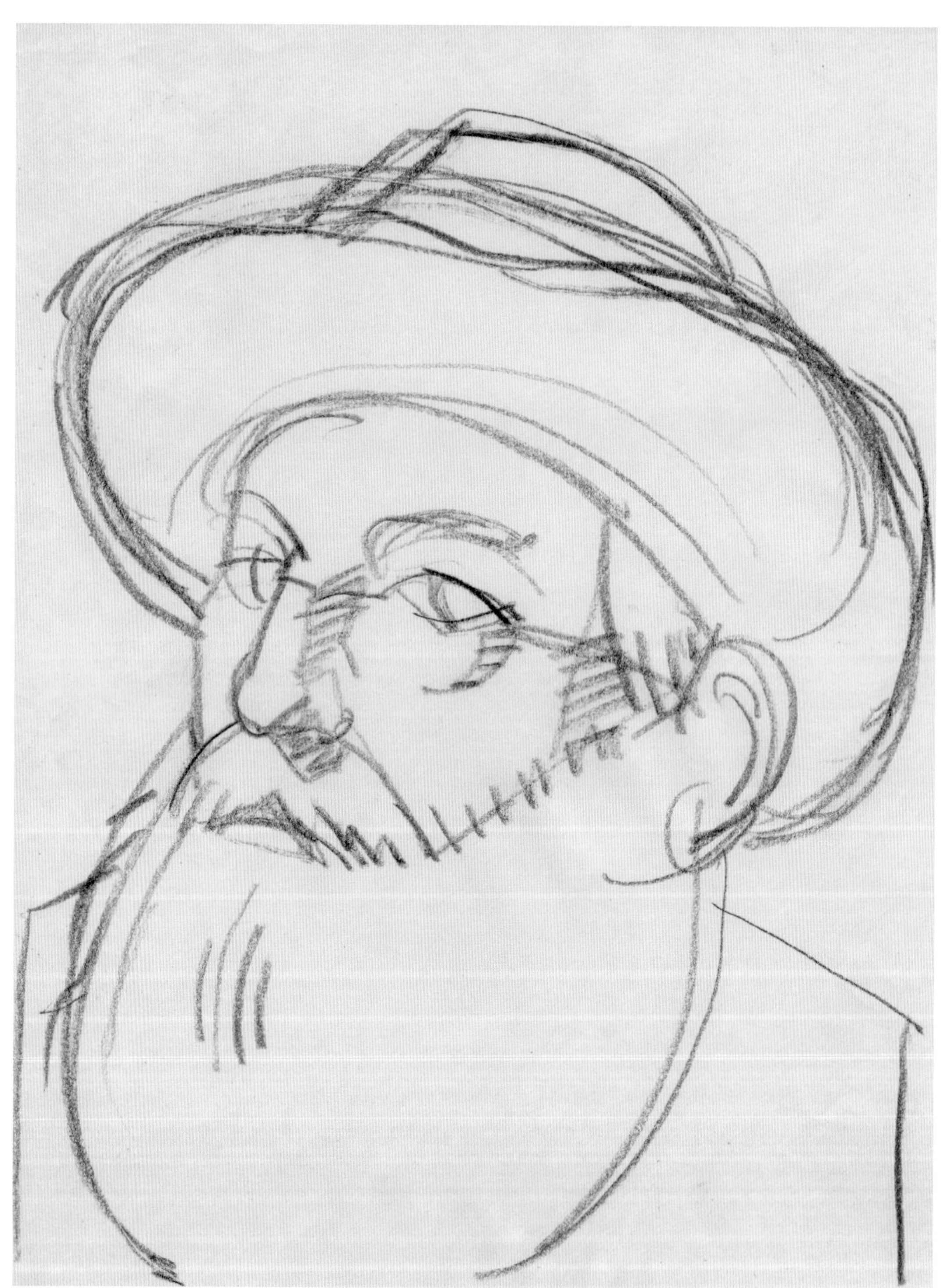

Early pencil sketch.

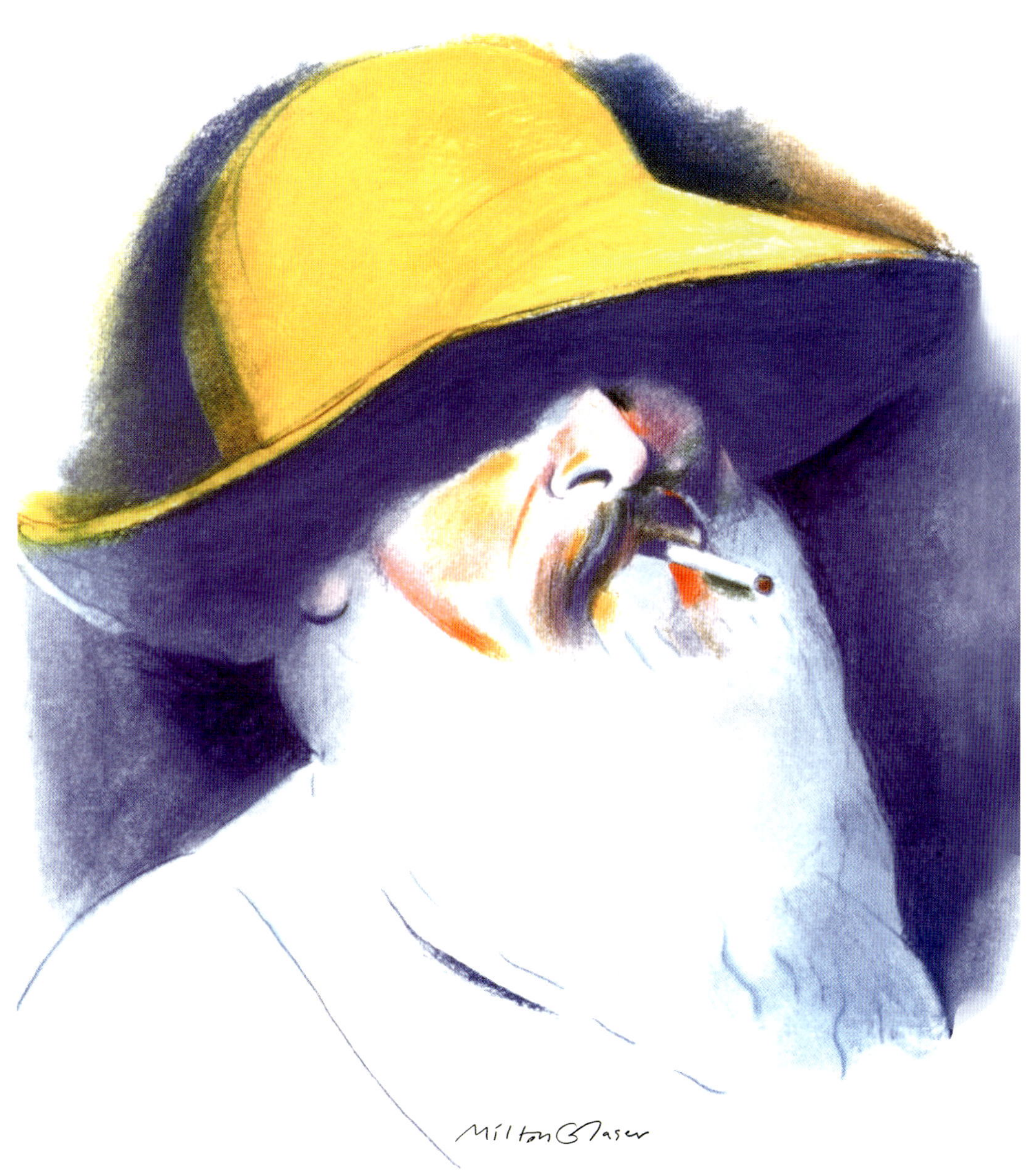

Final drawing.

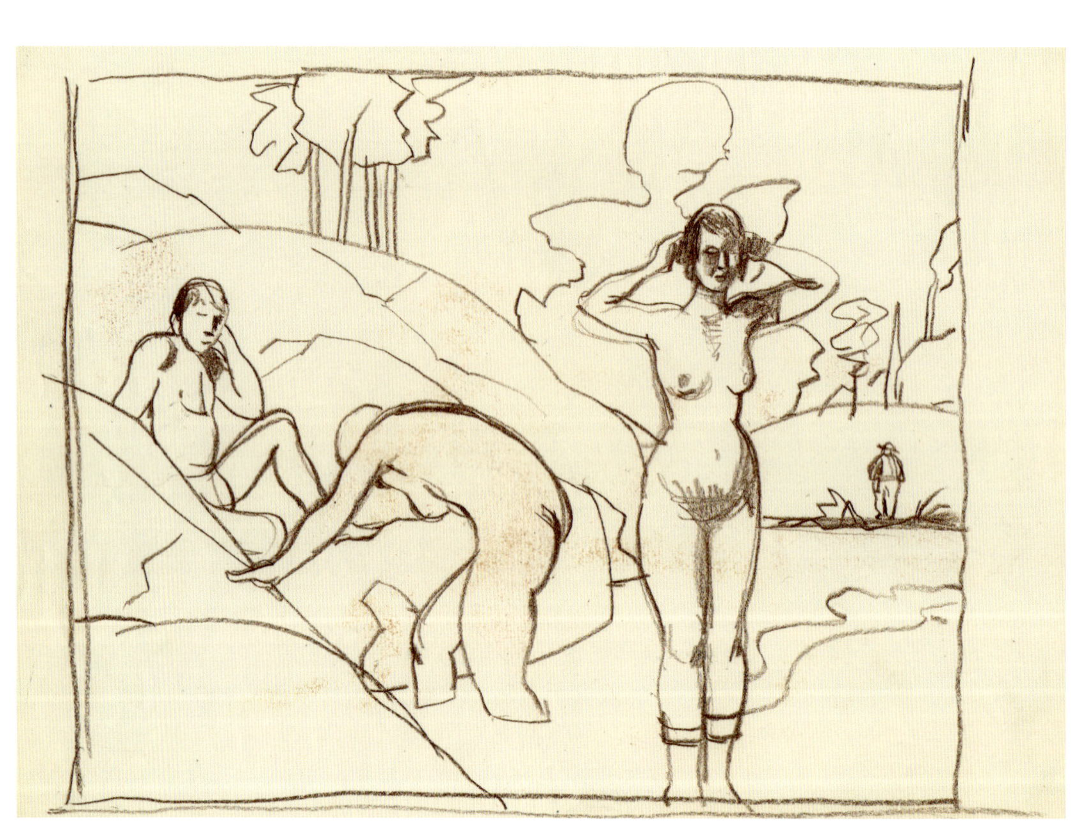

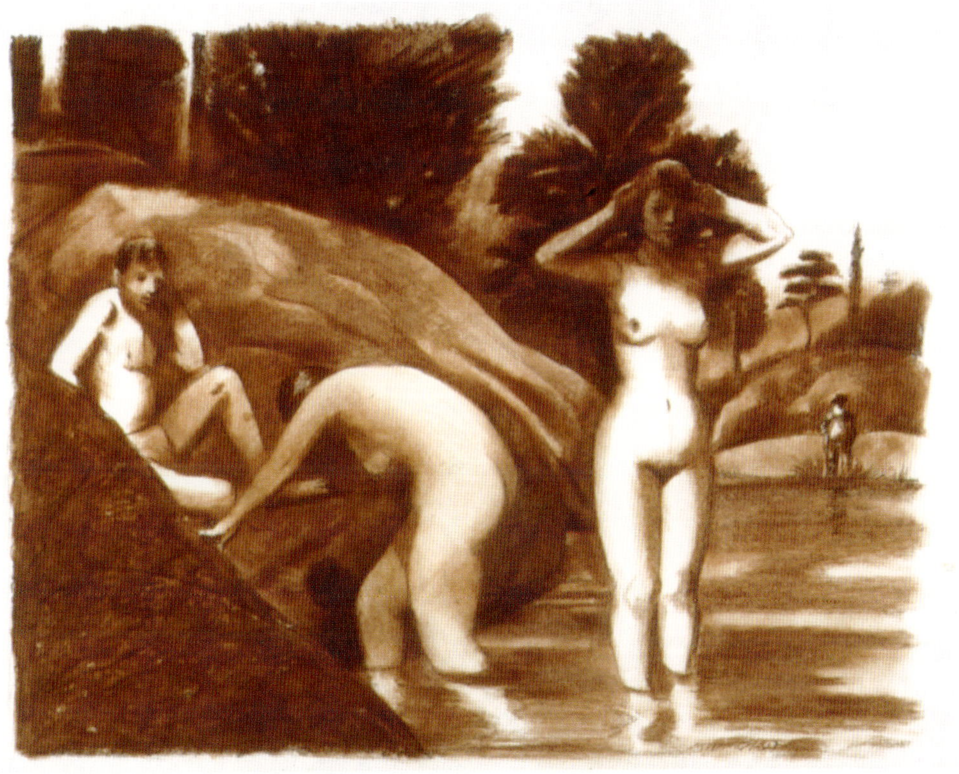

Three alternatives for a portrait of Nina Simone. The sketch had to be fully developed before I applied it. You could say that any of these is suitable for reproduction.

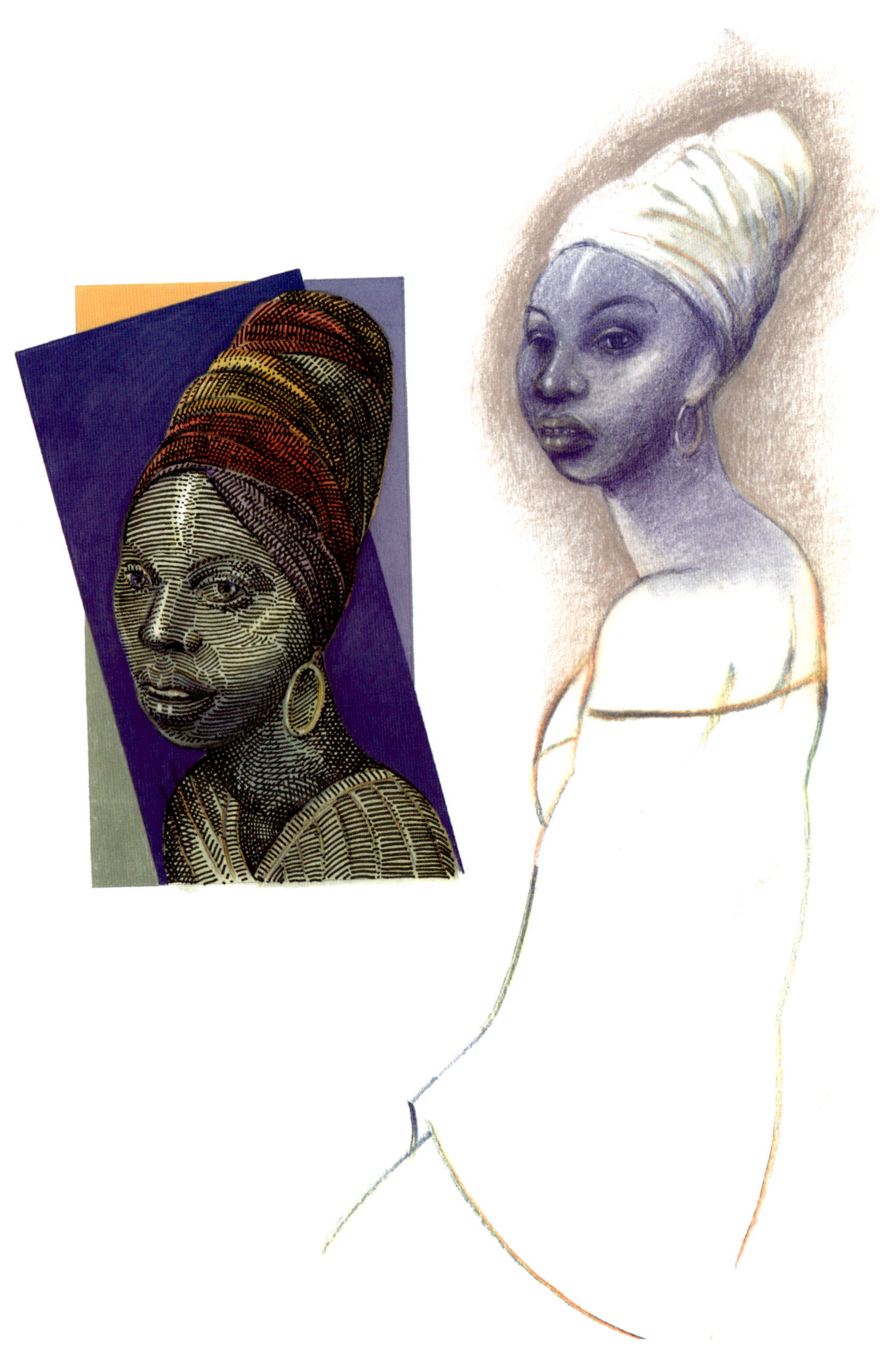

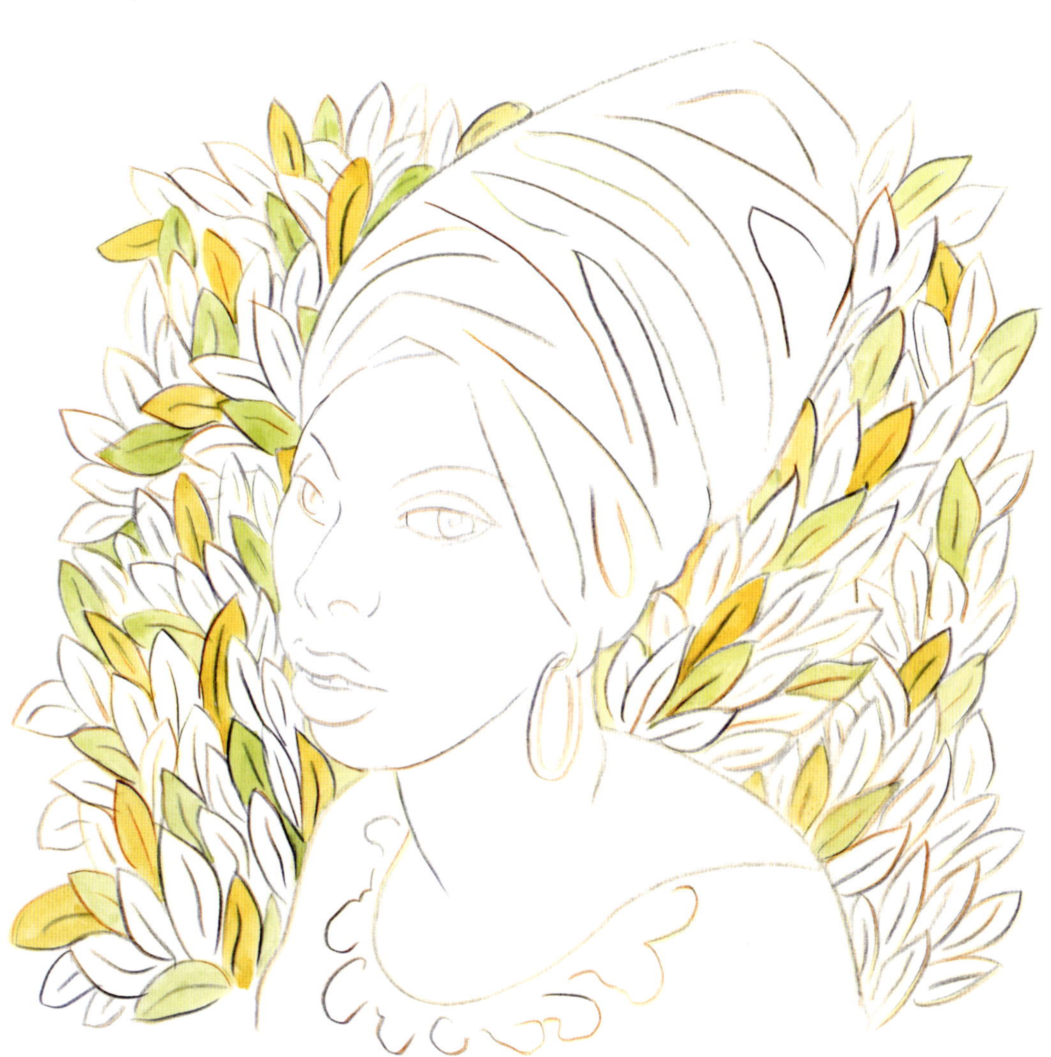

These were studies for a poster call for entries for the 1983 AIGA Book Show. Alternative light studies were reproduced in black and white.

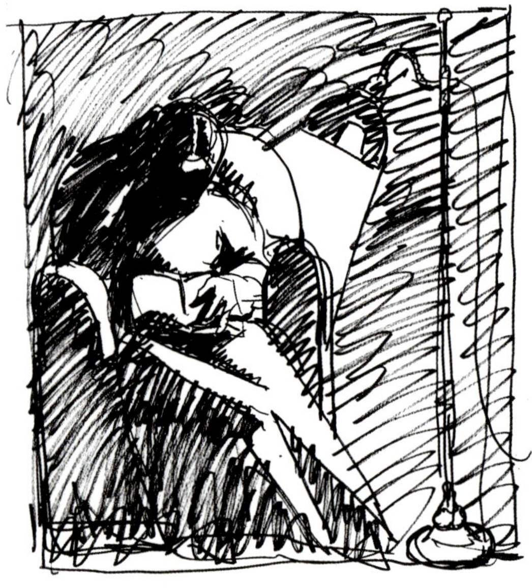 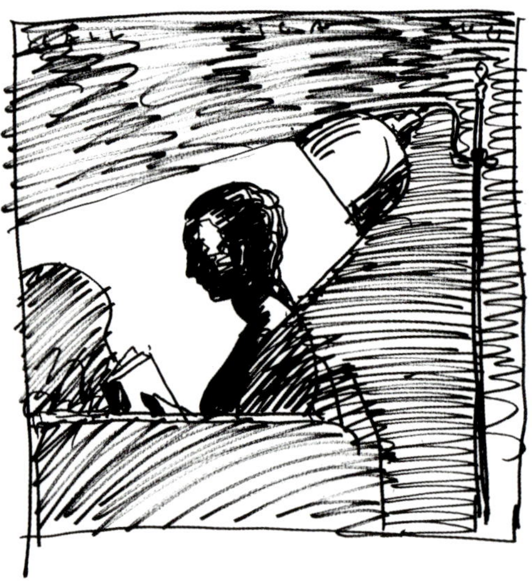

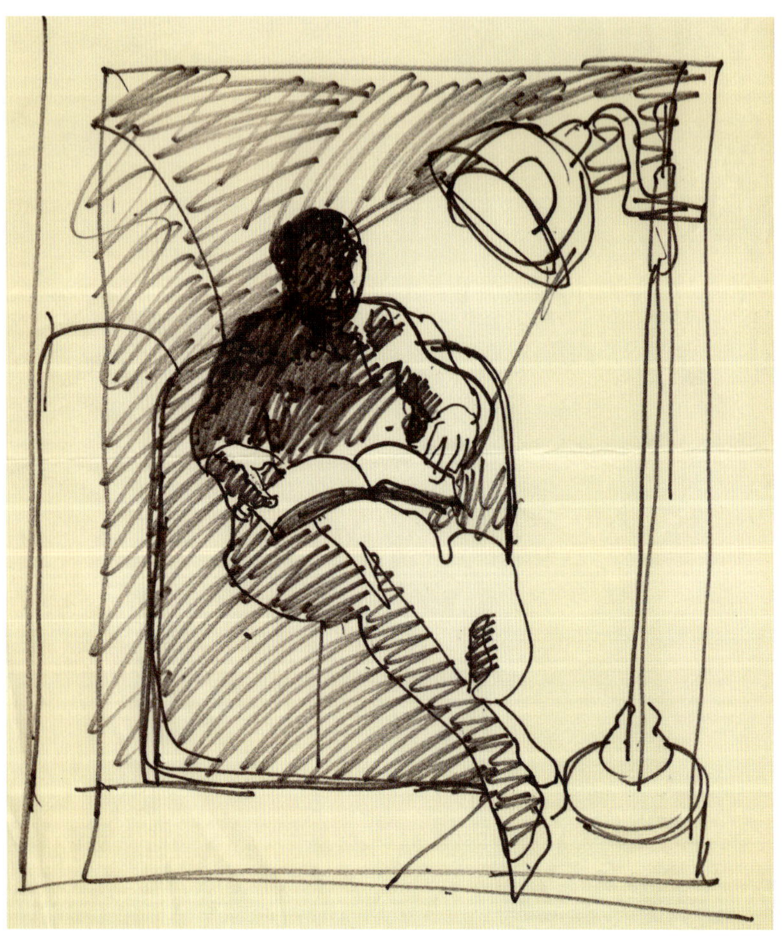

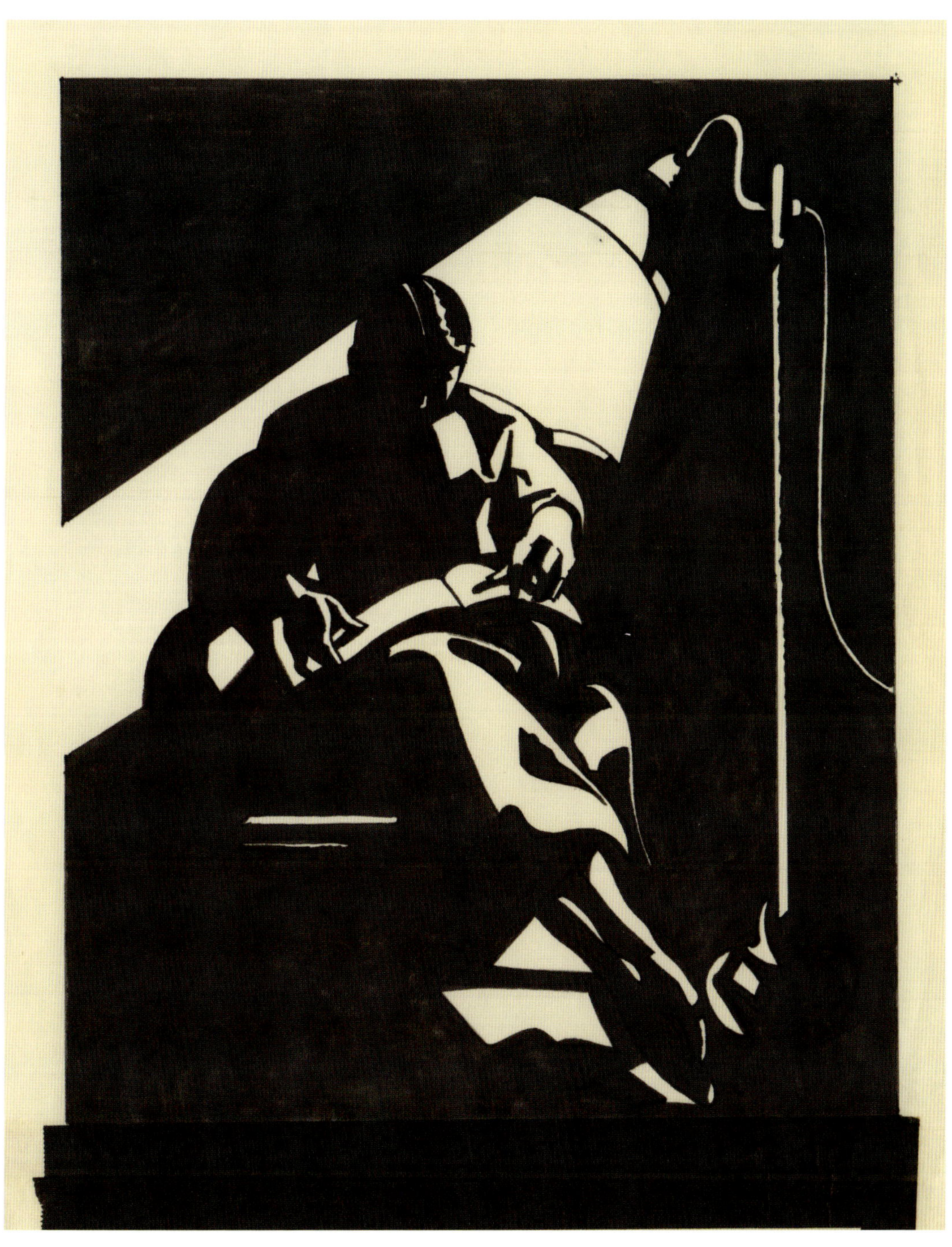

This drawing contains the essential elements of the finish, but its color has been modified.

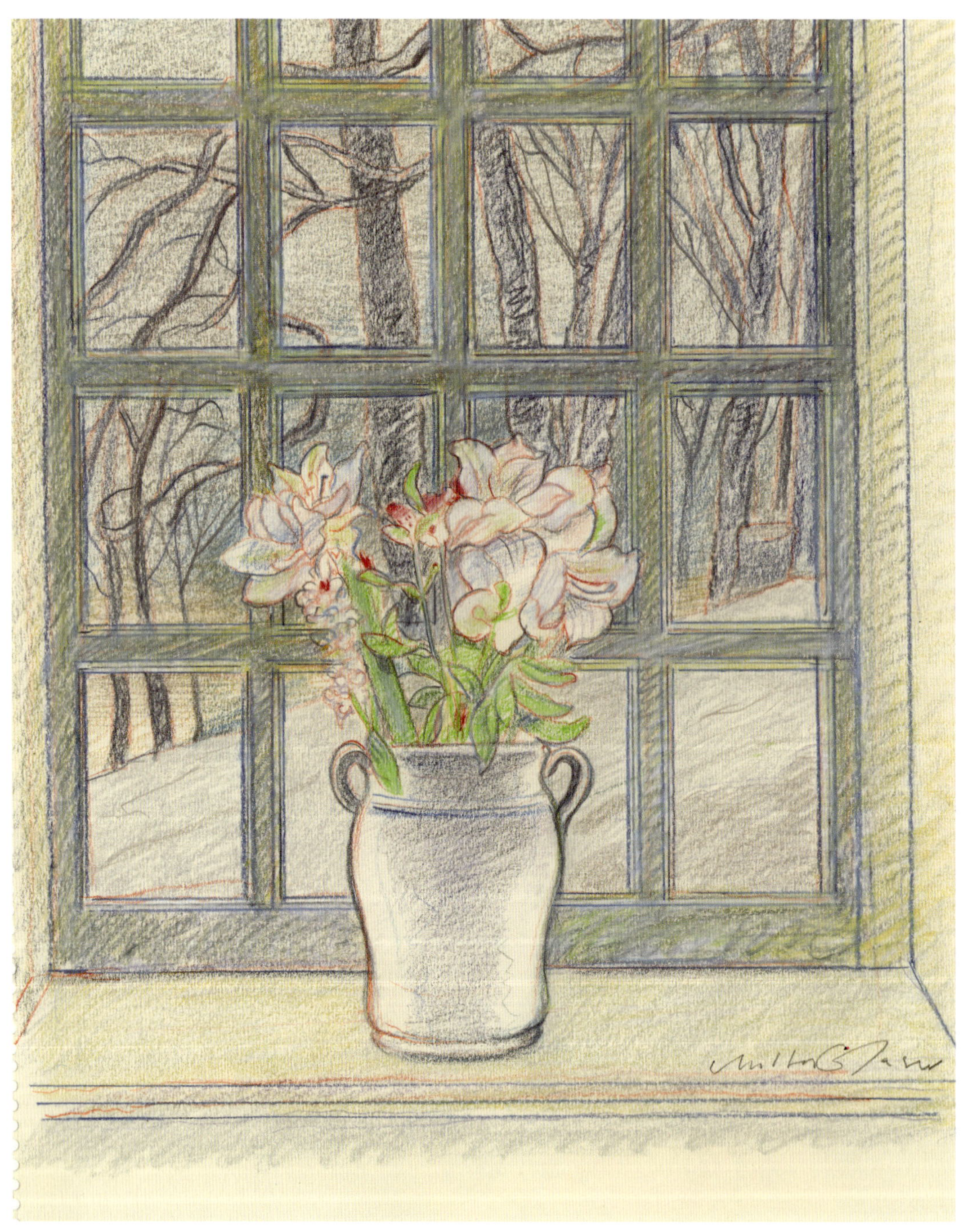

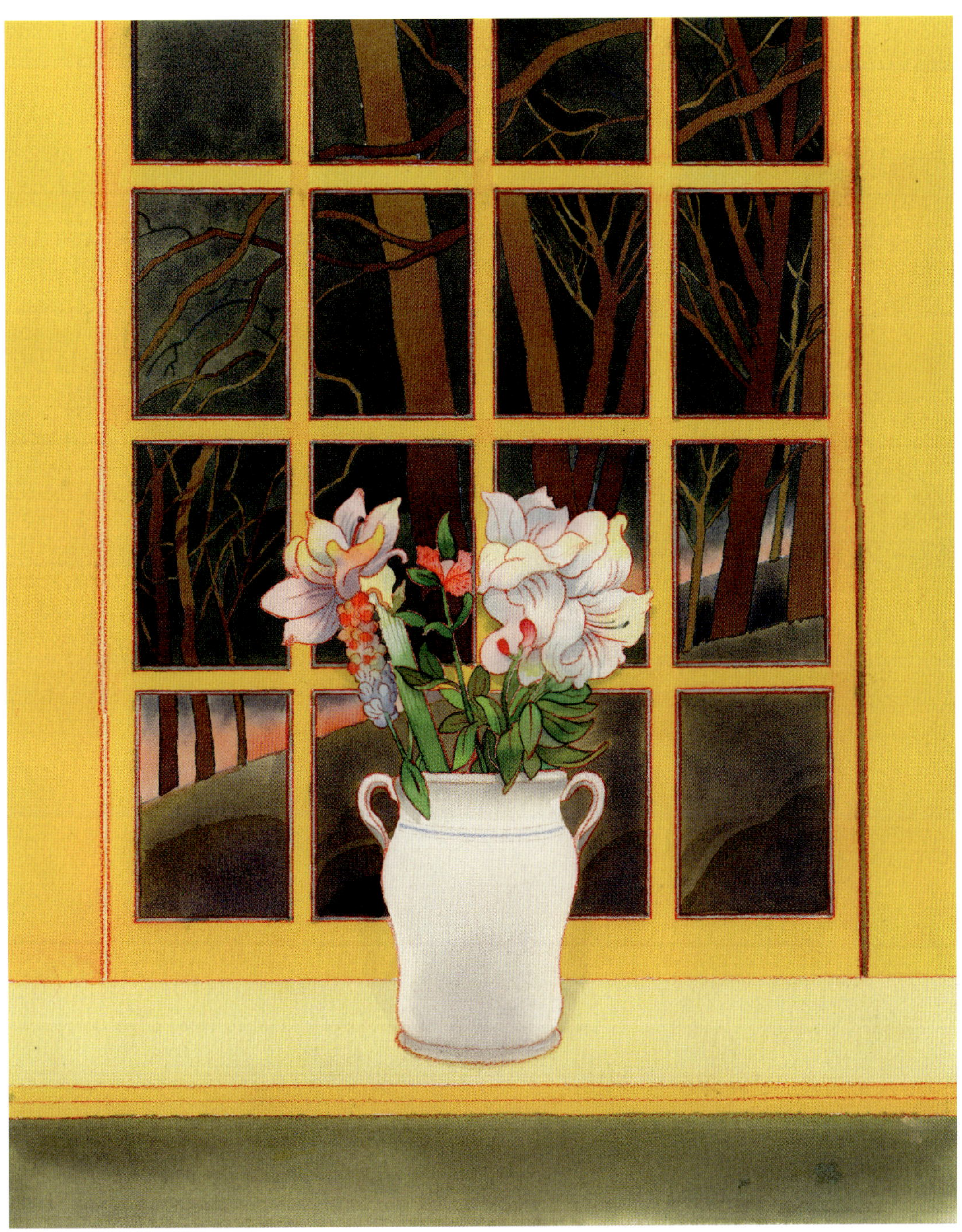

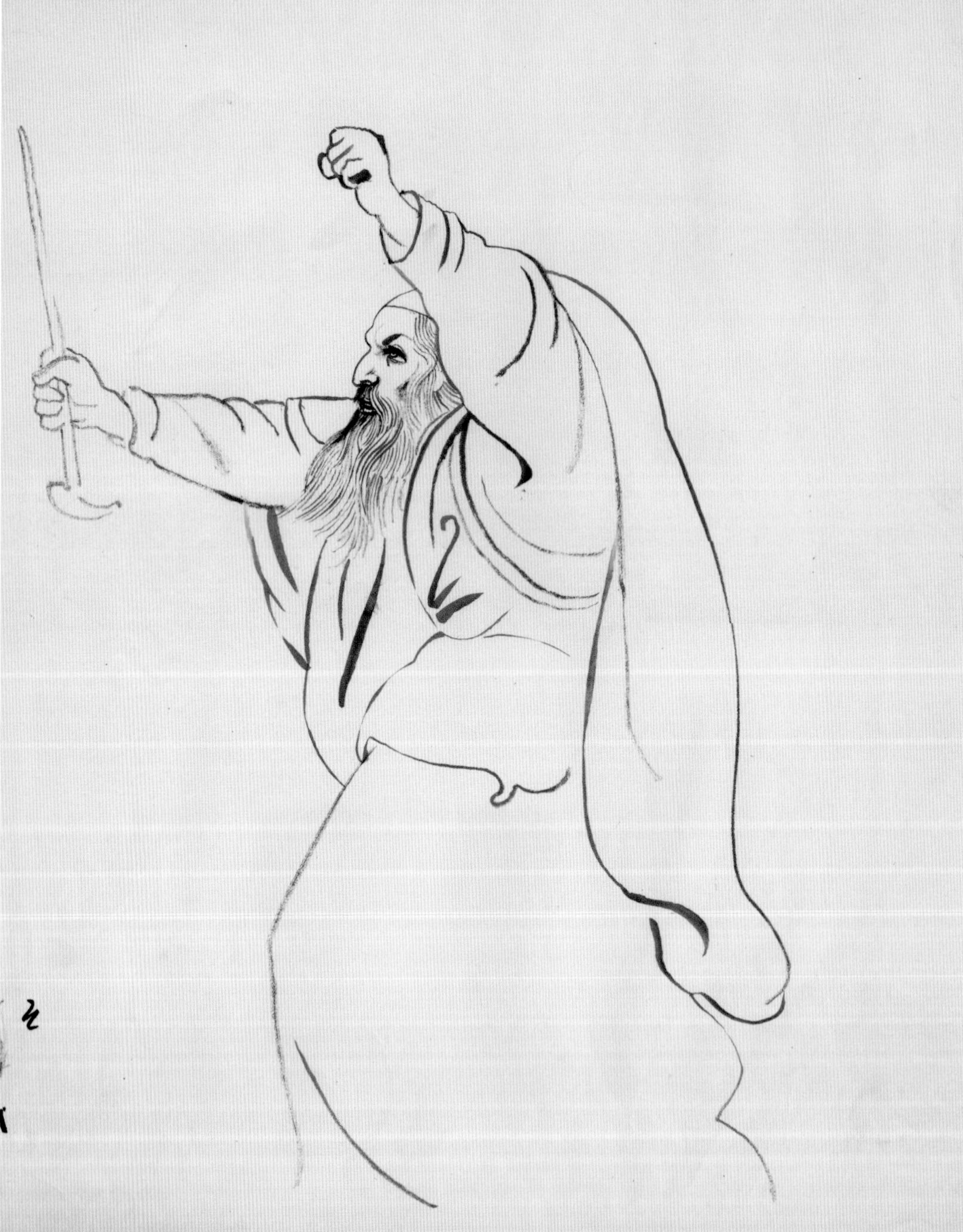

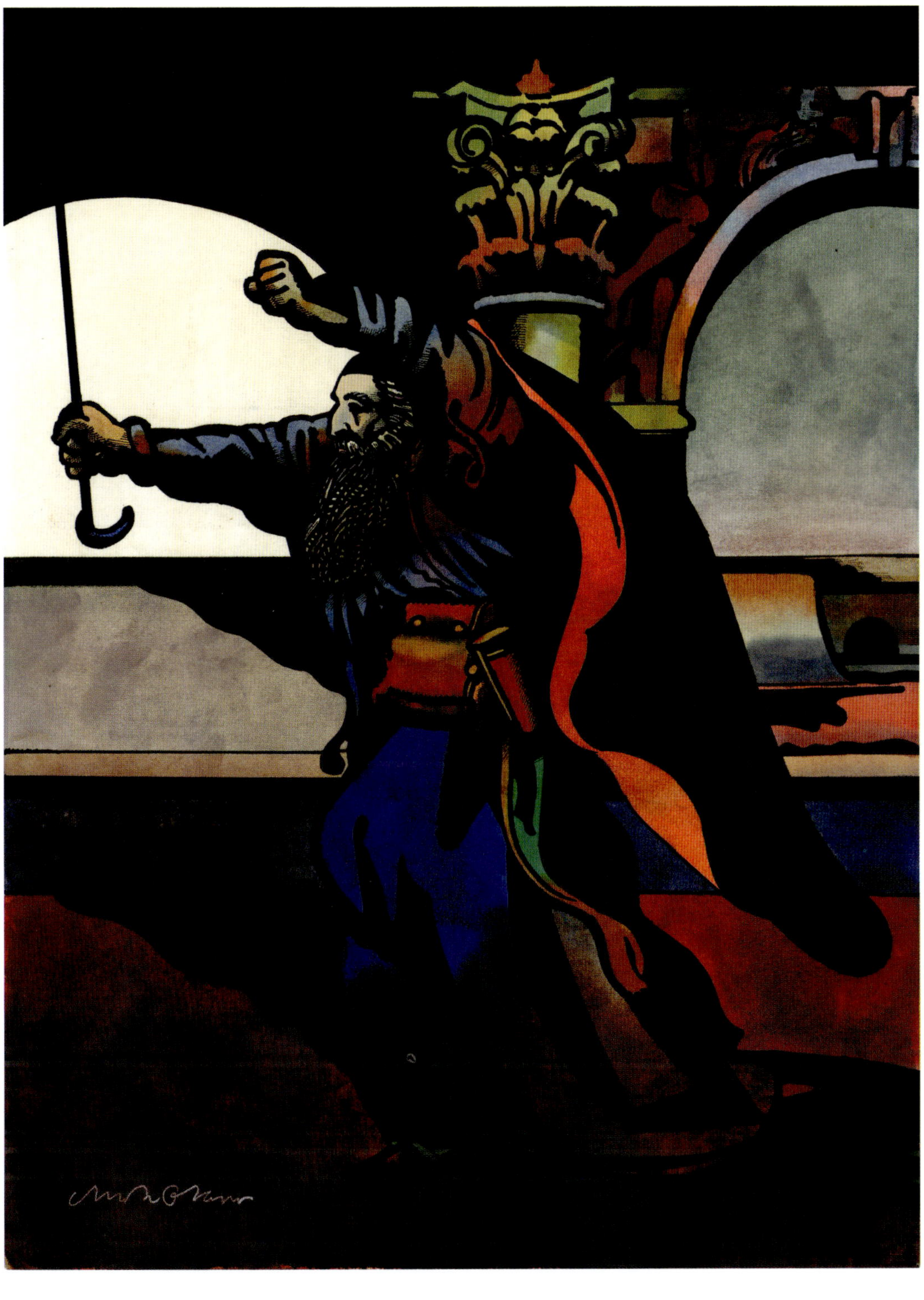

The intent of this poster was to attack the contempt that the president of the United States shows to immigrants by using the word "dreamer" negatively. The core idea that dreaming is human determined the final form that was implicit in the original rough drawing. How to represent the subject of dream is complex, but I attempted to do it expressively rather than logically.

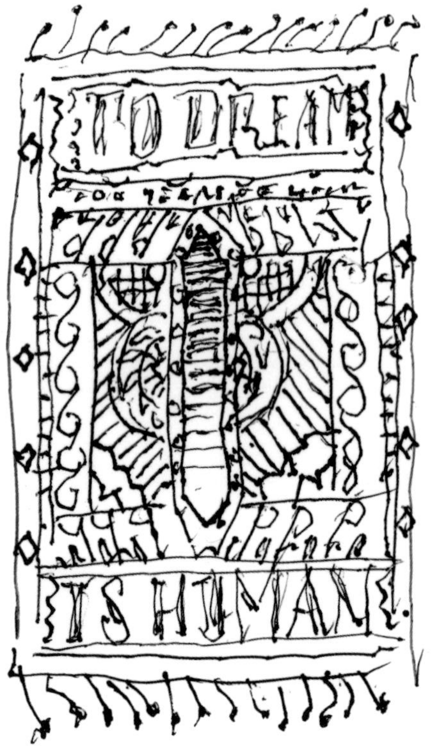

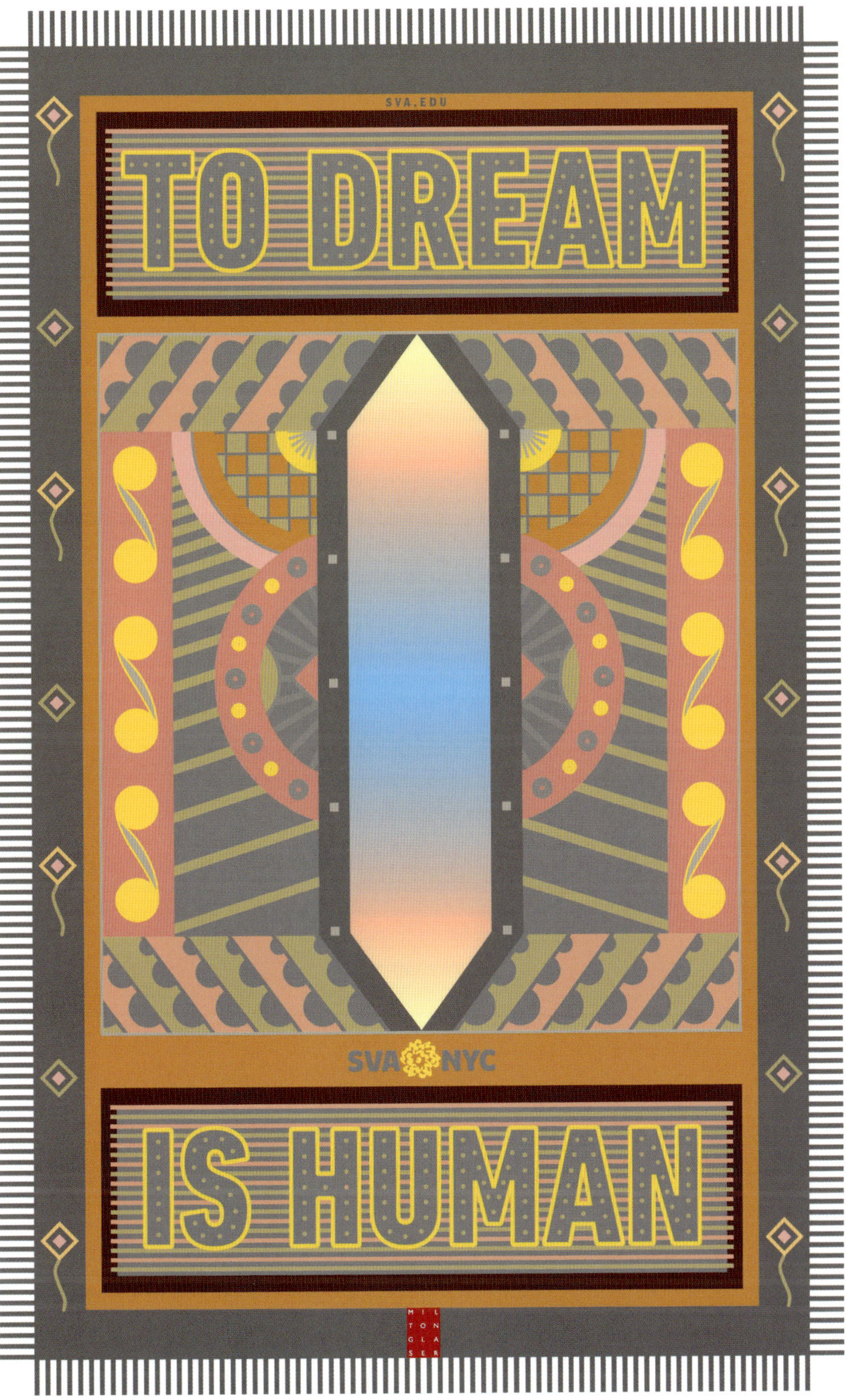
SVA.EDU
TO DREAM
SVA NYC
IS HUMAN
MILTON GLASER

The image on the left was an illustration for an antiwar poster. The image on the right was made five years later but reflects my memory of the original.

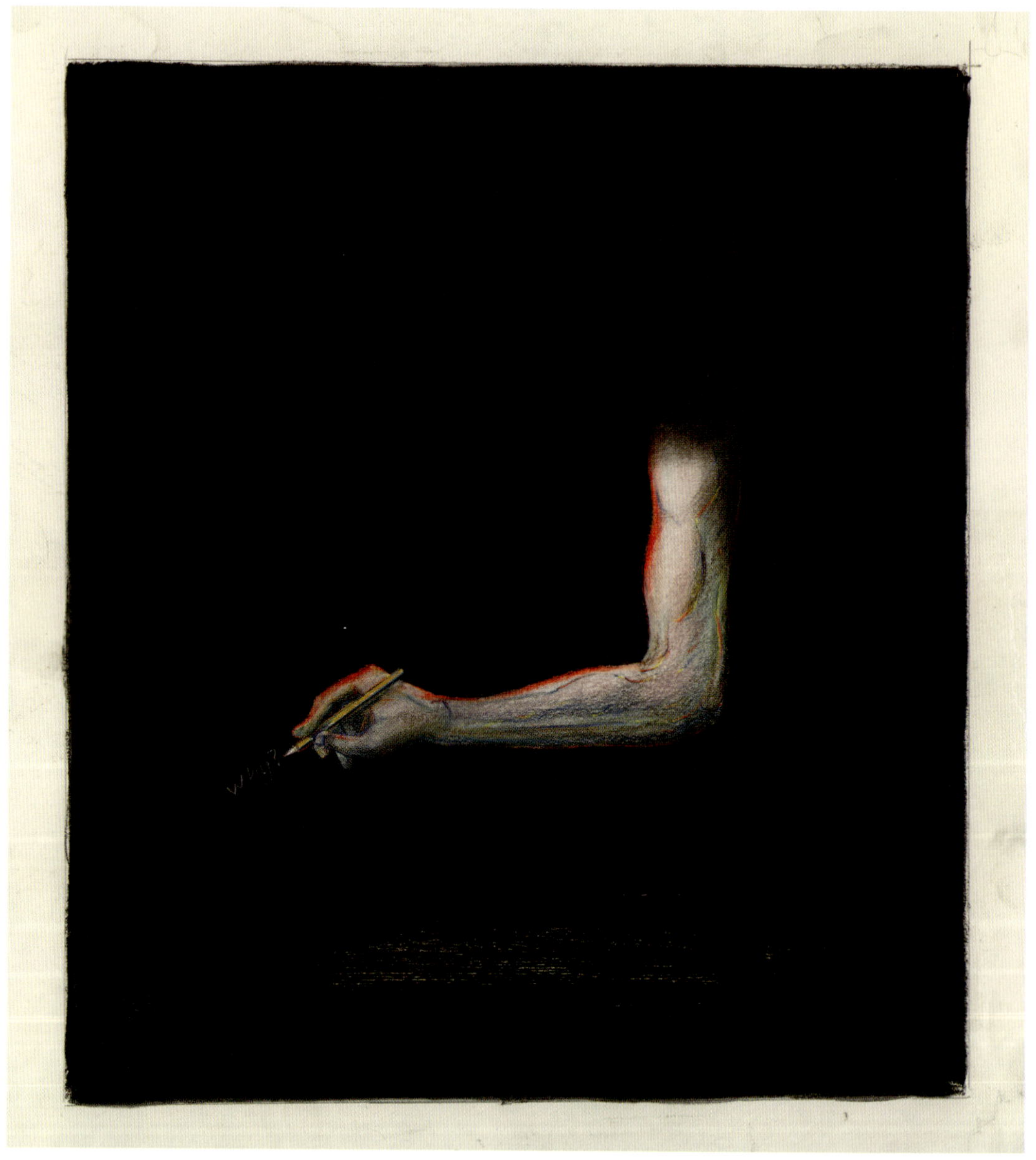

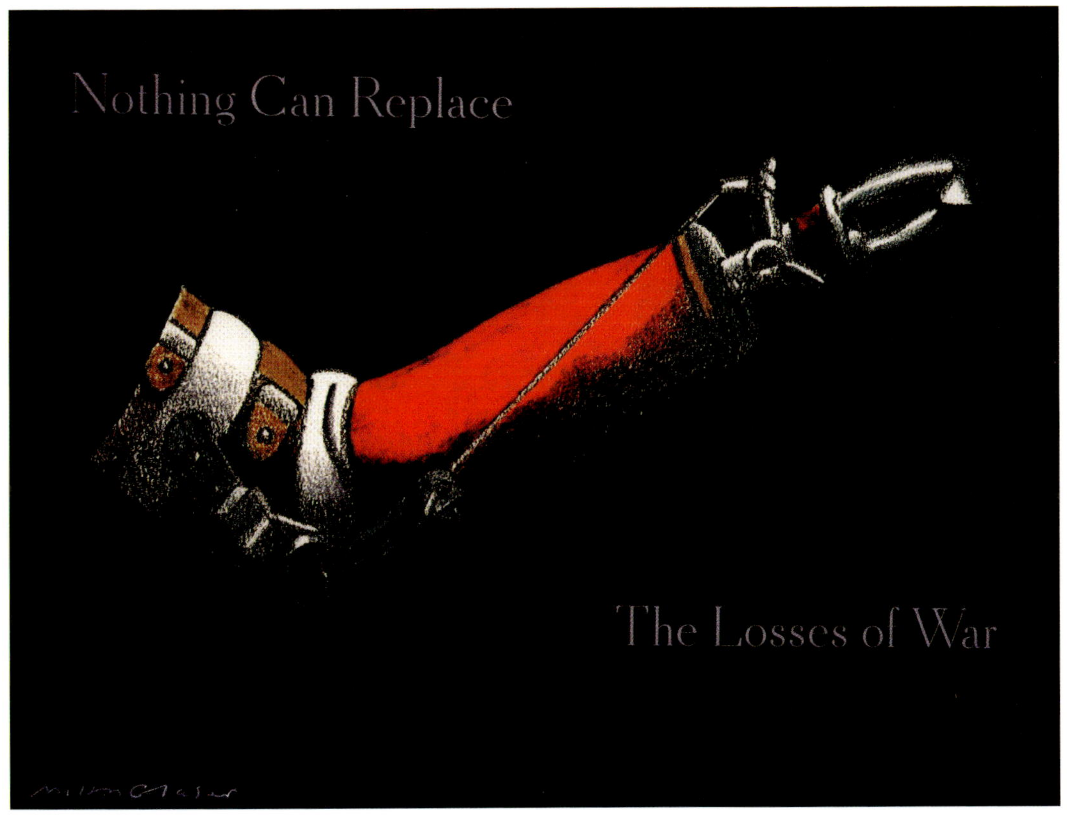
Nothing Can Replace
The Losses of War

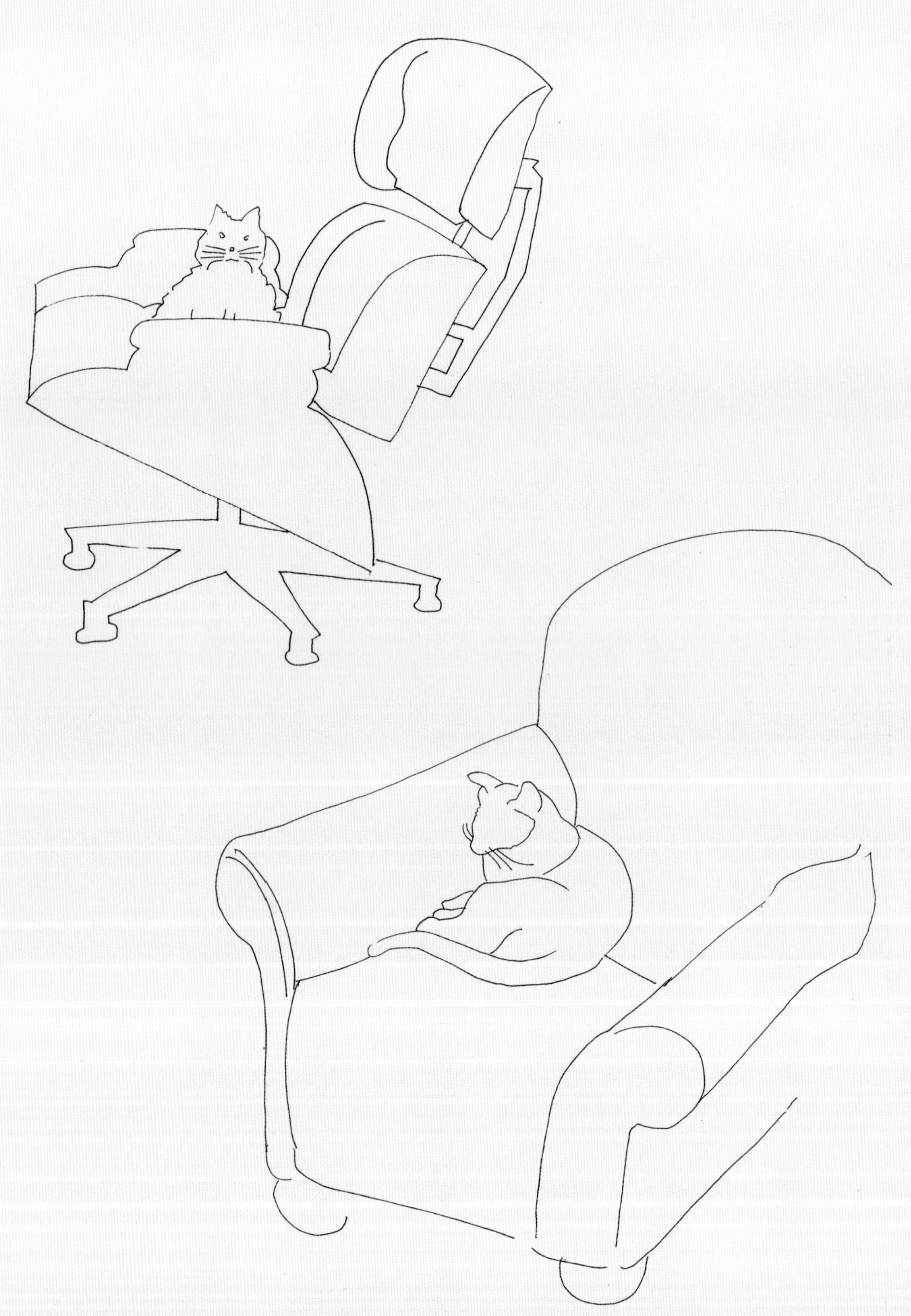

The Chair Fair

AN OPEN EXHIBITION OF CHAIRS DESIGNED DURING THE PAST TEN YEARS

Chairs are at once practical and metaphoric, everyday objects and expressions of individuality. The challenge of this program (manageable size and a universal client) has attracted designers, architects, and others: how to combine performance and personality? Everyone wants to design a truly new chair, the "better mousetrap" of the design professions. *Call for Entries:* Chairs submitted by architects, designers, artists, manufacturers, craftspeople and others are welcome; maximum of three chairs per entrant. Chairs must be designed within the last ten years, and fit within a 3' x 3' footprint. A jury of distinguished designers and artists will choose winners in several categories.

MADE POSSIBLE BY:

IDCNY
Domore Corporation
Furniture Consultants, Inc.
Knoll International
Herman Miller, Inc.
Steelcase Inc.
Atelier International
The Gunlocke Company
SunarHauserman

Registration via the official entry form is mandatory by 1 October 1986. Please read the form carefully for complete rules and conditions of entry. If no forms are available, write or call:

The Architectural League of New York
457 Madison Avenue, New York, NY 10022
212/753-1722

Sponsored by The Architectural League of New York at the International Design Center, New York (IDCNY) 30-20 Thomson Avenue, Long Island City, New York

Exhibition open 10 November–6 December 1986

JURORS:

Richard Artschwager, artist
Mario Bellini, architect and designer
Milton Glaser, designer
T. Merrill Prentice, Jr., sculptor and architect
Lella Vignelli, designer

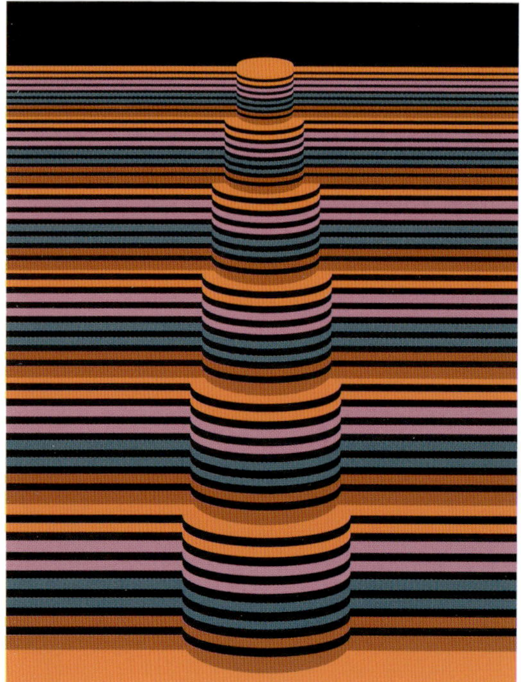

Preliminary computer variations.

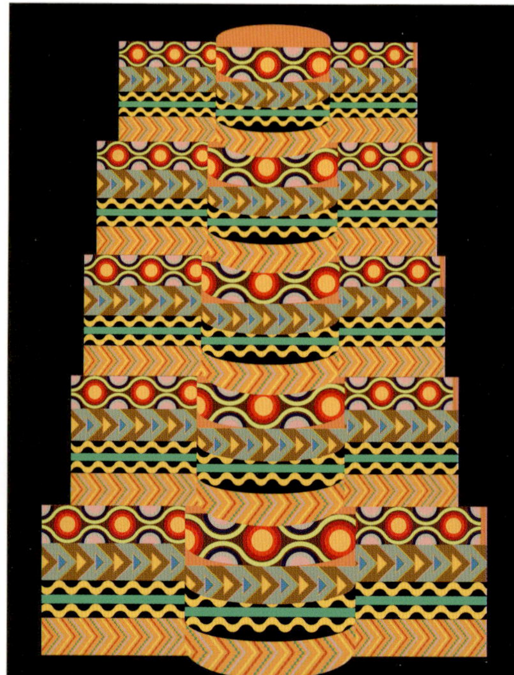

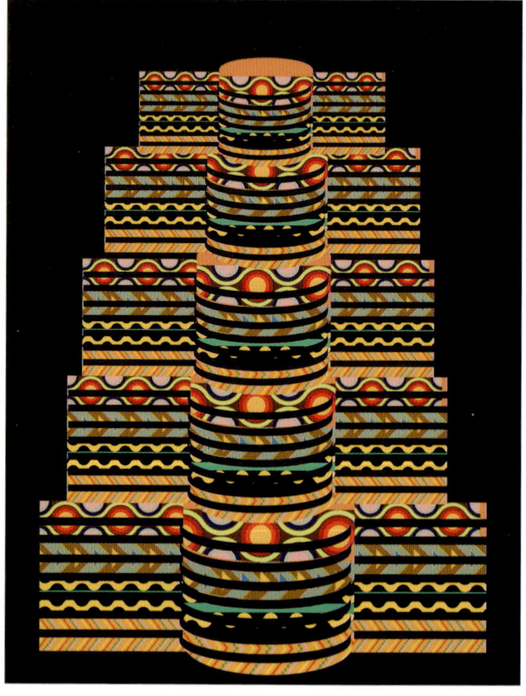

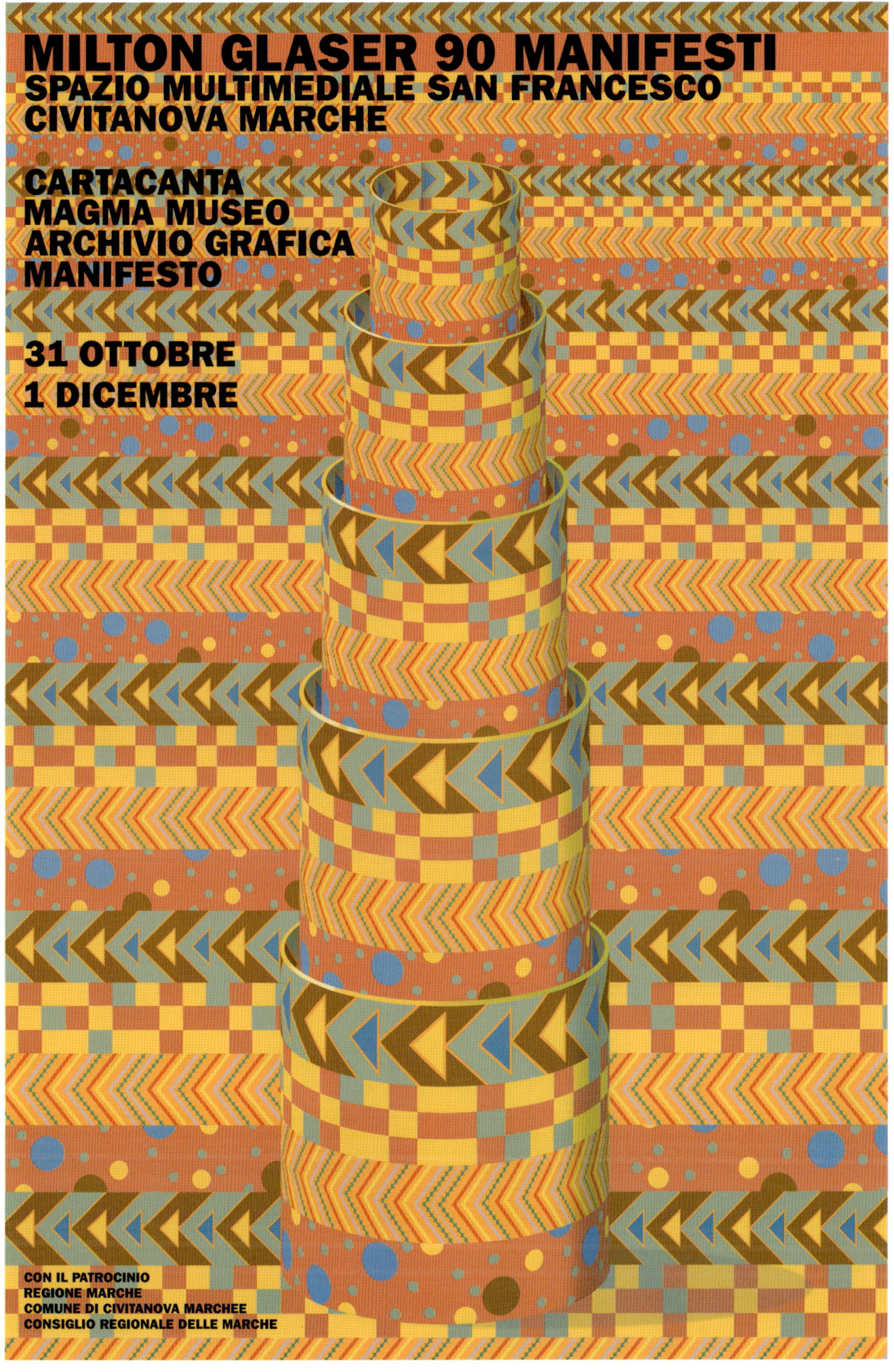
MILTON GLASER 90 MANIFESTI
SPAZIO MULTIMEDIALE SAN FRANCESCO
CIVITANOVA MARCHE

CARTACANTA
MAGMA MUSEO
ARCHIVIO GRAFICA
MANIFESTO

31 OTTOBRE
1 DICEMBRE

CON IL PATROCINIO
REGIONE MARCHE
COMUNE DI CIVITANOVA MARCHEE
CONSIGLIO REGIONALE DELLE MARCHE

The sketch of Pope Paul VI on the left is a bit unconventional in that it's not fuzzy. As I was working on this, I decided that it would be more interesting to show his full figure. Seeing him in his vestments really introduces a different spatial idea that makes him seem more intimate and closer to the viewer.

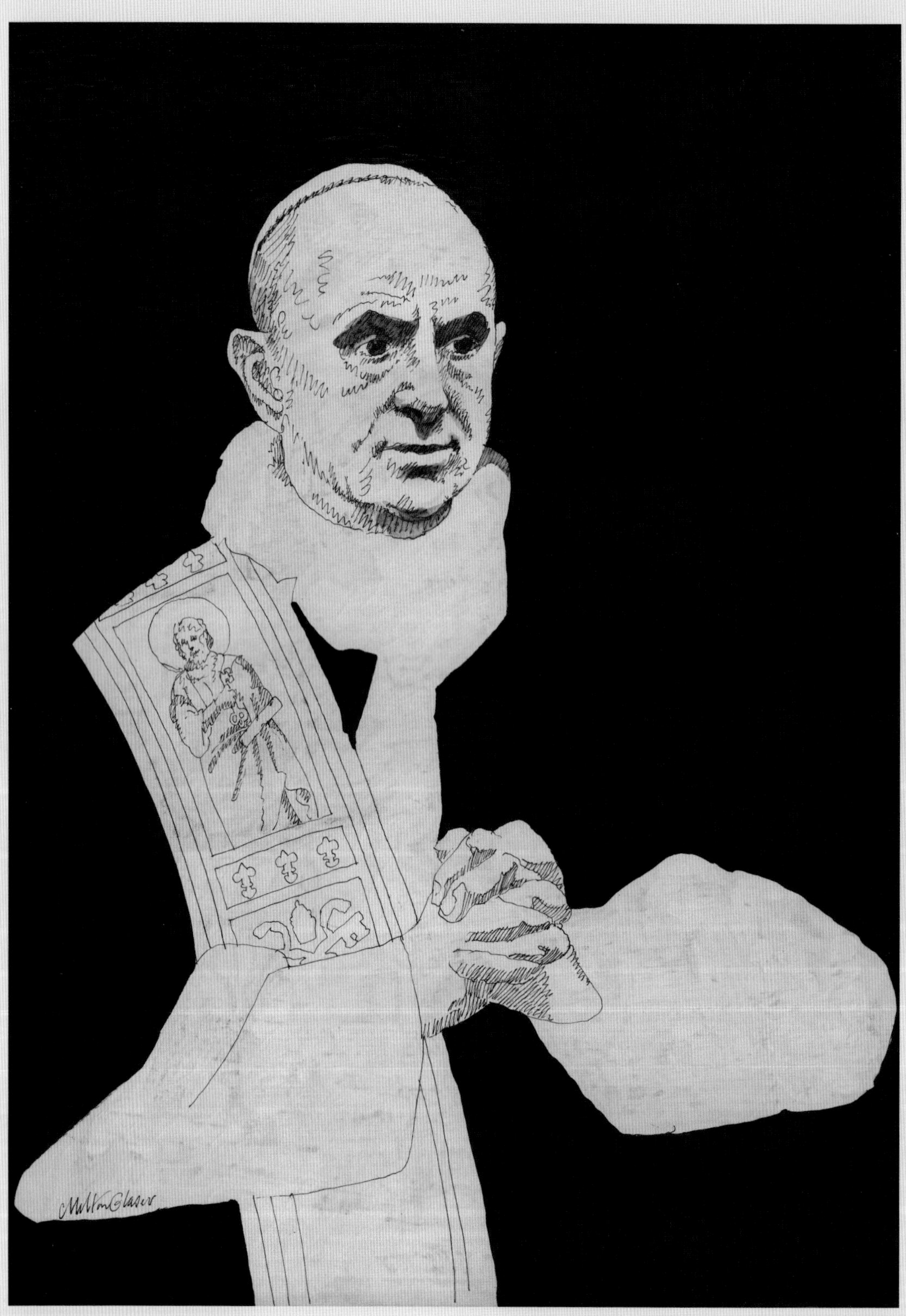

First study.

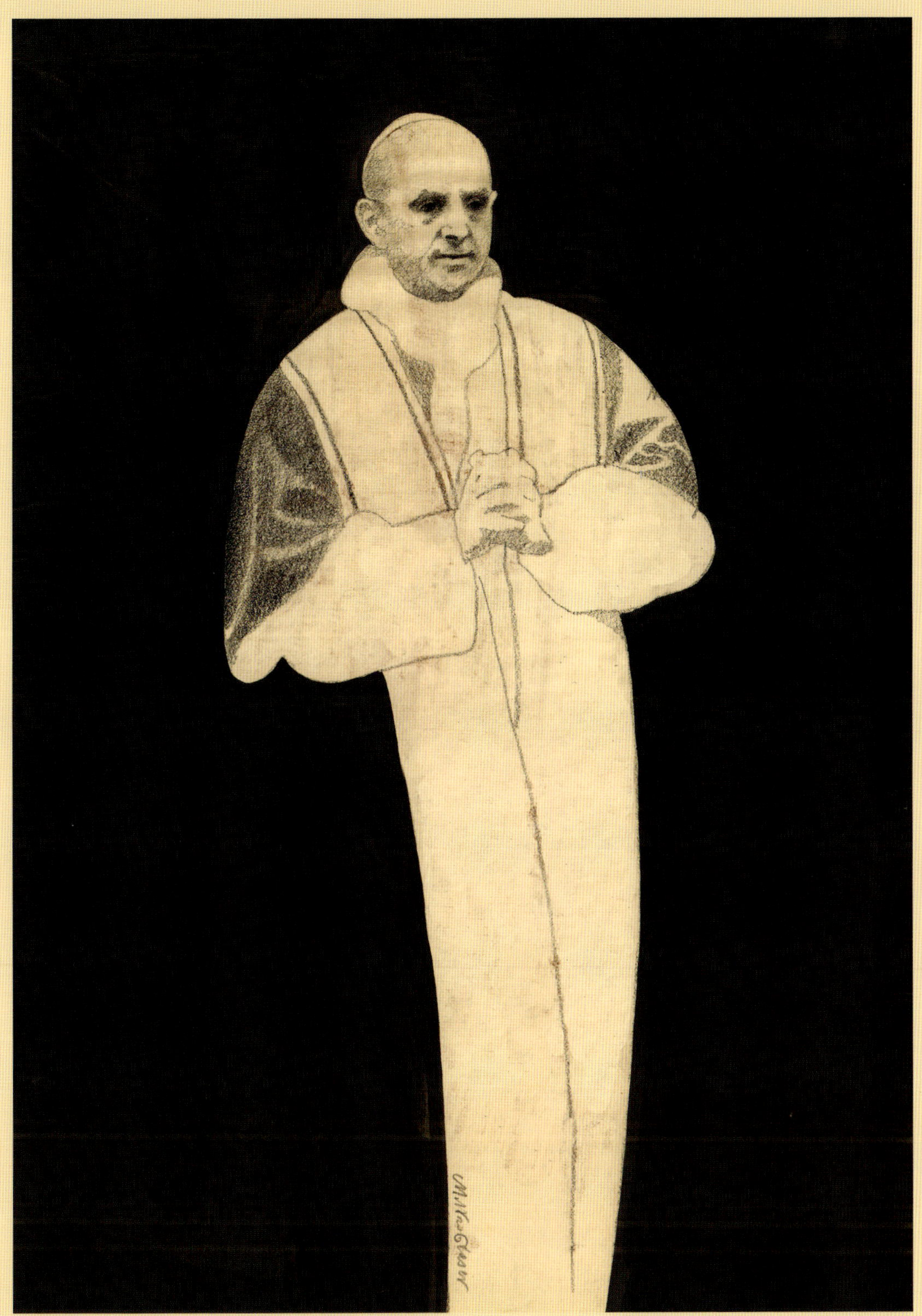

Final choice.

This is a study for a poster about painting in Italy, submitted to a poster competition in Japan. At first I used a Giorgio De Chirico–like tower in a landscape, but I thought it was too ambiguous. I made it more complex, though not necessarily better.

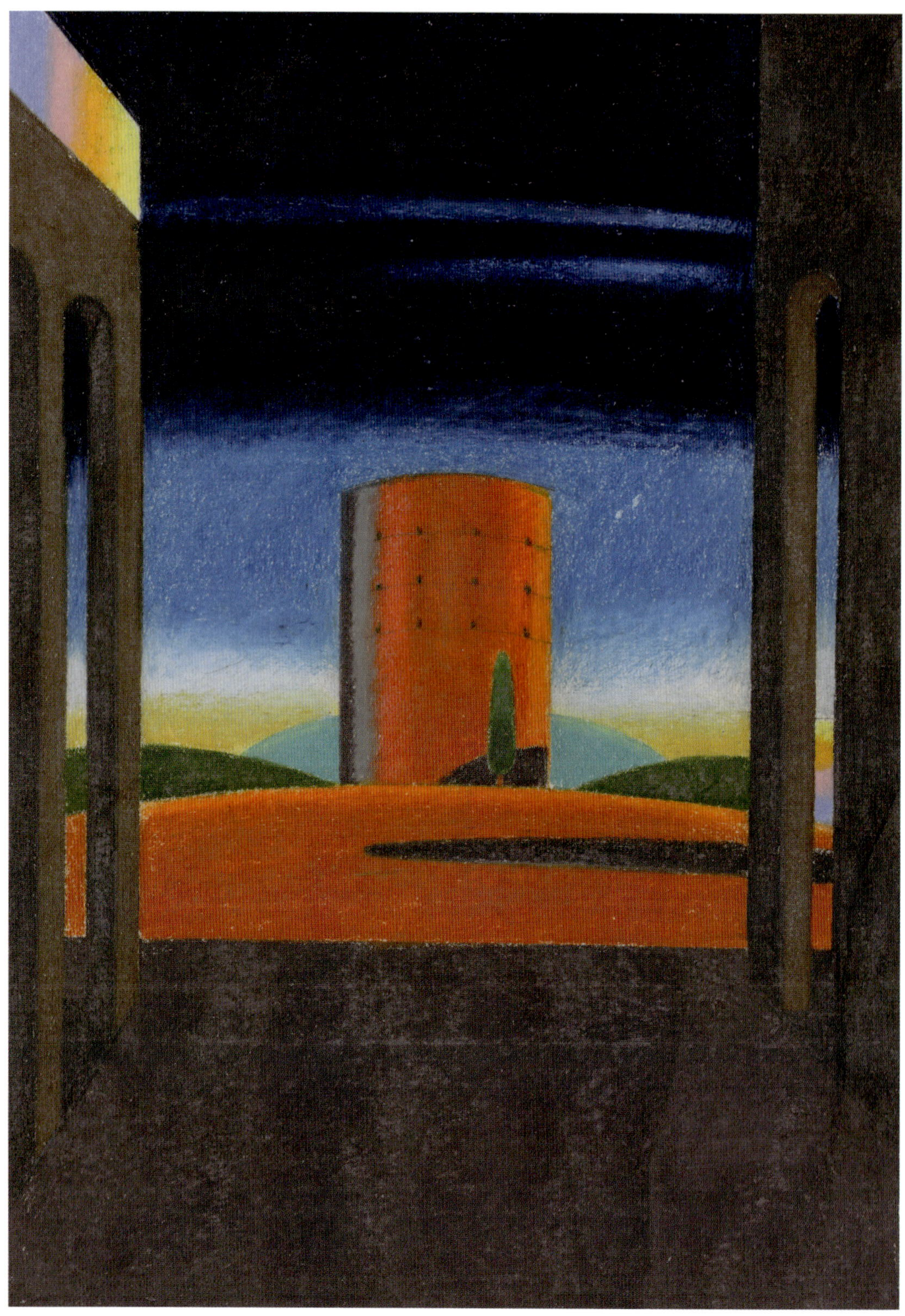

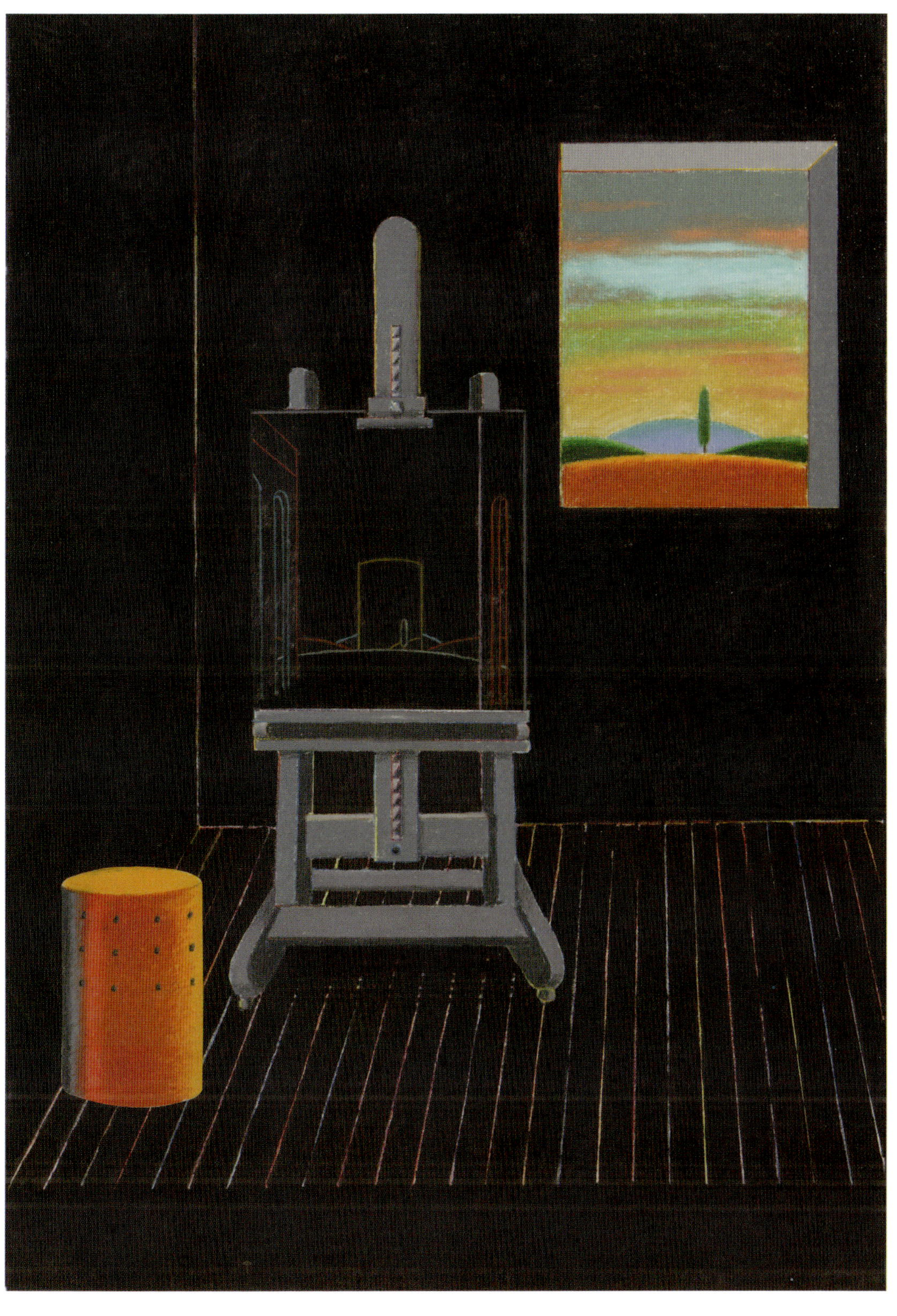

I wanted to do something with the word "poetry." I thought if I could transform the literal word I could mimic what poetry does, which is transform an initial idea into a different kind of content.

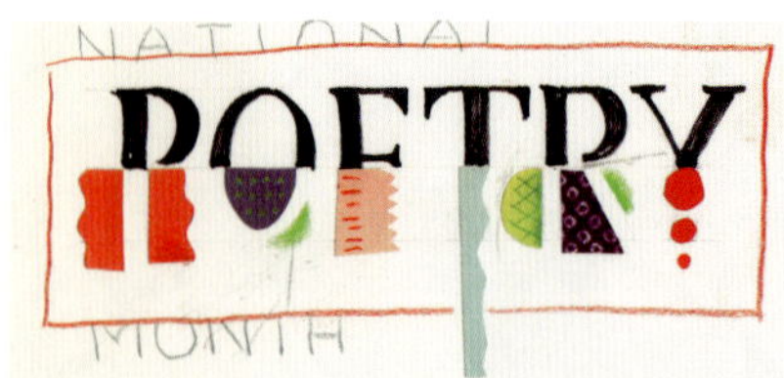

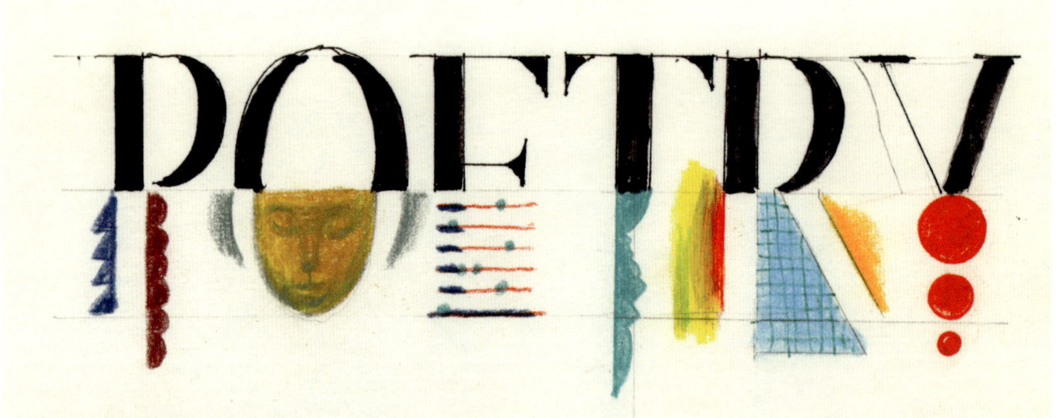

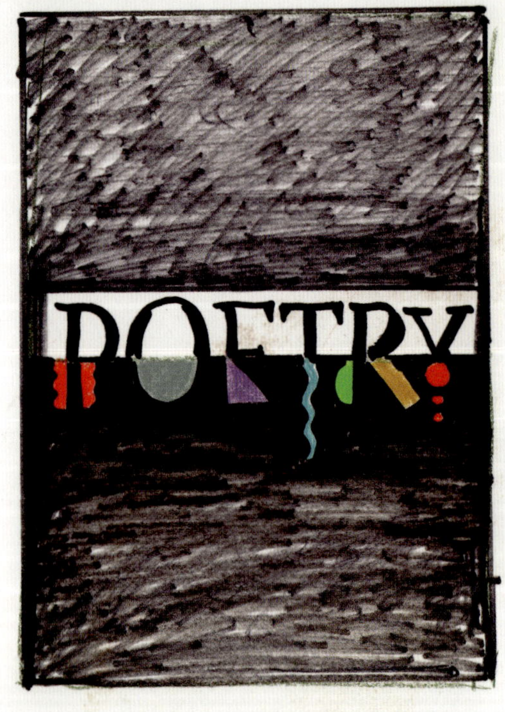

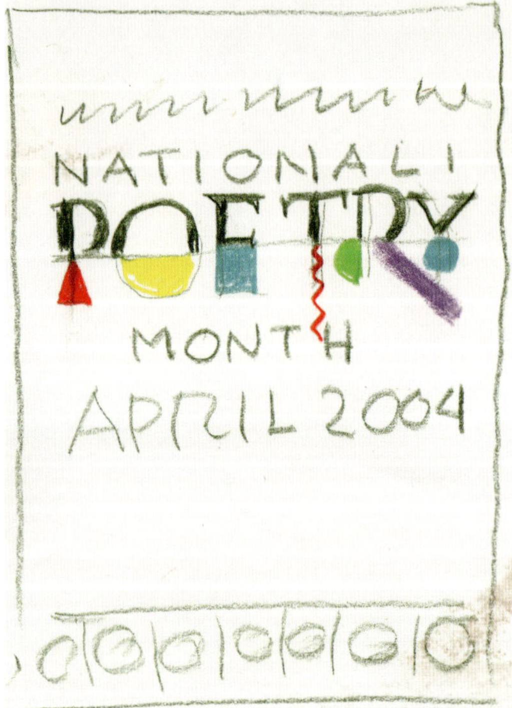

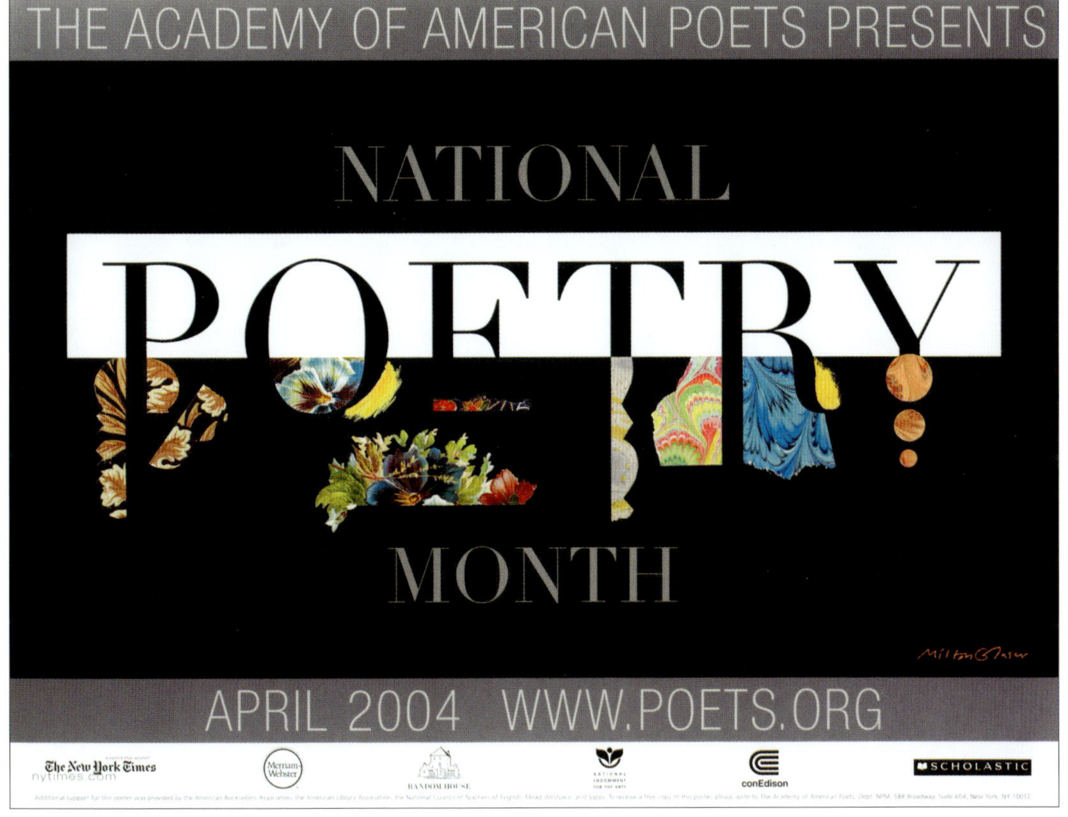
THE ACADEMY OF AMERICAN POETS PRESENTS
NATIONAL
POETRY
MONTH
APRIL 2004   WWW.POETS.ORG
The New York Times
nytimes.com
Merriam-Webster
RANDOM HOUSE
NATIONAL ENDOWMENT FOR THE ARTS
conEdison
SCHOLASTIC

<u>The idea was to link love and death for the AIDS campaign. The sketch shows the idea of the skull emerging from the intersecting hearts.</u>

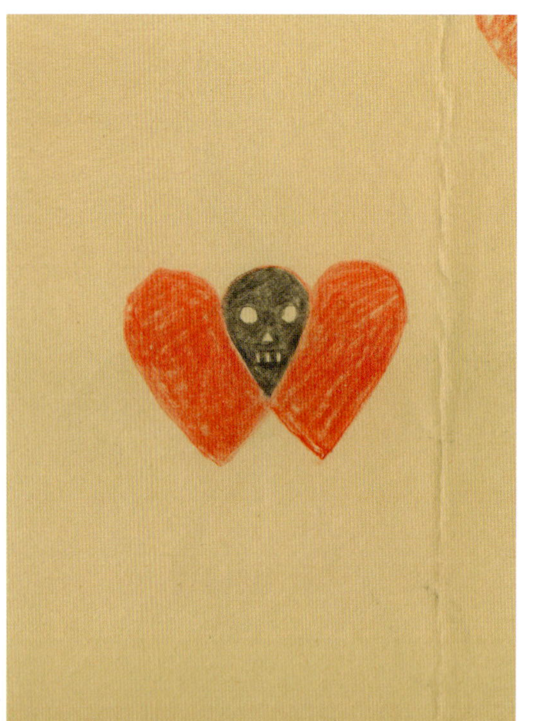

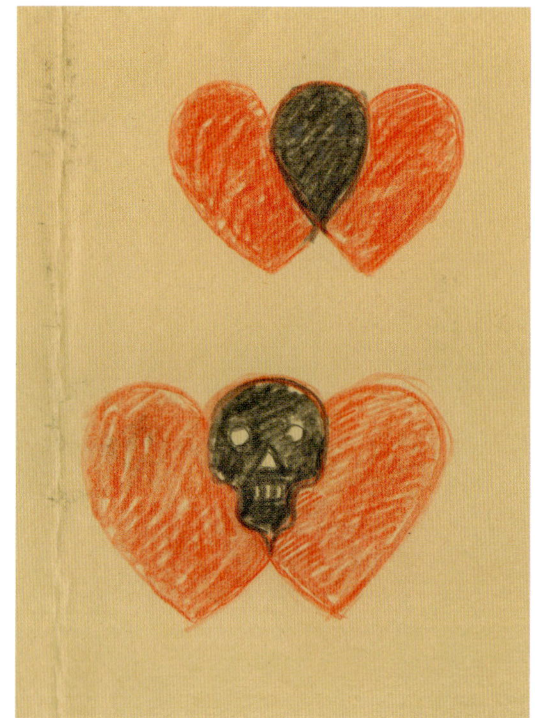

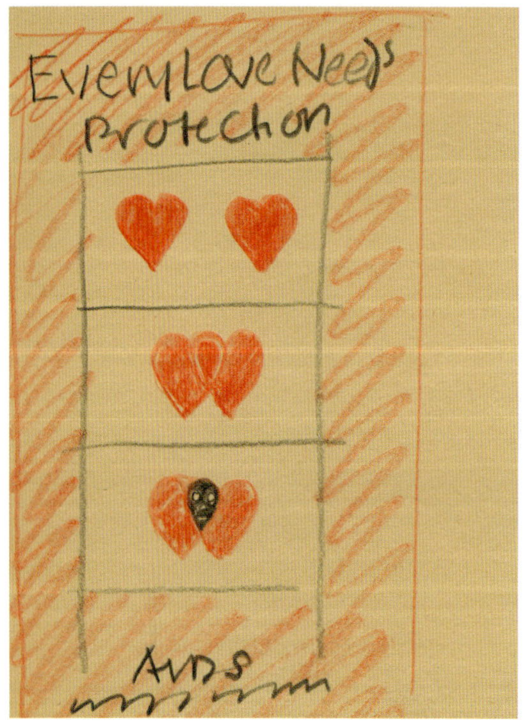

Sketches.

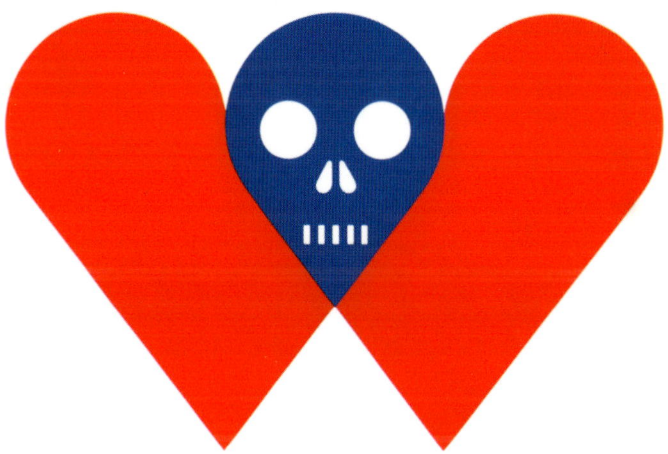

AIDS
A worldwide effort will stop it.

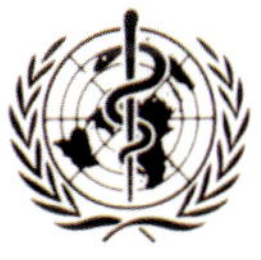

WORLD HEALTH ORGANIZATION
SPECIAL PROGRAMME ON AIDS

Very often the preliminary sketch has more visual content than the final. In this case, it is significantly more impressive. You're often modifying a sketch according to the understanding of the audience. But if you only work that way, you can never produce the extraordinary.

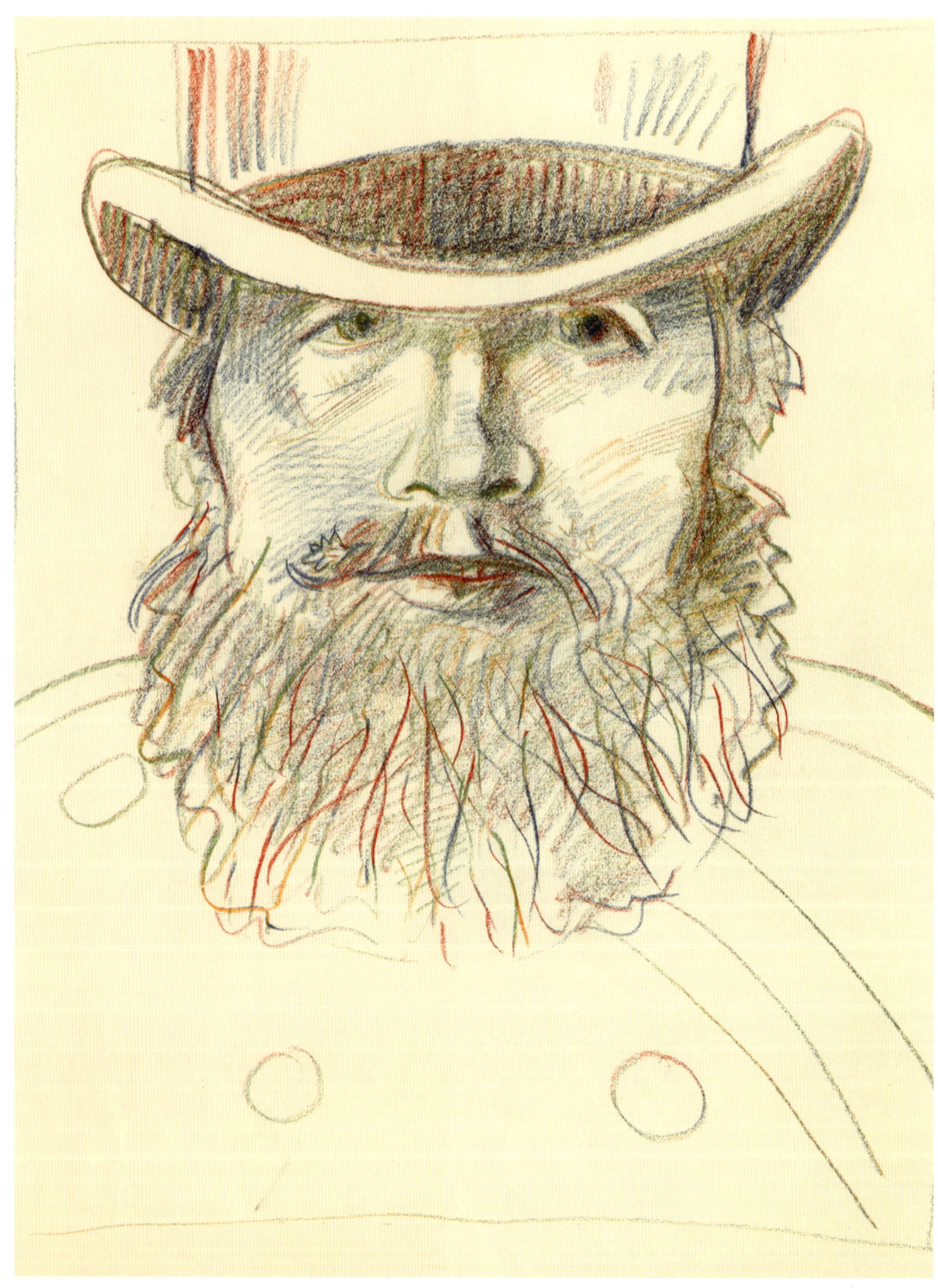

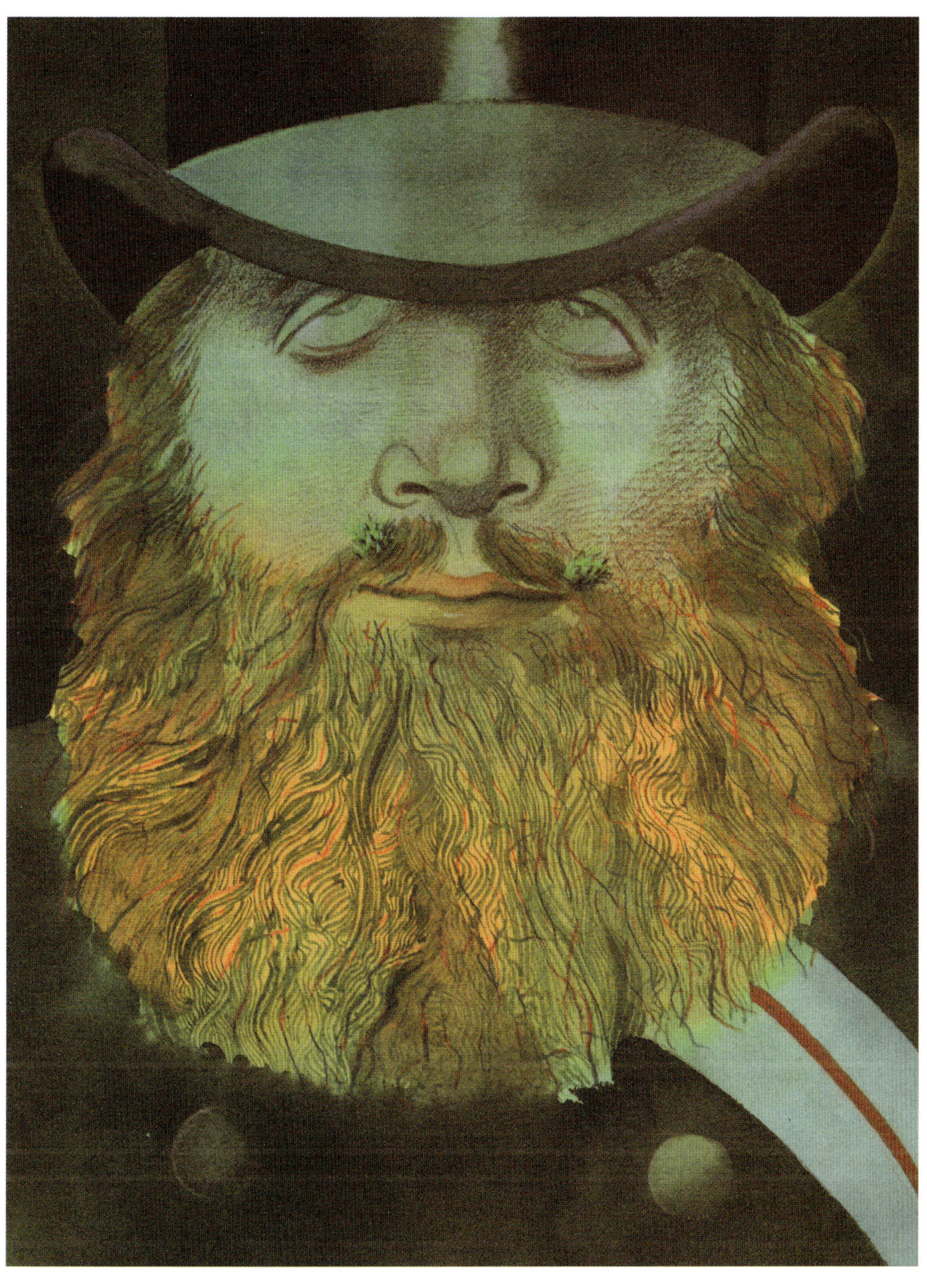

Here the character of the portrait changes in response to the medium. The linear drawing in pencil becomes something else when color and tonality are added.

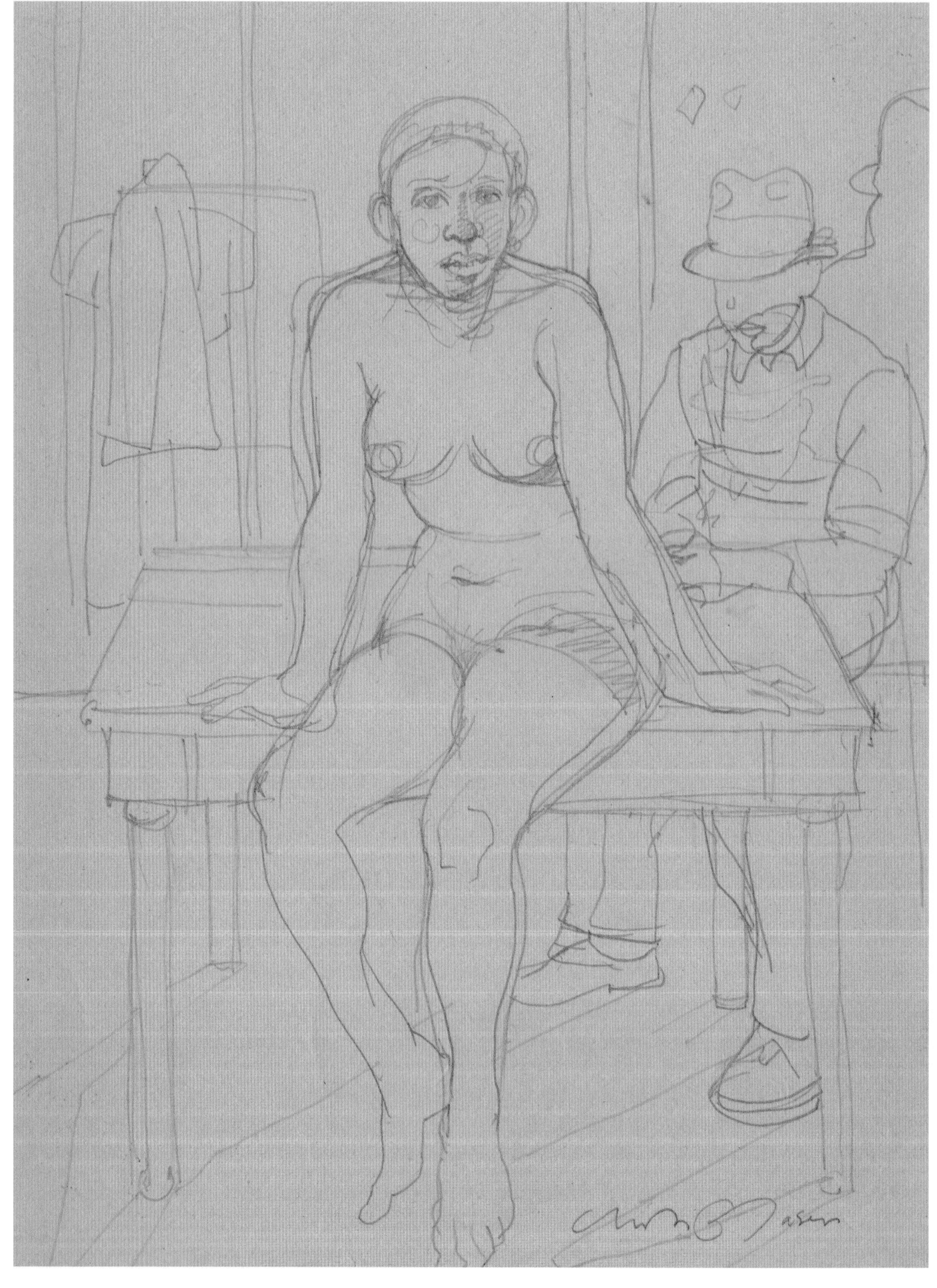

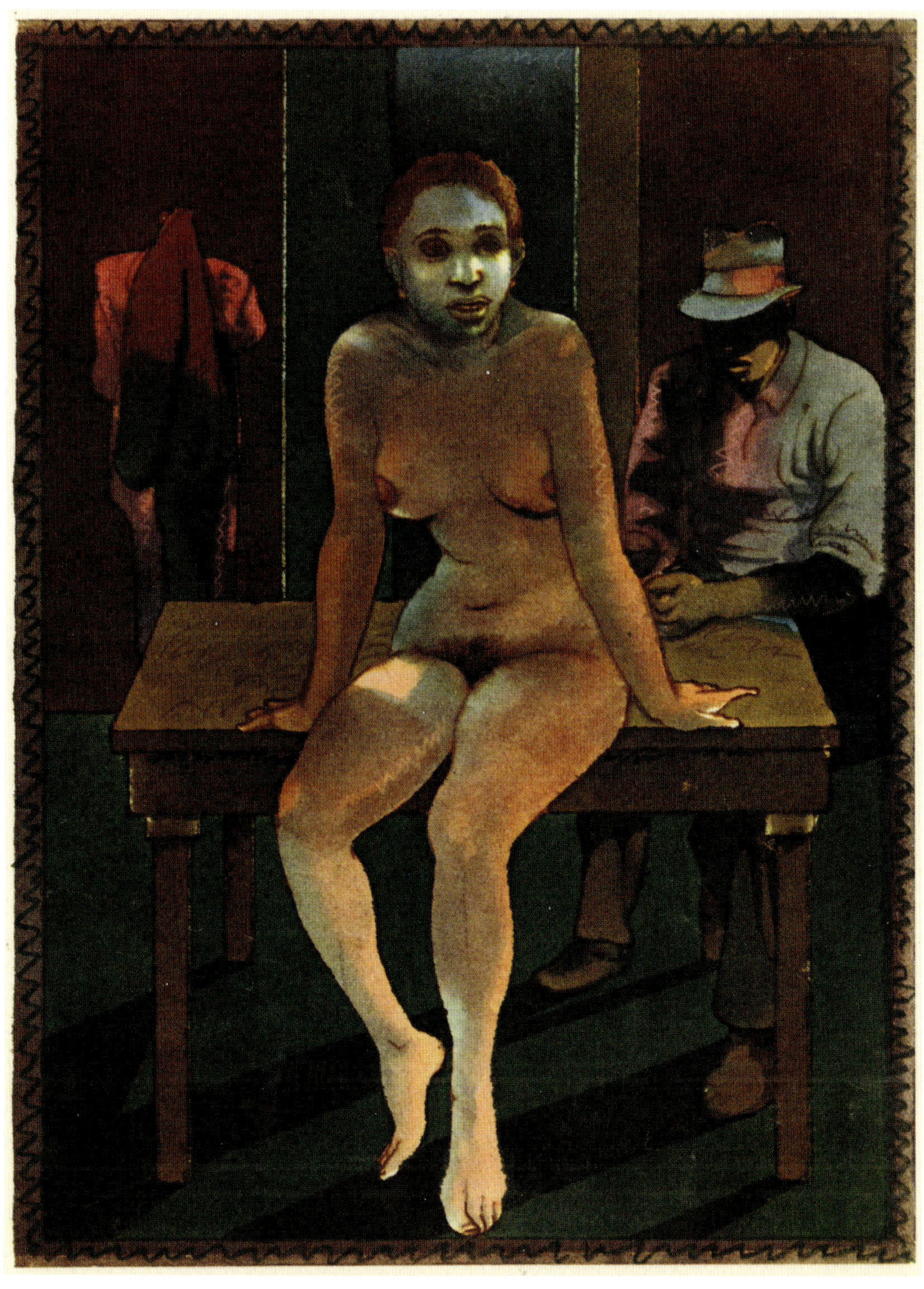

Nothing much is happening in either version, but the colored version seems portentous.

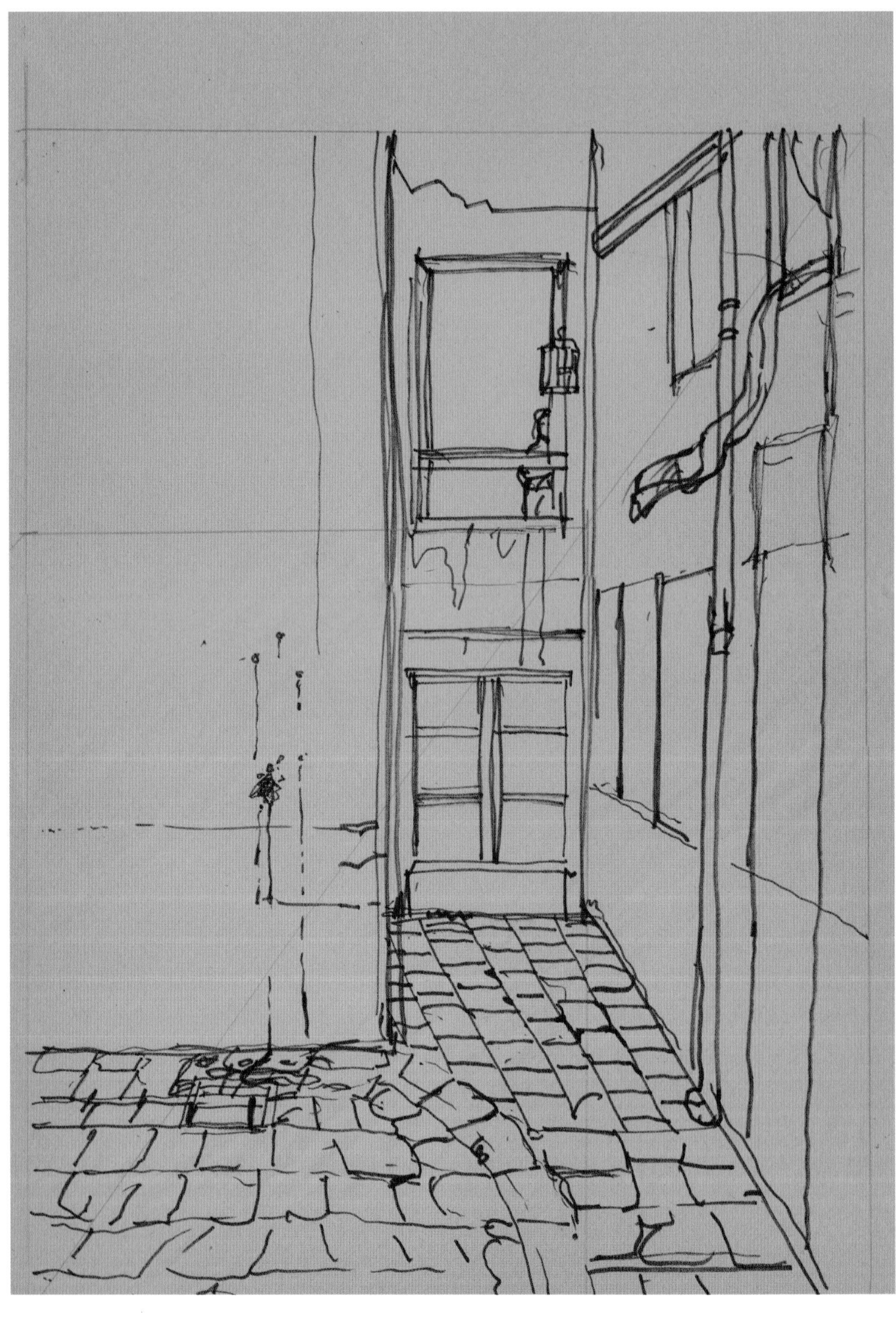

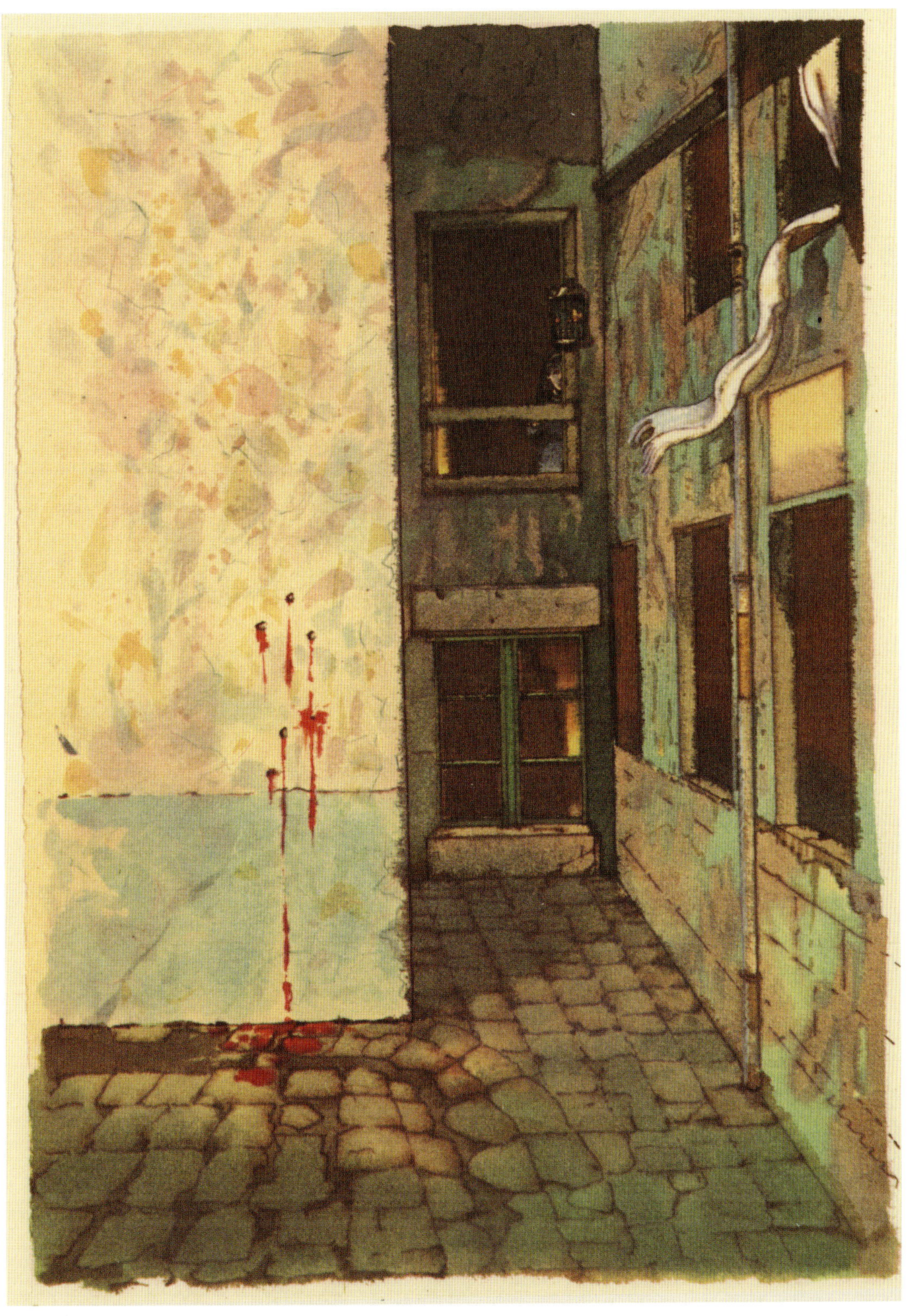

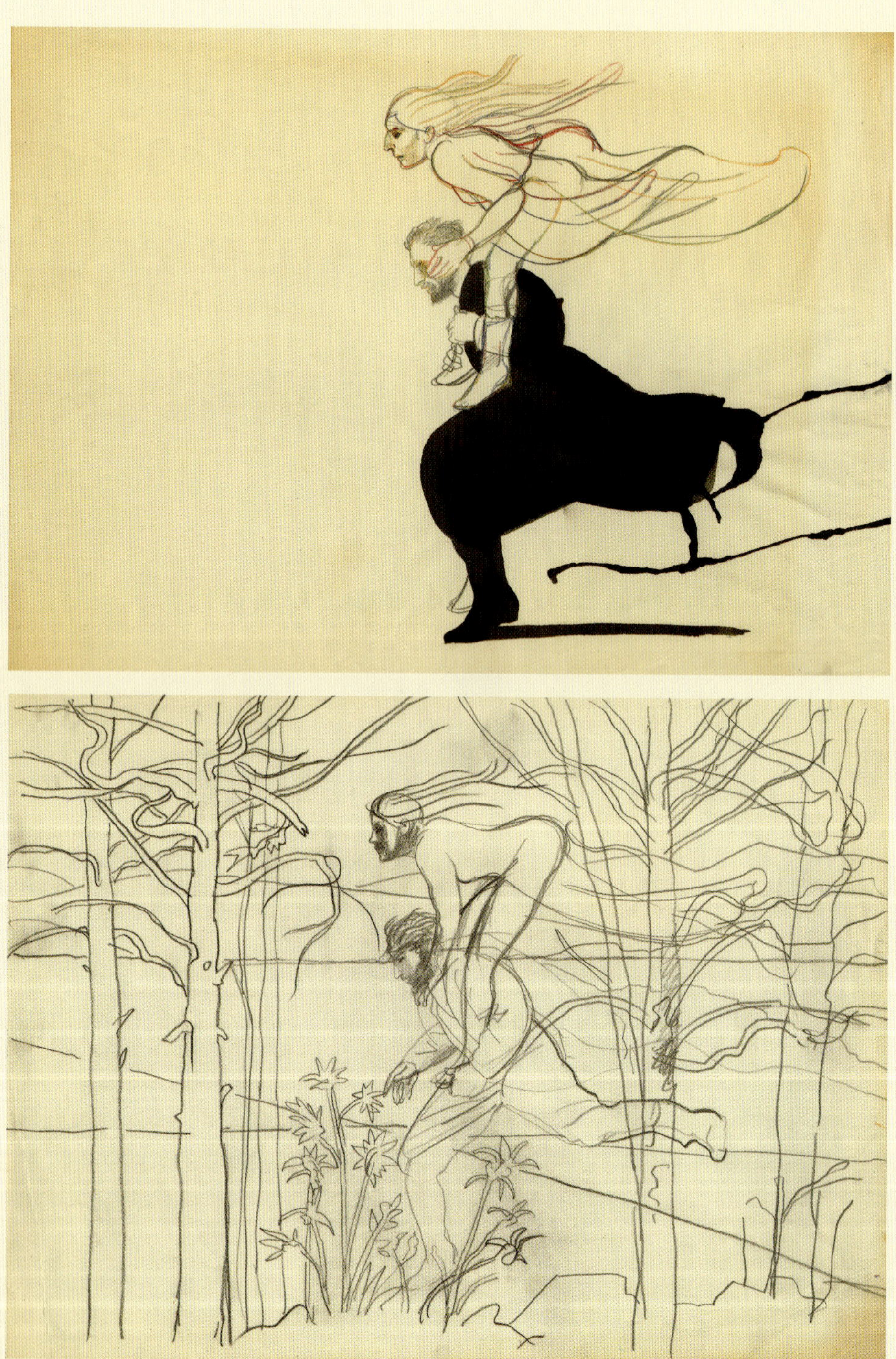

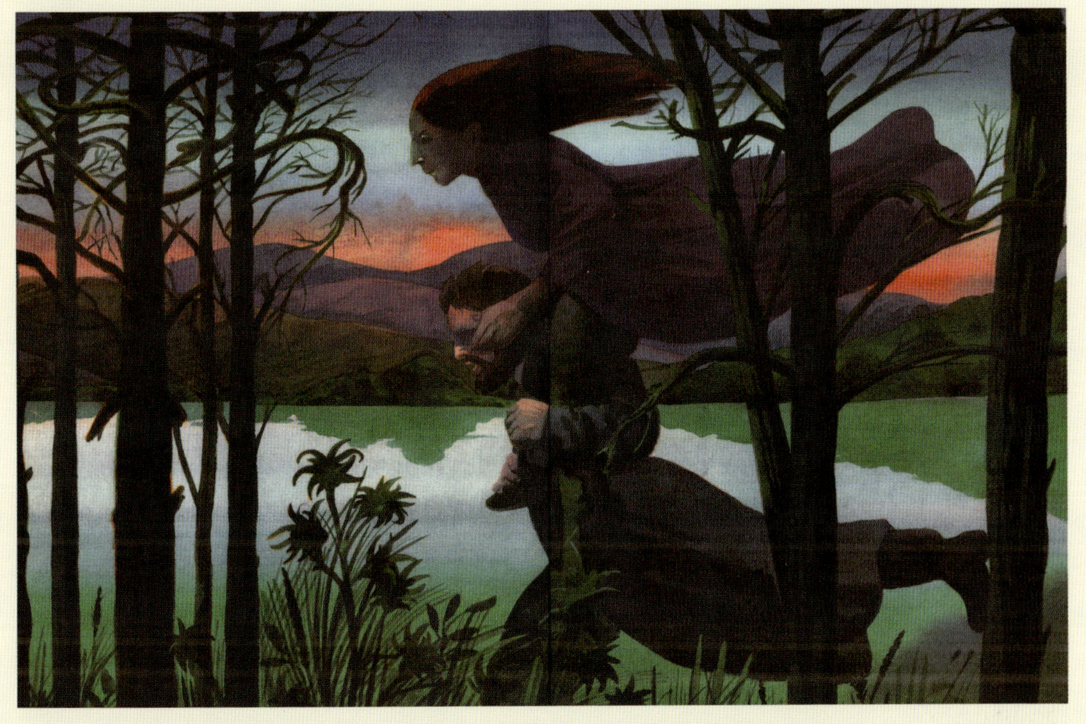

A cover for *New York* Magazine became the basis for a sculptural representation elegantly done by Nicolas Fasolino. It now lives on the counter of Russ & Daughters, a famous delicatessen on the Lower East Side of Manhattan.

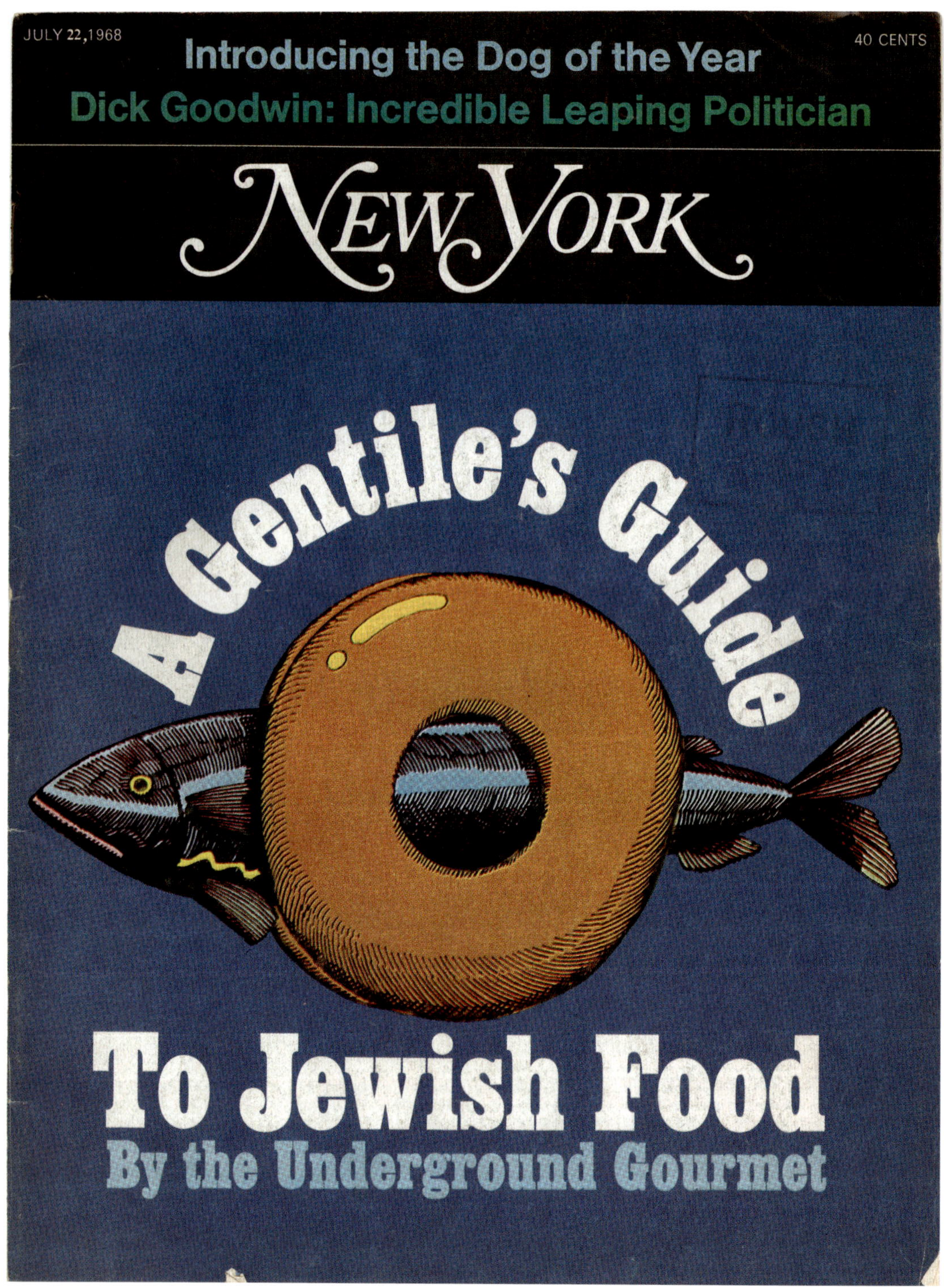

Original cover for New York *Magazine.*

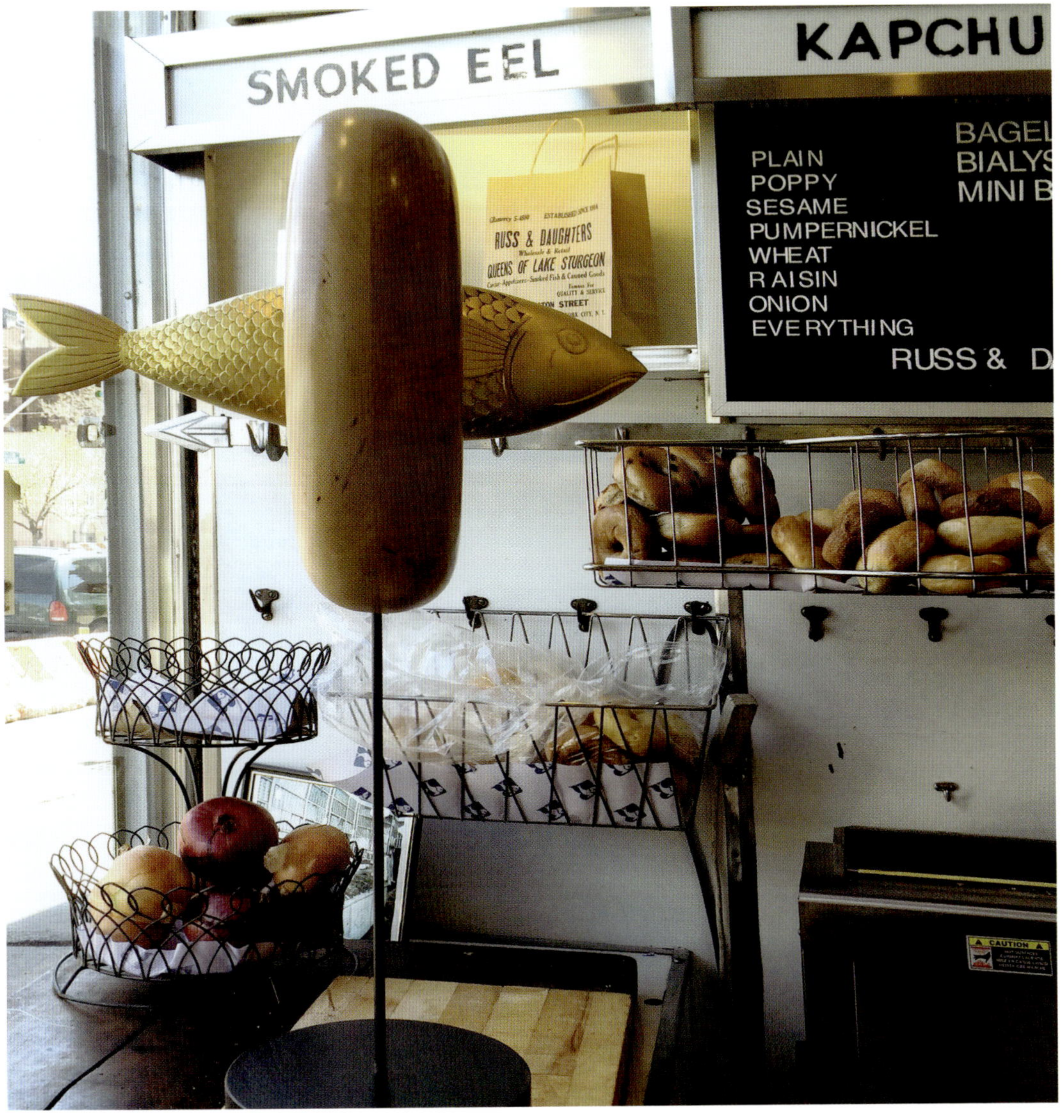

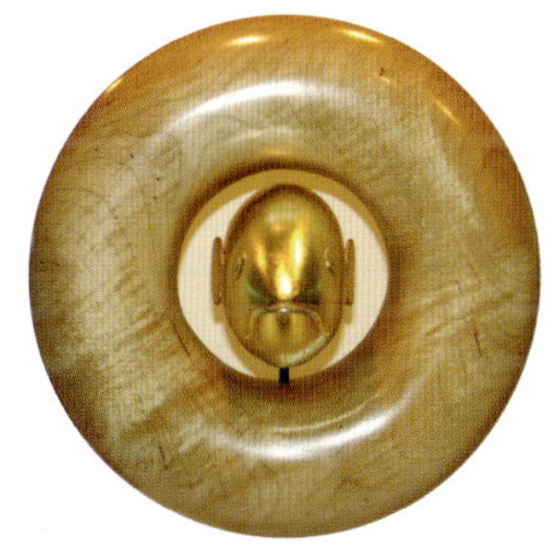

Installation at Russ & Daughters store.

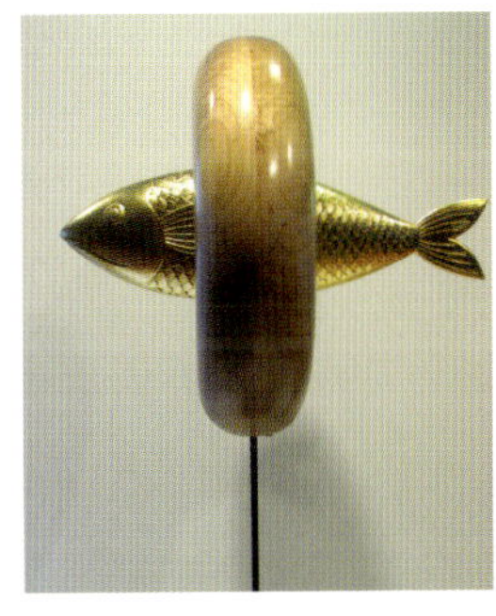

This is a portrait of the German writer Hermann Hesse, showing a black-and-white sketch and a color version. Even though the forms are the same, the color transforms everything.

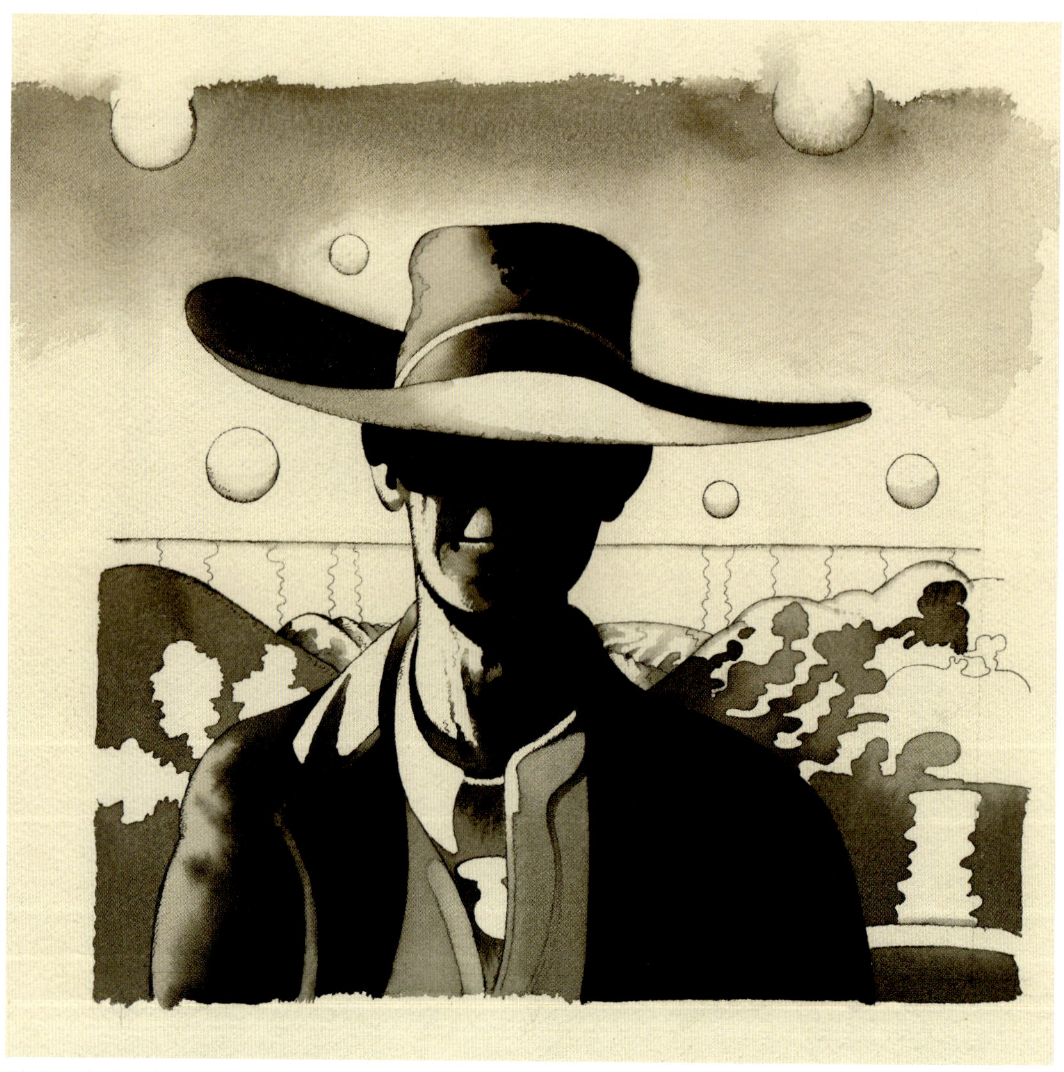

Black-and-white drawing. Ink wash.

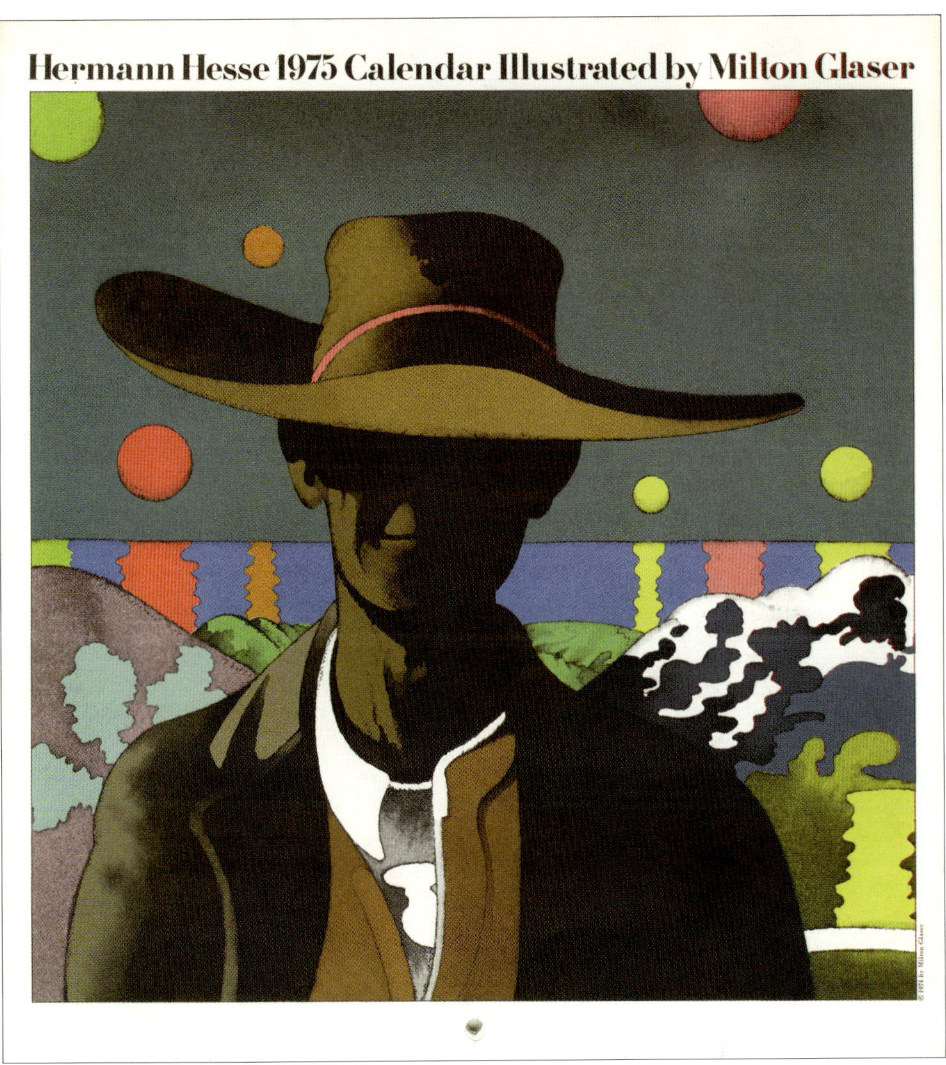

Finished illustration in color.

In some cases, the sketch is inspired by an outside influence. Here, I started with Piero della Francesca's superb painting of the Duke of Urbino. My interest is in looking at art history in the same way we look at nature, in that everything is usable for interpretation.

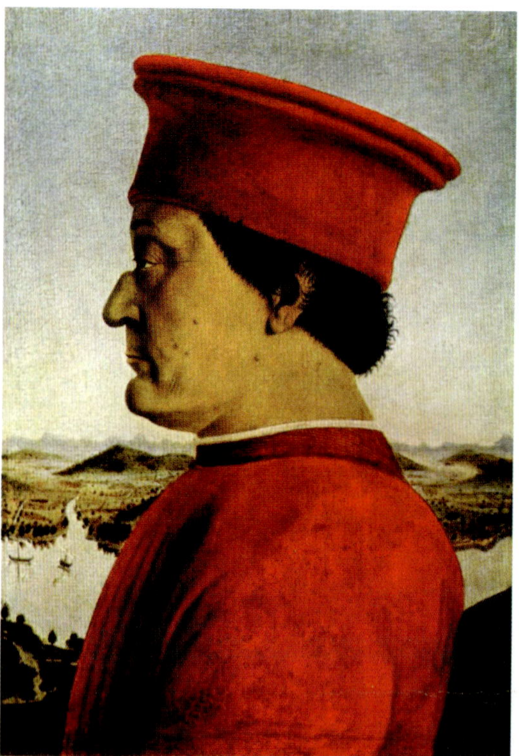

Original painting by Piero della Francesca.

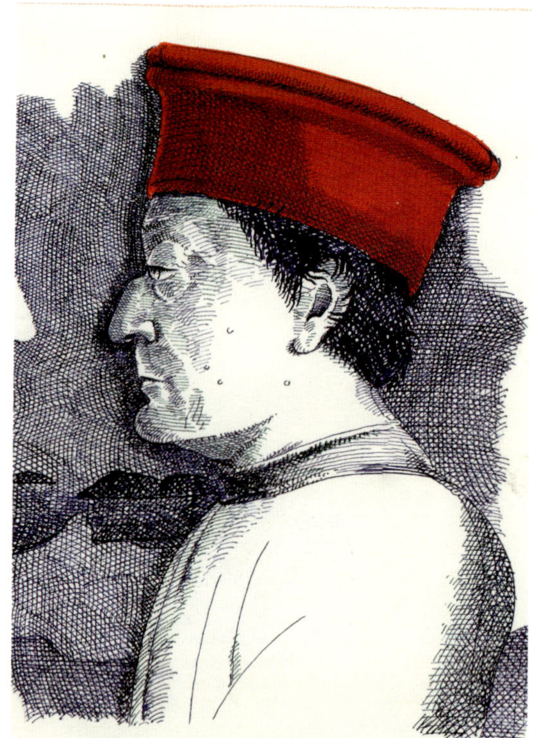

Pen and ink study.

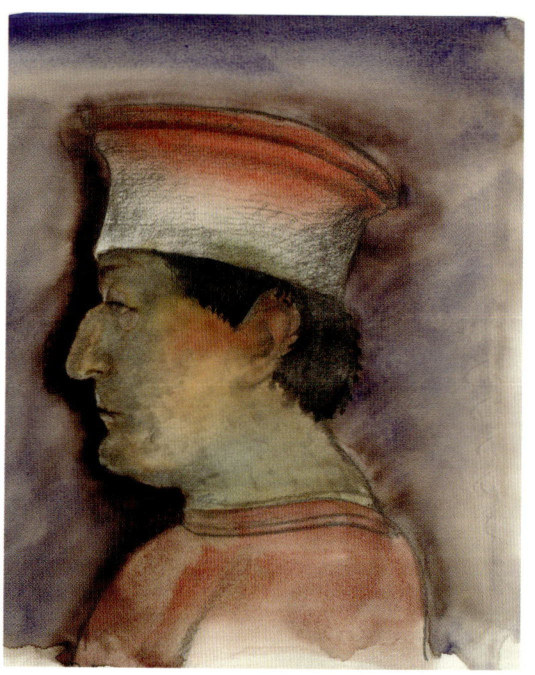

Watercolor study.

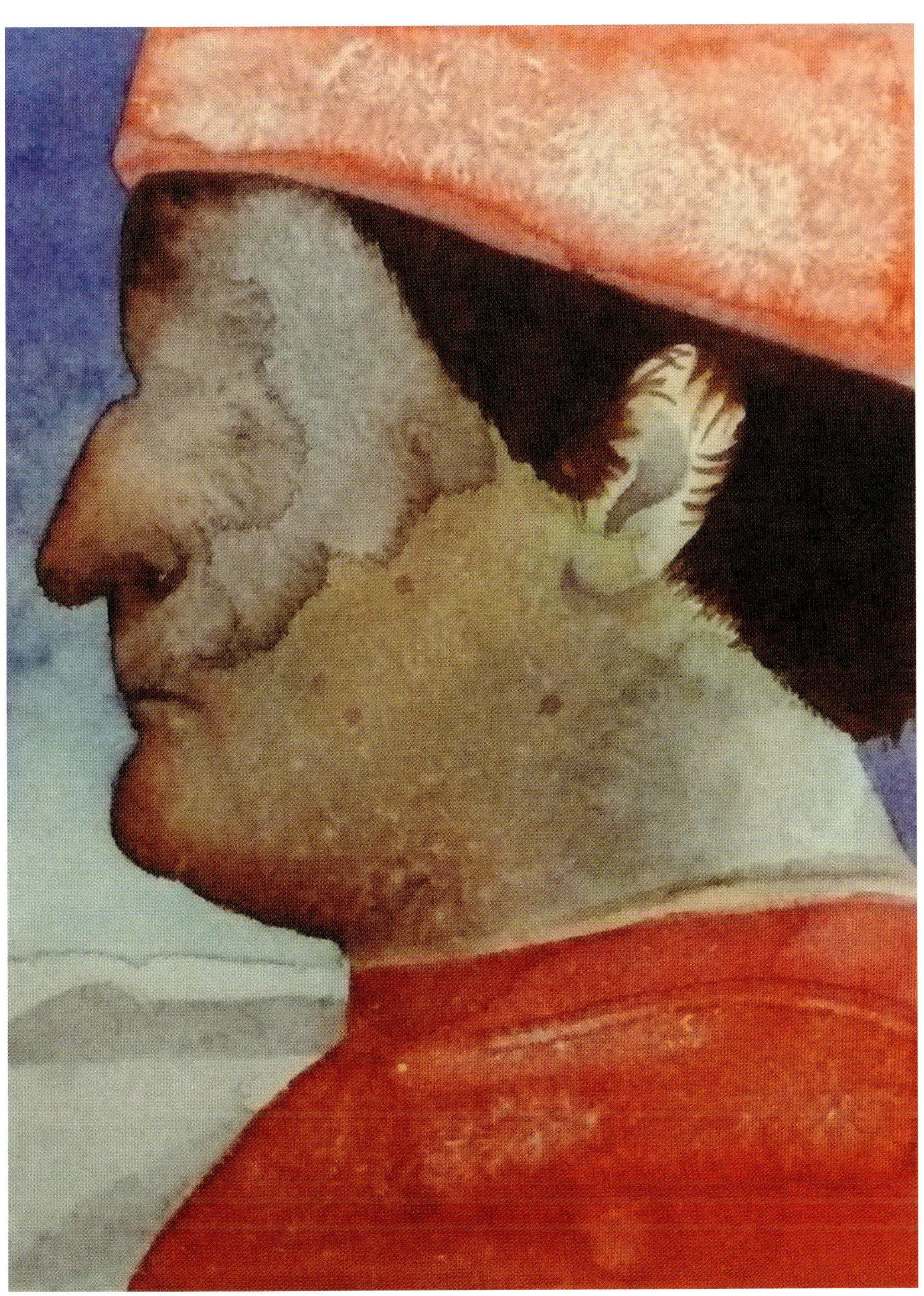

Final painting.

The core idea of using an "x" to represent both a letter and a number arose with the first sketch. That remained the central idea for the poster, expressing both the notion of the country of Mexico and the 25th anniversary of the Poster Biennial. The additional graphic elements were added to provide some visual interest that the original sketch lacked.

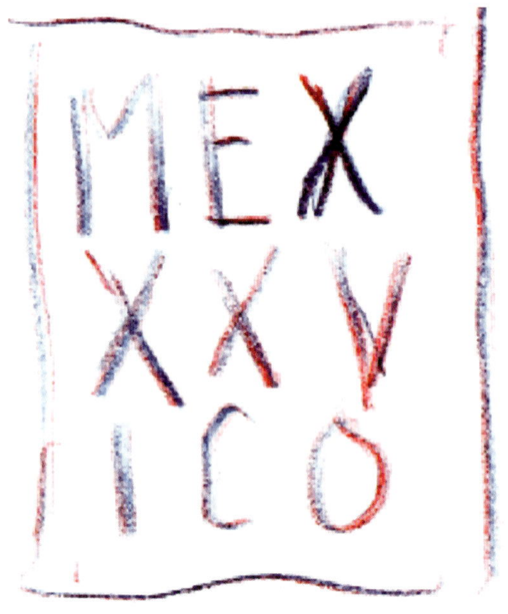

Initial sketch.

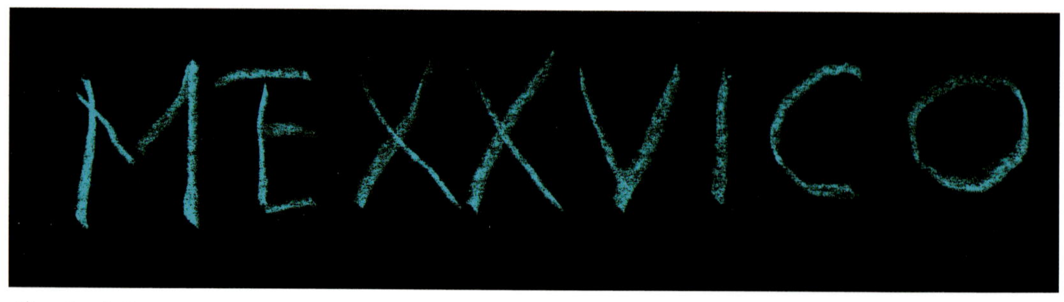

Alternative sketch.

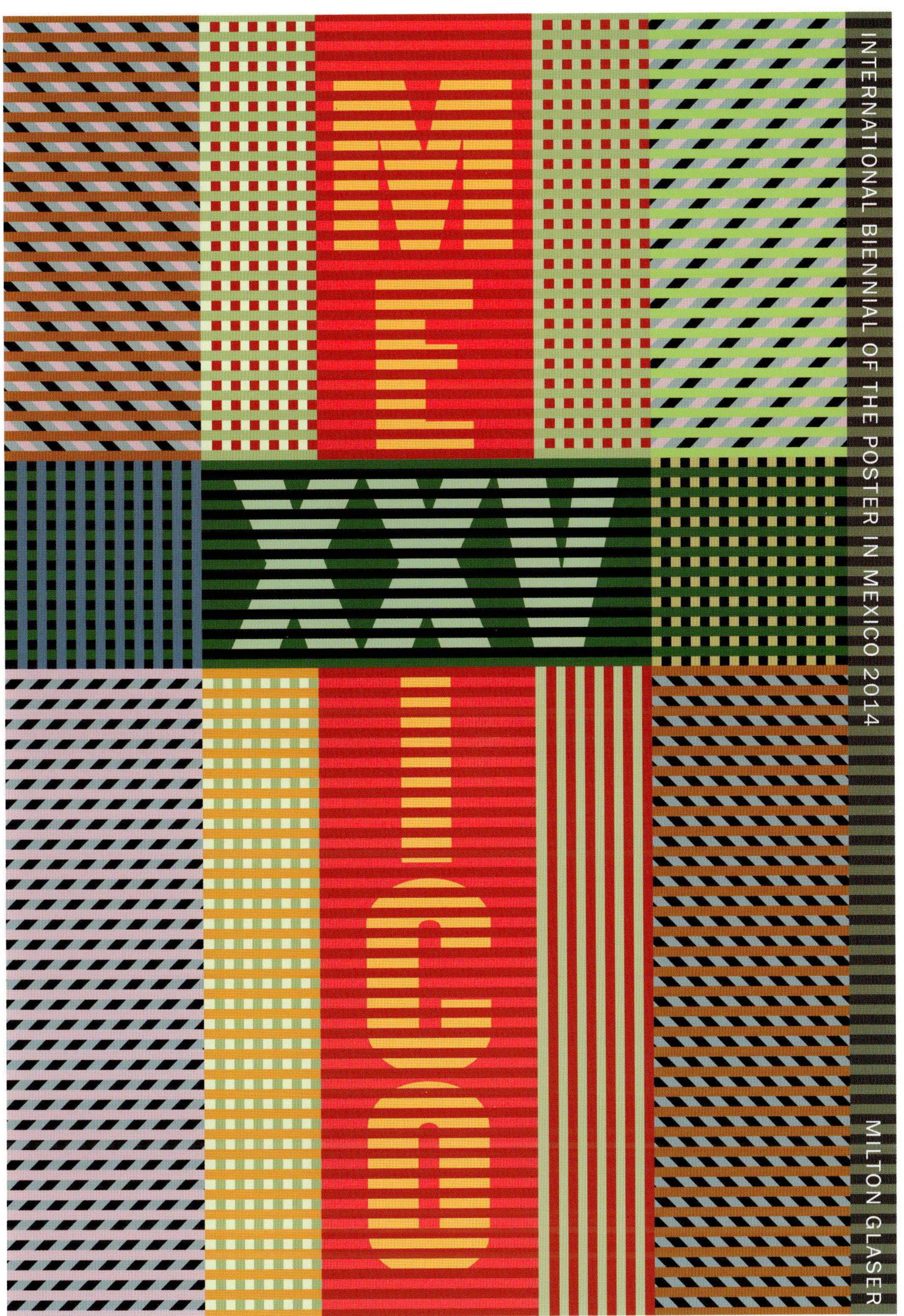

Final poster.

Submission of the original sketch of my Bob Dylan poster to the art director of Columbia Records, John Berg. He said, "Get rid of the harmonica," and he was right.

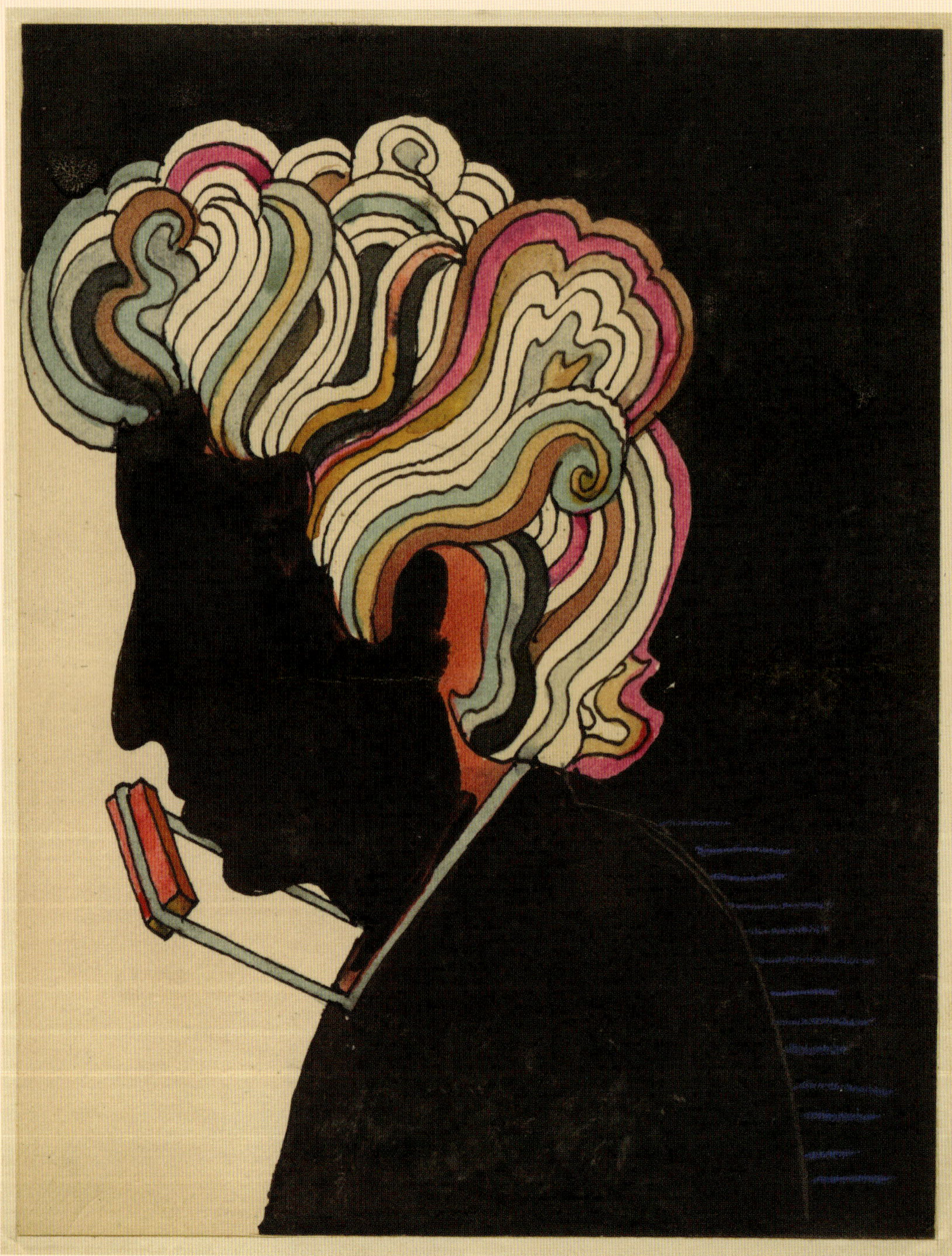

Sketch.

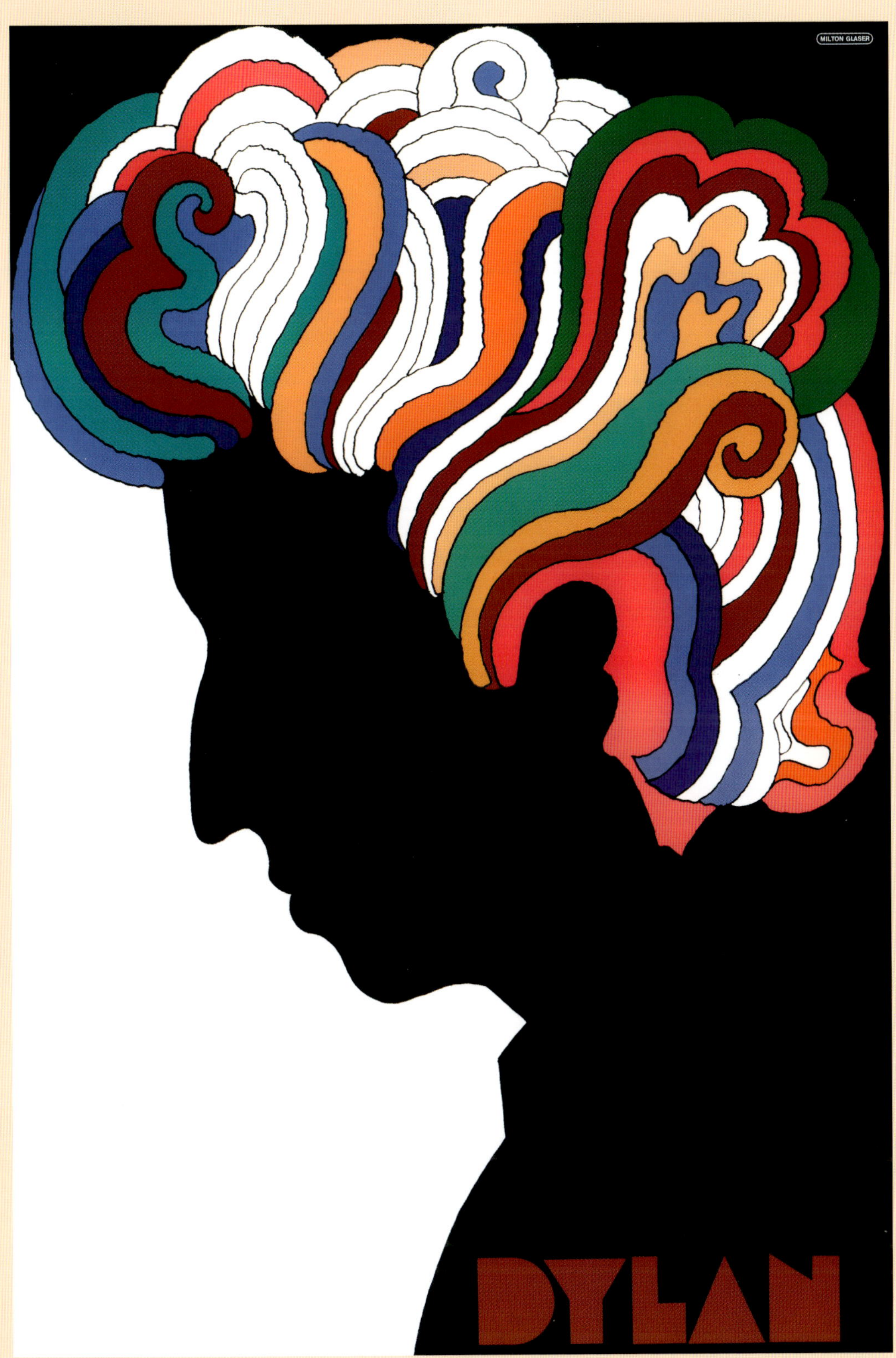
MILTON GLASER
DYLAN

Published by
Princeton Architectural Press
202 Warren Street
Hudson, New York 12534
www.papress.com

ISBN 978-1-61689-961-5

Design by Milton Glaser and Ignacio Serrano
Introduction and texts by Milton Glaser and Anne Quito
Assistance by Xiao Hua Yang and Ke Zhanger

Library of Congress Cataloging-in-Publication Data
available upon request from the publisher.